The Sixth
Amendment

The
Sixth Amendment
to the
Constitution
of the United States

A Study in Constitutional Development

by

Francis H. Heller
University of Kansas

GREENWOOD PRESS, PUBLISHERS
NEW YORK

Preface

The Constitution of the United States contains in its Bill of Rights a number of provisions designed to offer protection to persons accused of crime. Specifically, the Sixth Amendment lays down certain essential trial procedures to which "the accused shall enjoy the right." The terms of this amendment are perhaps not so easily remembered nor so frequently quoted as those of other provisions of the Constitution. Nor is their meaning, past or present, part of common knowledge. We live, however, in an era when the concepts of criminal law have been so widely extended[1] and federal jurisdiction over crime has been so widely expanded[2] that the fairness of criminal procedure in the federal courts may assume immediate importance for many a citizen.

This study will examine the origin and meaning of the procedural guarantees found in the Sixth Amendment. No pretension is made that the result might serve as a treatise on criminal procedure: Professor Orfield's recent volume[3] covers that subject with expertness and lucidity. The practitioner who seeks guidance for the presentation of criminal cases in the federal courts has access to such compendia as that by Housel and Walser.[4] This inquiry is directed solely at the antecedents and the implications of this one constitutional provision: the Sixth Amendment. It is not an annotation on that amendment: no effort has been made to collect everything ever said about it or to list all the cases in which it has been mentioned. Rather it has been the intention to present an outline of whence this provision came and of what it has meant and what it means today, and to determine to what extent it has been adapted to changing times and conditions. The endeavor of the following pages is to offer, as the subtitle suggests, "a study in constitutional development."

In substance, the material in these pages was collected and prepared as a doctoral dissertation at the University of Virginia. At that stage I had the benefit of the encouragement and the criticisms of Professors James Hart and George W. Spicer. A revised version, enlarged primarily in interpretation and analysis, was read by Professor Robert E. Cushman of Cornell University. A number of colleagues at the University of Kansas have examined the study in its present form. Professor Clyde K. Hyder has done much to improve my style and preserve consistency throughout the manuscript. To each and all of them I am properly indebted.

Portions of Chapter IV have previously been published in the *Cornell Law Quarterly*. The editors of that journal have kindly consented to their use here.

FRANCIS H. HELLER

Lawrence, Kansas
July, 1950

Contents

The Sixth Amendment

"In all criminal prosecutions the accused shall enjoy the right to a speedy and public trial, by an impartial jury of the State and district wherein the crime shall have been committed, which district shall have been previously ascertained by law, and to be informed of the nature and cause of the accusation; to be confronted with the witnesses against him; to have compulsory process for obtaining witnesses in his favor, and to have the Assistance of Counsel for his defence."

Amendment VI, Constitution of the United States.

Chapter I

Background in English Law

The story of criminal law and its enforcement is one of gradual evolution from the archaic standards of "a tooth for a tooth" and tribal retribution to the elaborate codes of the twentieth-century state, its highly organized police system, its penitentiaries and parole boards. Among our Anglo-Saxon forebears criminal law was hardly deserving of that name: its nature was still so primitive that there was no distinction between crimes and torts; physical force was still the predominant method of redressing wrongs, and outlawry and the feud were the recognized remedies of the age.[1] Already, however, the community's interest in peace and order had resulted in the emergence of a non-violent alternative to the feud by payment of a compensation (*bot* or *wergild*) to the injured person, or in case of murder to the deceased's family. "It is this system of bot and wer, resting upon the blood feud and upon outlawry, which is the groundwork of Anglo-Saxon criminal law."[2]

Yet there were also present among the Angles and Saxons those elements and institutions which would eventually give rise to our modern law of crimes. The earliest reports on the Germanic tribes indicated that among them compensation for an offense was due not only to the injured man but also to the king, or other person having authority, or to the community.[3] In this custom was contained the germ of the idea which is a necessary condition precedent to the growth of a criminal law: that a wrong committed not only affects the injured individual but concerns the peace and order of the entire community.[4]

Another factor conducive to the growth of criminal law lay in the increasing number of offenses which could not be atoned for by compensation with money. There apparently always had been a few offenses in this category, usually those which for moral or religious reasons were repugnant to the community. Their number increased sharply with the acceptance of Christianity and the growing integration of political society, and eventually it came to be thought that such "unemendable" offenses should be dealt with by the king.[5]

A further cause which led to the evolution of criminal law was the more definite organization of the state. Duties of the subject became more specific and mandatory. Royal power began to insist on fulfillment of these duties and backed its commands with threats of punishment. Clerical influence furthered these tendencies by its exaltation of the royal office as the guardian of law and order, and the maintainer of justice and equity.[6]

But the great and sudden development of the criminal law did not set in until after the Norman conquest. The judicial procedures which the Normans found prevailing among the Anglo-Saxons were largely of ritual character and attended with varying degrees of church sanction.[7] Men's ideas of a trial were dominated by the primitive ideas which centered around the old processes of ordeal, battle, or compurgation. These were, in essence, but means of securing a divine decision. As one writer has rather caustically commented:

Trial by Battle and Trial by Ordeal were both methods of decision which should commend themselves to all but an accused person on account of their fine, bluff, open-handed, Anglo-Saxon characteristics. Trial by Battle, beginning as it did with invocation, combined the attraction of a prize fight with those of a religious ceremony. Trial by Ordeal was more popular among prosecutors because it eliminated the unpleasant chances of battle. The accused person, being bound hand and foot, was thrown into a pond. If he 'swam', as it was expressed, he was taken out and dealt with as guilty. If he sank and drowned, his innocence was manifest and he was buried with all decency and respect. . . . A not unreasonable dissatisfaction was felt among the criminal classes which at that time constituted the bulk of the population.[8]

There is evidence, however, that there may have been cause for dissatisfaction among the injured parties too. There were other, less drastic versions of the ordeal which offered a chance of escape to the guilty and innocent alike. In the ordeal by fire, involving the lifting and carrying of a red-hot iron weight, and in the ordeal by hot water, where the accused plunged his hand into a kettle of boiling water, tricks and ruses were possible. The ordeal by water, mentioned above, was not always carried out in a manner that necessarily resulted in the death of the accused; at least one account relates that the water involved was only hip-deep and that the test consisted in remaining submerged for the period required for a fleet runner to recover an arrow shot over the accused's head. The clergy had the benefit of a special form of ordeal which was virtually tantamount to a guarantee of impunity: this was known as the ordeal of the morsel, and the proof of innocence lay in the accused's ability to swallow without choking a morsel of bread. Trial by battle, brought to England by the Normans, lost much of its punitive value by the spreading use of hired champions. Compurgation frequently resulted in inaction as oath-helpers were pitted against oath-helpers.[9] A more rational, more reliable method of proof was badly needed.

The urgency of this need was accentuated by the successive elimination of the old procedures. By the assize of Clarendon (1166) compurgation was ruled out in many cases.[10] But it was the Church which precipitated the crisis in English legal procedure that was to lead to eventual pre-eminence of the trial jury. In 1215, Pope Innocent III forbade the clergy to perform any religious ceremony in connection with the ordeal.[11] The elimination of the religious sanction attached to ordeals deprived that method of proof of the divine aspects with which it had been associated, and practically abolished it as a trial procedure. In the vacuum so created the method of trial by jury now expanded and prospered.

The origin of the English jury system was for a long time a subject of scholarly dispute, but in the latter part of the nineteenth century new light was thrown on the controversy by the researches of Heinrich von Brunner,[12] whose findings have since been generally accepted.[13]

Contrary to the older view, the origin of trial by jury is to be found not in ancient popular custom but in royal prerogative. This "palladium of English liberties is . . . in its origin rather French than English, rather royal than popular, rather the livery of conquest than the badge of freedom."[14] The vigorous royal power built up by the Frankish rulers included an institution, known as the inquest, for discovering the extent of the king's rights in the community, especially in fiscal matters.[15] Royal officers would convene the best and oldest men in each neighborhood and compel them to answer on oath whatever questions might be addressed to them in the king's name. Mostly these pertained to land holdings and the royal title to real estate. The Norman duke who conquered Britain used this method to compile his Domesday Book. The inquest as a prerogative procedure of the crown was thus at first an administrative rather than a judicial proceeding; it was "the regular means whereby the . . . kings evaded the technicalities and rigor of folk-law in determining the rights of the crown."[16] Then Henry II, endeavoring to establish a royal monopoly in the administration of justice, put this royal remedy at the disposal of all his subjects. Before the twelfth century was at an end, the inquest in one form or another—sometimes called an assize, sometimes a jury—had become part of the normal procedure in almost every kind of civil action.[17]

In the trial of criminal cases Henry II also made the inquest a regular procedure. Maitland has suggested that this particular form of the inquest, the sworn testimony of selectmen as to the occurrence of crime in the community, may have made its way into England in the century before the Norman conquest, but little is known of any use of it until Henry ordained its general utilization for the detection of crime.[18] It is, of course, the forerunner not of the trial jury but of the grand jury of our day. This jury of presentment, by its indictment, created a presumption of guilt which only the customary modes of proof could erase. Sir James F. Stephen says that "their accusation was practically equivalent to a conviction, subject only to the chance of a favorable termination of the ordeal."[19] This one chance of escape however, was suddenly eliminated as the result of the papal ban on the participation of clergy in ordeals. "The law then hardly knew what to do."[20] The judges of the thirteenth century had no substitute ready to take the place of that supernatural test of which Innocent's decree had deprived them. Yet there had to be some remedy to traverse the *prima facie* proof of guilt established by the presentment. The defendant was asked to "put himself upon the country," that is, to accept the verdict of the neighborhood through its representatives on the jury. Originally the submission to this form of trial was purely voluntary; a prisoner who refused to plead before such a tribunal could not be tried at all. But by the Statute of Westminster I (1275) a potent means of persuasion was brought into play. Chapter 12 of that statute provided that "notorious felons who are openly of evil fame and who refuse to put themselves upon inquests of felony at the suit of the king before his justices, shall be remanded to a hard and strong prison . . . ." Such confinement was frequently attended by various forms of violent persuasion as, for instance, the barbarous form of torture, reported by one scholar, wherein the accused was placed between two boards and stones and weights were piled on him until he accepted trial by jury or expired in his obduracy.[21]

Initially the jury which passed on the question of guilt was the same body which had proffered the presentment. The legal historians find it difficult to determine the exact point of time when a second and different jury came into general use as a tribunal before which the truth of the presentment made by the first could be tested. This result seems certainly to have been reached by the end of the thirteenth century. Sir James F. Stephen states that two separate and distinct juries were known at the time Britton wrote (believed to be 1291-92).[22] In 1352, 25 Edward III, Stat. 5, c. 3 recognized the existence of two different bodies of jurors when it allowed the accused to challenge any prospective members of the trial jury who had served on the jury of presentment.[23]

This early trial jury differed from our modern institution in many respects but most importantly in the fact that the jurors were not selected because they were open-minded and free of bias; nor were they expected, as are their modern successors, to render a verdict based solely on what they had heard and seen in the courtroom. On the contrary, they were expected to be already familiar with the facts when the trial began and to announce a verdict based on their own personal knowledge of crime and defendant. It was the jurors' duty, upon being summoned for jury service, to make inquiry into the facts of the case to be tried, to sift the information and then, in court, to state their conclusion in terms of guilt or innocence. The jury thus was, in a sense, a body of witnesses who found a verdict upon their own knowledge, however acquired, of the facts.[24]

The developments which transformed the trial jury from witnesses into judges of evidence in court are obscured in history:[25]

The transition was gradual, so gradual that it cannot be described with details and exactitude. As population grew more dense and social life more complex, the jury of neighbors no longer had ready access to the facts; it tended to rely upon evidence, which the litigants themselves were in the best position to provide.[26]

It is only with the completion of this change that the trial jury as we know it was truly born. At least as far as civil cases were concerned, this process of change appears to have been completed by the middle of the fifteenth century.[27]

In criminal trials the introduction of witnesses in court and the hearing of sworn evidence by them was much slower in gaining recognition. The King was not merely one of the parties to a private squabble; his prerogative almost necessarily required that the proceedings be heavily weighted in his favor. In Sir Thomas Smith's account of the ordinary course in a trial for felony, written in 1565, there is no mention of any evidence for the accused; only evidence for the prosecution is invited: "After the inquest is full [the crier] said in a loud voice: 'If any can give evidence or can say anything against the prisoner let him come now, for he standeth upon his deliverance.' "[28] In *Throckmorton's Case*, a trial for treason in 1554, a witness for the defendant, Fitzwilliams by name, was summarily dismissed from the court and was not permitted to speak.[29] Again, in *Udall's Case* in 1590, in a trial for felony, the defendant offered to produce witnesses on his behalf, and it was declared that because their testimony would be against the Queen's majesty they could not be heard.[30] The practice of denying the accused the benefit of witnesses in his favor appears to have been generally accepted. Thus Chief Justice Coke, referring to certain "slander of the Jesuits against our common law," which included the statement that it denied the accused the benefit of witnesses and of counsel while counsel and sworn witnesses were allowed for the king and against the accused, made no denial but merely asserted that under English practice the judge would take ample care of the prisoner's interests.[31]

It was in Coke's time, however, that public sentiment began to force a softening of the rules with regard to witnesses. In 1606, the House of Commons against opposition of the Crown and the House of Lords forced the passage of the statute 4 James I, c. 1, s. 5 and 6, which permitted in the trial of certain felonies the introduction of witnesses for the accused "for the better information of the consciences of the jury and justices." But in 1679, Chief Justice Scroggs still announced as the rule that "in no capital case against the king can the witnesses for the prisoner be sworn."[32] Similarly Sir Matthew Hale in his *Pleas of the Crown*: "Regularly the evidence for the prisoner in cases capital is given without oath, though the reason thereof is not manifest."[33] Not until after the Glorious Revolution did the defendant attain the right to have his witnesses heard under oath.[34]

The inequality in the provision of professional legal advice persisted even longer. In civil cases and on the trial of charges of misdemeanor, the parties were entitled to the aid of counsel in eliciting facts from the witnesses and in presenting their case to the court and the jury. But from an early period persons accused of treason or felony were refused the help of counsel. Holdsworth reports that "the manner in which the accused was either deprived of or hampered in his liberty of defense . . . [was] not only tolerated but even applauded by a large body of public opinion . . . because the government was so weak and its enemies so strong that it was felt, not without reason, that it must take every advantage of its enemies."[35]

Not until after the Revolution of 1688 did the stability of the government enable it to become more generous, and counsel was then permitted to appear on behalf of persons accused of treason.[36] But the spirit in which the criminal law was being administered becomes plainly apparent from the case of Sir William Parkins, who was tried for high treason after the passage of this remedial statute but one day before it was to take effect. He asked to be allowed counsel and quoted the preamble of the new law to the effect that such allowance was just and reasonable. Lord Holt, in denying the prisoner's request, declared that he had to administer the law as he found it, and could not anticipate the operation of an Act of Parliament, not even by a single day. Parkins was duly convicted and executed.[37] And not until 1836 was the privilege of counsel extended to persons accused of felonies other than treason.[38]

Nor was the prisoner originally entitled to receive a copy of the indictment which in form and in fact was a presentment to the King on which the King took action. This rule was changed as to treason by 7 Wm. III, c. 3 (1695), but continued to apply in general felony trials. Holdsworth suggests that "there can be little doubt that [the rule] was retained because, taken in connection with the rule that the prisoner could not be advised by counsel, it prevented him from taking some of those captious objections to the indictment which . . . were possible . . . ."[39]

Yet while the Crown was thus assured of procedural advantages intended to enable it to cope with the lawlessness of the age the balance continued to be maintained by the public character of the trial and, eventually, by the independence of the jury.[40] Initially, when the jury was still in the nature of witnesses, the civil juror who "found wrong" was liable to be "attainted." Subsequently when the jury was required to render a unanimous verdict,[41] all the jury were held equally liable.[42] For centuries the great check upon juries in civil cases lay in these proceedings of attaint, in which the original parties and also the first jury were parties, and where a larger jury, made up of knights or other persons of greater status than the members of the first jury, passed again on the same issue, and if they found contrary to the first finding, thereby convicted the first jury of perjury.[43] In criminal cases attaint apparently did not lie: the defendant, who had either in fact or, in later years, by presumption of law consented to be tried by the jury, was thereby precluded from impugning their findings. The King, however, in view of the advantages secured him in other procedural matters, had small need of the attaint in criminal cases.[44] The means of control of the jury available to the court were still of such stringency as to assure compliance where it was desired. The court always assumed the power to punish such forms of misconduct in jurors as separating, or eating or drinking before they had returned a verdict;[45] and fines and punishment were readily meted out to the juror who incurred the displeasure of the Crown or of the court. This was "too convenient a doctrine not to find acceptance with the Tudor sovereigns."[46] Thayer quotes from Hudson's treatise on the Star Chamber[47] that "in the reigns of H. VII., H. VIII., Queen Mary and the beginning of Queen Elizabeth's reign, there was scarce one term pretermitted but some grand inquest or jury was fined for acquitting felons or murderers; in which case lay no attaint."[48] These were welcome precedents for the Stuart kings. Even after the abolition of the Star Chamber, jurors continued to be rebuked and fined for failure to find as directed by the court.

But the practice was incurring increasing disapproval and in 1667 was formally condemned by resolution in the House of Commons.⁴⁹ At last, three years later, the jury was freed of court domination by the decision in *Bushell's Case*.⁵⁰ Edward Bushell was one of the jurors who acquitted William Penn and William Mead, who had been indicted for holding an unlawful assembly in the streets.⁵¹ As the verdict was against the magistrate's direction he fined each of the jurors and, on Bushell's refusing to pay the fine, committed him to jail. Bushell thereupon sued out a writ of *habeas corpus* and was set free by Chief Justice Vaughan, whose opinion marks the end of court fines or punishment for intractable jurors. "Since that time no juryman has been called in question for giving a verdict according to his own judgment."⁵² The jury had become independent judges of fact.

Chapter II

Colonial Experiences and the Adoption of the Sixth Amendment

The adventurers and settlers who landed at Jamestown and Plymouth Rock in the opening years of the seventeenth century were not men learned in the law nor, indeed, particularly sympathetic with the practices and methods of the law. The system of courts which they had known in England was one of arbitrariness and harshness. "It is difficult to realize," says one writer,

the unfairness, the brutality, the almost savage satisfaction in conviction and execution that characterized criminal prosecutions in England up to well along in the nineteenth century. You may recall the denunciation of the English Judges by John Bright given by Henry Adams, in his *Education*: "For two hundred years," he said, "the judges in England sat on the bench condemning to the penalty of death, every man, woman and child who stole property to the value of five shillings and during that time not one judge remonstrated against the law."[1]

The first execution ordered among the colonists is striking evidence regarding the stringency of the criminal law of the realm as it then existed: for a rather insignificant act of insubordination "James Read the Blacksmith" was condemned to be hanged within a few months of the initial Jamestown landing.[2] The law as it stood had little to recommend it to the individualists of the New World.

That the English law should follow the colonists to their new homes was apparently intended by the Crown, for the Elizabethan patents to Gilbert[3] and Raleigh[4] already contain statements to the effect that the colonists settled under these grants should possess the same constitutional rights as were enjoyed by Englishmen in the homeland. The first Virginia charter by James I in 1606, recited that

we do for Us, our Heirs and Successors, Declare by these Presents, that all and every the Persons, being our Subjects, which shall dwell and inhabit within every or any of the several Colonies and Plantations, and every of their children, which shall happen to be born within any of the Limits and Precincts of the said several Colonies and Plantations, shall HAVE and enjoy all Liberties, Franchises, and Immunities, within any of our other Dominions, to all Intents and Purposes, as if they had been abiding and born, within this our Realm of *England*, or any other of our said Dominions.[5]

Similar language may be found in most of the later charters.

Among the rights of Englishmen, trial by jury had by then won undeniable recognition. Indeed, until Brunner's researches[6] exploded the theory, it was generally believed that trial by jury was an institution of such long standing as to antedate the Great Charter of King John. Thus, e.g., Story, in an oft-quoted passage, asserted that

It seems hardly necessary in this place to expatiate upon the antiquity or importance of the trial by jury in criminal cases. It was from very early times insisted on by our ancestors in the parent country, as the great bulwark of their civil and political liberties, and watched with an unceasing jealousy and solicitude. The right constitutes one of the fundamental articles of Magna Charta, in which it is declared, "*nullus homo capiatur, nec imprisonetur, aut exulet, aut aliquo modo destruatur, etc.; nisi per legale judicium parium suorum, vel per legem terrae;*" no man shall be arrested, nor imprisoned, nor banished, nor deprived of life, etc., but by the judgment of his peers, or by the law of the land.[7] The judgment of his peers here alluded to, and commonly called in the quaint language of former times a trial *per pais,* or trial by the country, is the trial by jury, who are called the peers of the party accused, being of the like condition and equality in the state. When our more immediate ancestors removed to America, they brought this great privilege with them, as their birthright and inheritance, as a part of that admirable common law, which had fenced round and interposed barriers on every side against the approaches of arbitrary power.[8]

We know today that this statement was doubly in error. It appears well established at present that trial by jury was not known in its present form or function when the barons forced King John's signature at Runnymede.[9] This, however, does not diminish the significance of the belief generally held in the seventeenth and eighteenth centuries that trial by jury was among the fundamental rights guaranteed by the Great Charter. Considering the almost religious veneration accorded to that document by the great majority of the people both in England and in this country,[10] it is more important to recognize the fact that our ancestors associated trial by jury with this renowned mainspring of liberty than to insist that in so doing they were guilty of historical error.

It may be more significant that modern research has led to another correction of Justice Story's statement. The varied reception which trial by jury received among the early colonists took on added significance as historical scholarship compelled a reexamination of the traditional juristic theory which assumes a wholesale transfer of the common law from the mother country to the colonies.[11] Thus the development of jury trial in America reflects the fact that there was at first "a period of rude, untechnical popular law,"[12] an attempt by laymen to order their affairs by themselves in an atmosphere of pronounced hostility toward the legal profession and their methods.[13] The jury trial of colonial days is, therefore, not a rigid copy of its English prototype but rather the result of variegated experiences, experimentation, and adaptation. The different practices so established were sufficiently divergent to allow only the most general statement with regard to jury trial to be included in the Constitution framed at Philadelphia, lest local customs be offended.[14]

Juries were impanelled from the earliest period on. Reinsch, after extensive research in the Massachusetts Colonial Records, found evidence of a jury trial a few months after Winthrop's arrival.[15] And the only extant item of legislation of the first five years of the Plymouth Colony is an ordinance of 1623 which provides among other things "that all criminal facts . . . shall be tried by the verdict of twelve honest men, to be impanelled by authority, in form of a jury upon their oaths."[16] The Massachusetts Body of Liberties (1641) confirms this public policy with the declaration in Article 29 that "in all actions at law, it shall be the libertie of the plaintiff and the defendant, by mutual consent, to choose whether they will be tried by the Bench or by a Jurie . . . the like libertie shall be granted to all persons in Criminal cases."[17] But Reinsch notes [18] that the system was by no means unquestionably accepted and, for a time, seems to have had a very insecure tenure. Thus only one year after its apparent guarantee in the Body of Liberties the retention or rejection of jury trial was the subject of a special commission of inquiry; and it seems that juries may even have been abolished for a time, as a 1652 resolve decrees that "the law about juries is repealed and juries are in force again."[19]

In Connecticut, the jury system was modified by elimination of the unanimity requirement. Upon continued failure to agree, a simple majority of the jury could decide the issue, and in case of equal division the magistrate could cast his vote to break the tie.[20] In the New Haven Colony the institution of jury trial was at first altogether discarded.[21] Rhode Island, like Connecticut, used a modified form of jury trial.[22]

In New York, the jury came into use immediately upon the occupation by the English. The Charter of Liberties of 1683, the first statute enacted by the colonial legislature after New Amsterdam became English and framed expressly for the colony by the Duke of York, secured a jury trial to all its inhabitants.[23] In practice, however, and particularly during the early period, jury trials were very informal, more after the manner of simple arbitrations, and verdicts were often rendered in alternative form.[24]

In both parts of [New] Jersey, East and West, trial by jury found recognition in the early fundamental laws. In West Jersey, where Quakerism predominated and Penn's influence was strong, the charter provisions demonstrate clearly the popular aversion to the legal profession; thus chapter XXII of the Charter of Fundamental Laws of 1676 reads:

That the tryals of all causes, civil and criminal, shall be heard and decided by the virdict [sic] or judgment of twelve honest men of the neighborhood, only to be summoned and presented by the sheriff of that division, or propriety where the fact or trespass is committed;

and continues immediately:

that no person or persons shall be compelled to fee any attorney or councillor to plead his cause, but that all persons have free liberty to plead his [sic] own cause, if he please.... [25]

The trend toward popular, nontechnical administration of justice is also apparent in the terms of the provision in the same charter guaranteeing public trials,[26] and in the predominant position of the jury "in whom only the judgment resided," whose verdict was beyond control or direction by the judges, and who could themselves pronounce judgment if the judges should refuse to do so.[27] Provisions similar to those of West Jersey are to be found in the Fundamental Constitutions for the Province of East Jersey (1683):

That no person or persons within the said Province shall be taken and imprisoned, or be devised of his freehold, free custom or liberty, or be outlawed or exiled, or any other way destroyed; nor shall they be condemn'd or judgment pass'd upon them but by lawful judgment of their peers: neither shall justice nor right be bought or sold, defered [sic] or delayed, to any person whatsoever: in order to which by the laws of the land, all tryals shall be by twelve men, and as near as it may be, peers and equals, and of the neighborhood, and men without just exception.... And in all courts persons of all perswasions [sic] may freely appear in their own way, and according to their own manner, and there personally plead their own causes themselves, or if unable, by their friends, no person being allowed to take money for pleading or advice in such cases.[28]

These articles reflect the same tenor as those of Pennsylvania, whose system of colonial codes showed from the first a desire for settled legal relations and a solicitude for fairness and stability. The "Laws agreed upon in England" for Penn's dominion (1682) decree public trials[29] by a jury of twelve,[30] and guarantee the defendant's right to have his case heard in court.[31] But it would be misleading to judge from this that the methods of criminal procedure in colonial Pennsylvania were more formally anchored than in the other colonies. Indeed, the very exercise of criminal jurisdiction appears to have been placed in dispute by the provision, which appears in the two earliest Frames of Government, that criminals might be tried by the General Assembly through impeachment proceedings.[32] And such trials as took place in the courts were most informal in nature. Juries numbered six or seven members, whose verdict was reached by majority decision. An informal statement of the matter at issue was made, and though some technical language was used, there was little discrimination, even the distinctions between civil and criminal cases not being clearly drawn. "The administration of justice was rather founded upon the ideas of the magistrate than on any rules of positive law."[33]

A similar informality and uncertainty of proceedings appears to have prevailed in the early period in the Carolinas,[34] until the proprietors undertook to impose their control through the celebrated Fundamental Constitutions.[35] The pertinent articles of this document are illustrative of the reactionary tendencies for which the instrument is noted. They included, e.g., a provision that "no landgrave or cazique shall be tried for any criminal cause in any but the chief justice's court, and that by a jury of his peers";[36] an elaborate, graduated scale of property qualifications for jury service;[37] discontinuance of the common law requirement of an unanimous verdict, thus easing the way for conviction of the accused;[38] and, as in other colonies, a prohibition against the employment of professional counsel, by a clause which opens with the statement that "it shall be a base and vile thing to plead for money and reward."[39] To what extent the Fundamental Constitutions became operative is not fully known. However, it may be assumed that their effect may not have been too far-reaching, particularly in view of the absence of any system of circuit courts in the colony. In South Carolina, for example, all judicial business was centered in the city of Charleston; the colonial court sat there and no courts were open anywhere else in the province. Such lawyers as were in practice resided in Charleston only. The result was that large sections of the colony were virtually without administration of justice and hence depended for the maintenance of law and order on self-appointed associations of "regulators."[40]

More details are available to the general reader with regard to the administration of justice in colonial Virginia than any other of the New World settlements.[41] These accounts further illustrate the informality of the early period, the temporary emergence of popular, nontechnical justice, accompanied as in the other colonies by manifestations of strong opposition against the professional lawyer. The courts of Virginia initially exercised many powers and discharged many duties of a nonjudicial character, a practice which even today has not entirely disappeared. On the other hand, the legislative branch of the colonial government was equally ready to exercise judicial functions.[42] Thus the first House of Burgesses on August 3, 1619, heard and adjudged a criminal complaint by Captain William Powell against his servant Thomas Garnett.[43] Nor were the proceedings in the courts of Virginia always in full conformity with the law of England. Although the Instructions of King James (1606) provided specifically that in all capital cases the question of guilt or innocence should be decided by "twelve honest and indifferent persons sworn upon the Evangelists,"[44] we find in 1630 trials being conducted before juries of thirteen and fourteen members.[45] More importantly, jury trials in Virginia differed from those in the mother country with respect to the requirement that the jury be drawn from the vicinage. As all cases involving loss of life or limb had to be tried before the General Court in Jamestown, it was frequently difficult, if not impossible, to secure jurors from the neighborhood where the crime had been committed. For some time, the jury seems to have been selected from among the bystanders at the court at Jamestown, but by statute (2 Hen. 63-64) in 1662 the problem was met by providing that the sheriff of the accused's county was to summon six freeholders from the neighborhood for jury service (for the inducive fee of twenty pounds of tobacco per day), while the other six members of the panel would be selected from the court's bystanders as had been the custom.[46] A strict property qualification further limited the number of those eligibles for jury service.[47]

The consolidation of governmental power in the colonies which was generally accomplished in the closing years of the seventeenth century and during the reign of Queen Anne also brought about greater stability in the administration of justice. Professional lawyers assumed their place and gained recognition in colonial society.[48] Except in Delaware, the bench, as in England, became the exclusive domain of those trained in the law.[49] Many of those lawyers had received their training at the Inns of Court in London[50] and brought with them, applied, and enforced the procedural modifications enacted in England after the Revolution of 1688.[51] Thus these reforms, the new liberality as to witnesses and counsel for the accused, became associated in the minds of the people with the aims of greater freedom that had caused the overthrow of the Stuarts and Tories. No longer could the royal prerogative overawe the courts; indeed, it was the aim now, as declared for Pennsylvania, "that all Criminals shall have the same Privileges of Witnesses and Council [sic] as their Prosecutors."[52]

To the American colonists the meaning of this sentence was not what it would have been to their English cousins. For early in the eighteenth century the American system of judicial administration adopted an institution which was (and to some extent still is) unknown in England: while rejecting the fundamental juristic concepts upon which continental Europe's inquisitorial system of criminal procedure is predicated, the colonies borrowed one of its institutions, the public prosecutor, and grafted it upon the body of English (accusatorial) procedure embodied in the common law.[53] Presumably, this innovation was brought about by the lack of lawyers, particularly in the newly settled regions, and by the increasing distances between the colonial capitals on the eastern seaboard and the ever-receding western frontier. Its result was that, at a time when virtually all but treason trials in England were still in the nature of suits between private parties, the accused in the colonies faced a government official whose specific function it was to prosecute, and who was incomparably more familiar than the accused with the problems of procedure, the idiosyncrasies of juries, and, last but not least, the personnel of the court. The balance would continue to be weighted in favor of the Crown unless extreme vigilance was practiced to safeguard the precarious privileges so recently granted to the accused.

Thus when the Continental Congress declared[54] "that the respective colonies are entitled to the common law, and more especially to the great and inestimable privilege of being tried by their peers of the vicinage, according to the course of that law," the common law so appealed to must be understood to include not only trial by a jury of twelve men of the vicinage but also publicity of the proceedings, and the right to witnesses and to the assistance of counsel; in short, all the recognized rights of the accused. The denial of these rights was among the grievances complained of in the Declaration of Independence.[55] The inviolability of these rights was asserted in the constitutional documents of most of the new states, which, while differing in details and degree of emphasis, sounded a common note in including, among the fundamental rights of the individual, guarantees against arbitrary practices in criminal proceedings, safeguards to counteract the might of government when it called the individual lawbreaker before the bar of justice.

The Declaration of Rights of the new state of Maryland (1776), after reiterating, in language borrowed from the Continental Congress's declaration of 1774, the right of its inhabitants to the common law of England and trial by jury, proclaimed "that the trial of facts where they arise, is one of the greatest securities of the lives, liberties and estates of the people," and then enumerated the rights which every man had in criminal proceedings: to be informed of the accusation against him; to receive a copy of the indictment in time to permit him to prepare his defense; to be allowed counsel; to be confronted with the witnesses against him; to have process for his own witnesses; to examine the witnesses, for and against him, on oath; and to have "a speedy trial by an impartial jury, without whose unanimous consent he ought not to be found guilty."[56]

In North Carolina, the first state constitution, in its Declaration of Rights, stated

that, in all criminal proceedings, every man has a right to be informed of the accusation against him, and to confront the accusers and witnesses with other testimony, and shall not be compelled to give evidence against himself,

and

that no freeman shall be convicted of any crime, but by the unanimous verdict of a jury of good and lawful men, in open court, as heretofore used.[57]

The New Jersey constitution of 1776 echoed the words of Pennsylvania's Charter of 1701 in its Article XVII:

That all criminals shall be admitted to the same privileges of witnesses and counsel, as their prosecutors are or shall be entitled to;

while in Article XXII it guarantees

. . . that the inestimable right of trial by jury shall remain confirmed as a part of the law of this State, without repeal, forever.[58]

South Carolina furnishes a telling example of the high esteem in which Magna Carta was held at the time, in a single brief article of its constitution which obviously was intended to parallel the wording of the Great Charter:

That no freeman of this State be taken or imprisoned, or disseized of his freehold, liberties or privileges, or outlawed, exiled, or deprived of his life, liberty, or property, but by the judgment of his peers or by the law of the land.[59]

Georgia included in its constitution of 1777 two disconnected paragraphs, one of which stated the inviolability of the right to trial by jury, while the other guaranteed a trial within the county of commission.[60] John Jay's constitution for the state of New York (1777) assured the accused's right to counsel and affirmed that

. . . trial by jury, in all cases in which it hath heretofore been used in the colony of New York shall be established and remain inviolate forever.[61]

Earliest in point of adoption, the Virginia Bill of Rights as framed by George Mason presents in one compact article (Article 8) a detailed list of rights extended to the criminally accused. "In all capital or criminal prosecutions," this article reads,

a man hath a right to demand the cause and nature of his accusation, to be confronted with the accusers and witnesses, to call for evidence in his favour, and to a speedy trial by an impartial jury of twelve men of his vicinage, without whose unanimous consent he cannot be found guilty; nor can he be compelled to give evidence against himself.[62]

The most detailed provisions are those contained in the Declaration of Rights of Massachusetts (1780) and the largely identical language of the Bill of Rights of New Hampshire (1784). Elaborately and circumspectly phrased, these documents in essence guaranteed the accused the right to know the nature of the accusation, to decline self-incrimination, to present his own evidence, to meet the witnesses against him, and to have the assistance of counsel; and in words that hark back to Magna Carta they reaffirmed the right to trial by jury or by the law of the land. In each instance, a separate article limited criminal trials to the vicinity where the alleged offense had taken place.[63]

The New Hampshire articles numbered almost three hundred words; while South Carolina used less than fifty words to cover the same subject. This numerical difference alone is indicative of the diversity of substance to be found among the several states. As the perception and interpretation of the common law varied in the several states, as criminal procedures were more or less fair or arbitrary, so differed the sense of urgency with which the inhabitants of the different states viewed the problem of protecting the accused. Hence it is not surprising that the delegates who convened at Philadelphia in the spring of 1787 made no effort to embody details of criminal procedure in the document they were about to propose to the nation. The original Virginia Plan contained no references whatsoever to the procedure to be had in criminal cases. The New Jersey Plan, however, with an eye toward the preservation of the rights of the states in judicial matters, proposed

that no person shall be liable to be tried for any criminal offense, committed within any of the United States, in any other state than that wherein the offense shall be committed, nor be deprived of the privilege of trial by jury, by virtue of any law of the United States.[64]

A similar provision was included in Alexander Hamilton's draft;[65] and Pinckney's outline suggested the same two guarantees, and in addition would have stipulated that trials should be open and public.[66]

The Committee on Detail adopted the essence of these suggestions and embodied them in its draft constitution as section 4 of Article XI, in language resembling Pinckney's draft:

The trial of criminal offences (except in cases of impeachment) shall be in the State where they shall be committed; and shall be by Jury.[67]

Without much debate, this section was amended in Committee of the Whole in order to "provide for trial by jury of offenses committed out of any State."[68] It was in this amended form that the provision was sent to the Committee on Style, which, without further change, incorporated it in the Judiciary Article of the final document as the third clause of the second section.[69]

The opponents of the proposed Federal Constitution not only protested the absence of a specific Bill of Rights[70] but also claimed that those guarantees already included were inadequate in nature and scope. The jury trial clause of Article III was thus subjected to severe criticism in the debates over the ratification of the Constitution. The attack on this provision used several different approaches. First, those advocating rejection of the proposed document pointed to the appellate jurisdiction of the federal courts and predicted that it would, "in its operation, destroy the trial by jury. The verdict of an impartial jury will be reversed by judges unacquainted with the circumstances . . . ."[71] But the most vocal objections were aimed at the lack of a narrowly drawn vicinage requirement and of an explicit provision saving the right to challenge prospective jurors. In the Virginia convention, Patrick Henry exclaimed that he would have preferred to see trial by jury left out altogether "than have it so vaguely and equivocally provided for."[72] With the forceful eloquence for which he was so justly famed Henry declared that

this great privilege . . . is prostrated by this paper. Juries from the vicinage being not secured, this right is in reality sacrificed. All is gone . . . Why do we love this trial by jury? Because it prevents the hand of oppression from cutting you off . . . . Has not your mother country magnanimously preserved this noble privilege upwards of a thousand years? . . . And shall Americans give up that which nothing could induce the English people to relinquish? The idea is abhorrent to my mind . . . .[73]

Grayson, seconding Henry's attack, cited the example of Rome to show that abandonment of trial by jury would lead to servitude. "It may be laid down as a rule," he stated, that, where the governing power possesses an unlimited control over the venue, no man's life is in safety. . . . The idea which I call true vicinage is, that a man shall be tried by his neighbors. But the idea here is, that he may be tried in any part of the state. . . . The jury may come from any part of the state . . . . The conclusion . . . is that they can hang any one they please, by having a jury to suit their purposes. . . .[74]

Similar language had earlier been heard in the Massachusetts convention, where Holmes had not only addressed himself to the deficiencies of the jury-trial provisions but also deplored the absence of other procedural safeguards:

It is a maxim universally admitted, that the safety of the subject consists in having a right to a trial as free and impartial as the lot of humanity will admit of. Does the Constitution make provision for such a trial? I think not; for in a criminal process, a person shall not have a right to insist on a trial in the vicinity where the fact was committed, where a jury of the peers would, from their local situation, have an opportunity to form a judgment of the character of the person charged with the crime, and also to judge of the credibility of the witnesses. There a person must be tried by a jury of strangers; a jury who may be interested in his conviction; and he may, by reason of the distance of his residence from the place of trial, be incapable of making such a defense as he is, in justice, entitled to, and which he could avail himself of, if his trial was in the same county where the crime is said to have been committed. . . .

But what makes the matter still more alarming is, that the mode of criminal process is to be pointed out by Congress, and they have no constitutional check on them, except that the trial is to be by a jury; but who this jury is to be, how qualified, where to live, how appointed, or by what rules to regulate their procedure, we are ignorant as of yet; . . .

The mode of trial is altogether indetermined; whether the criminal is to be allowed the benefit of counsel; whether he is to be allowed to meet his accuser face to face; whether he is to be allowed to confront the witnesses; and to have the advantage of cross-examination, we are not yet told. These are matters of by no means small consequence; yet we have not the smallest constitutional security that we shall be allowed the exercise of these privileges . . . .[75]

In rebuttal of these attacks the proponents of the new Constitution emphatically denied any intention of infringing or abolishing trial by jury, and John Marshall, speaking in the Virginia convention, even asserted that, by virtue of the constitutional provision, trial by jury would be more secure in the United States than in England, for "what part of their constitution is there that the Parliament cannot change?"[76] Various replies were made to those critics who had complained of the lack of a vicinage requirement. Madison suggested that it was impractical: "Suppose a rebellion in a whole district; would it not be impossible to get a jury?"[77] Pendleton in the Virginia convention and Gore in that of Massachusetts pointed out that the role of the jury was not, as contended, to judge character and personalities but to find a verdict on the facts presented in court; knowledge of the neighborhood was no longer essential to the performance of their functions.[78] In all available convention reports, wherever the question of jury trial was raised, allusion was also made to the fact that "it was only by reason of the diversity of practice in the various states that a more detailed constitutional provision was not used,"[79] that "the rule could not have been drawn more narrowly without changing the rule of some of the states."[80]

It may be doubted that the objections raised against the trial by jury clause of the original Constitution, as they are reflected in the existing records of the state conventions, would in themselves have been sufficient to bring about the addition of an amendment to the Constitution. Still these criticisms, part and parcel of the louder and wider clamor for a Bill of Rights, indicated that the public continued to demand the maintenance of a fair balance in criminal trials, and to that end the protection of the rights of the accused.

With the din of these debates still resounding, the nation turned to the establishment of its government, faced at the outset with the task of "impregnably fortifying . . . the characteristic rights of freemen . . . [in order that] public harmony be . . . advantageously promoted."[81] For, as was said in a leading Supreme Court opinion nearly four score years later,

so strong was the sense of the country of the importance [of these rights], and so jealous were the people that these rights, highly prized, might be denied them by implication, that when the original Constitution was proposed for adoption it encountered severe opposition; and, but for the belief that it would be amended so as to embrace them, it would never have been ratified.[82]

The preparation and introduction in the First Congress of the amendments that were to discharge this political obligation was undertaken by James Madison, who, while campaigning for Congress, had pledged himself to the support of a Bill of Rights to be added to the Constitution. Although himself not convinced of the constitutional necessity for such amendments, he was highly sensitive to their political desirability. "Amendments," he wrote to a political friend during this election campaign, "if pursued with a proper moderation and in proper mode, will not only be safe, but may serve the double purpose of satisfying the minds of well meaning opponents, and of providing additional guards in favour of liberty."[83]

In the formulation of the amendments to be proposed Madison was able to utilize the results of similar efforts in the several states. From five of the ratifying states and North Carolina there had come a total of 103 desired changes in the Constitution.[84] Four of the states had included provisions concerning trial by jury and rights of the accused among their proposals. Maryland had submitted a brief but flexible article:

That there shall be a trial by jury in criminal cases, according to the course of proceeding in the state where the offense was commited; and that there be no appeal from matter of fact, or second trial after acquittal; but this provision shall not extend to such cases as may arise in the government of the land or naval forces.[85]

In New York it had been proposed that among the rights "which cannot be abridged or violated" there should be included that (except in the government of the land and naval forces, and of the militia when in actual service, and in cases of impeachment) a presentment or indictment by a grand jury ought to be observed as a necessary preliminary to the trial of all crimes cognizable by the judiciary of the United States, and such trial should be speedy, public, and by an impartial jury of the county where the crime was committed; and that no person can be found guilty without the unanimous consent of such jury. But in cases of crimes not committed within any county of any of the United States, and in cases of crimes committed within any county in which a general insurrection may prevail, or which may be in possession of a foreign enemy, the inquiry and trial may be in such county as the Congress shall by law direct; which county, in the two cases last mentioned, should be as near as conveniently may be to that county in which the crime may have been committed;— and that, in all criminal prosecutions, the accused ought to be informed of the cause and nature of his accusation, to be confronted with his accusers and the witnesses against him, to have the means of producing his witnesses, and the assistance of counsel for his defense; and should not be compelled to give evidence against himself.[86]

The convention of Virginia had recommended the incorporation in the Constitution of the respective clause of their own Bill of Rights, with only two modifications, the addition of the right to counsel and a parenthetical clause exempting the land and naval forces from the operation of the section.[87] North Carolina made the same proposal in identical language.[88]

Madison correlated these various proposals, eliminating those most likely to meet with opposition,[89] and on June 8, 1789, introduced his amendments in the form of nine propositions in the House of Representatives.[90] Three of these proposals referred, in parts, to matters of criminal procedure.

By one amendment Madison proposed to expunge in its entirety the trial-by-jury clause of the original Constitution, which had met with such criticism in the Virginia and other conventions, and to replace it by a much longer and more detailed clause providing for trial by an impartial jury of the vicinage, guaranteeing the right to challenge, and affirming the requirement of a unanimous verdict for conviction "and other accustomed requisites."[91]

By another proposition trial by jury was to be protected against impairment by any state along with freedom of speech, press, and religion.[92]

Still another proposal was to insert[93] a section guaranteeing procedural safeguards other than jury trial. This proposition was drafted in these words:

> In all criminal prosecutions, the accused shall enjoy the right to a speedy and public trial; to be informed of the nature and cause of the accusation; to be confronted with his accusers and with the witnesses against him; to have compulsory process for obtaining witnesses in his favor, and to have the assistance of counsel for his defense,[94]

—language which, with only two changes, eventually was adopted as the Sixth Amendment.

On July 21, 1789, Madison's proposals were referred to a Committee of Eleven on which each state was represented by one member, Madison being the member from Virginia. This committee completed its work on July 28, and on August 13 the House, in Committee of the Whole, began consideration of the proposed amendments, examining each one separately.[95]

The proposed restriction on state action was discussed first, on August 17. Tucker of South Carolina was the principal speaker in opposition, while Madison defended the proposition, calling it "the most valuable amendment in the whole list. If there was any reason to restrain the government of the United States from infringing upon these essential rights, it was equally necessary that they should be secured against the State Governments." Livermore of New Hampshire moved to rephrase the resolution so as to read:

> The equal rights of conscience, the freedom of speech and the press, and the right of trial by jury in criminal cases, shall not be infringed by any state,

and in this form it was passed by the Committee of the Whole.[96]

On the same and the following day, the other two articles touching on criminal procedure were presented for consideration. The Committee of Eleven had changed the arrangement of these two articles by combining them into one proposition—the seventh—consisting of two clauses, to take the place of the deleted clause 3 of Article III, section 2.[97] The principal opposition to this proposition was furnished by Burke of South Carolina: on August 17 he moved to permit an accused to put off the trial to the next session of the court provided he made it appear to the court that the evidence of the witnesses, for whom process was granted but not served, was material to his defense; and on August 18, he moved to replace the word "vicinage" by "district or county within which the offense was committed"; this change, he maintained, would be in conformity with South Carolina practice. Both motions failed of passage, but a proposal by Livermore to secure to the criminal the right of being tried in the state where the offense was committed was accepted.[98]

The House of Representatives made no further changes in these articles and passed them, in the form agreed to by the Committee of the Whole, on August 20.[99] On August 22, they were referred to a Committee of Three (Benson, Sherman, Sedgwick) appointed to arrange the amendments, presumably to conform with the House decision to add the amendments as supplements rather than to change the text of the original document.[100] This committee reported on August 24, and the re-arranged amendments—seventeen in number—were ordered sent to the Senate on the same day.[101]

The Senate consideration of the amendments began on September 2 and lasted for one week.[102] Unfortunately Senator Maclay of Pennsylvania, whose Journal is the principal source of information on the proceedings of the Senate in the First Congress, was ill during the period the amendments were debated in the Senate,[103] and hence we are without knowledge of the Senate's action on, and individual senators' reaction to, the proposed amendments. Available records merely reveal that when the amendments were returned to the House on September 10, they contained several changes and deletions and were accompanied by a request for a conference of managers for the two houses.[104]

Madison reported this to Edmund Pendleton in a letter which identified the trial-by-jury provisions as a principal stumbling block. "The Senate," he wrote,

have sent back the plan of amendments with some alterations which strike in my opinion at the most salutary articles. In many of the States juries, even in criminal cases, are taken from the State at large; in others, from districts of considerable extent; in very few from the county alone. Hence a . . . [manuscript torn here] like to the restraint with respect to *vicinage*, which has produced a negative on that clause. . . . Several others have had a similar fate. The difficulty of uniting the minds of men accustomed to think and act differently can only be conceived by those who have witnessed it.[105]

On September 21, 1789, the House appointed as its managers for the conference Madison, Sherman, and Vining.[106] Again a letter from Madison to Pendleton is our sole source of information on the negotiations of the conference committee: "The Senate," reported Madison to Virginia's Chief Justice on September 23,

are . . . inflexible in opposing a definition of the *locality* of Juries. The vicinage they contend is either too vague or too strict a term, too vague if depending on limits to be fixed by the pleasure of the law, too strict if limited to the County. It was proposed to insert after the word Juries, "with the accustomed requisites," leaving the definition to be construed according to the judgment of professional men. Even this could not be obtained. The truth is that in most of the States the practice is different, and hence the irreconcilable difference of ideas on the subject.[107]

The conference committee apparently failed to achieve any compromise on the particular subject, for when their report was returned to the House on September 24, the criminal procedure article was still among the points of disagreement. The House insisted on its version, and by withdrawing its objections to all but one other of the Senate's changes succeeded in placing its phrasing of this article into the amendments. It was in this form that the article was submitted to, and ratified by, the states.[108]

Any attempt to trace the exact development of the finished product, to ascribe with definitive certainty the authorship of specific words, or to place the responsibility for its ultimate form and arrangement, continues to the present to be frustrated and hampered by the complete lack of information on the proceedings in the Senate. Among Madison's original propositions, three, as we have seen, were related to the subject of criminal procedure. After minor changes by the Committee of Eleven they were adopted by the House and sent to the Senate. The Committee of Three, whose task it had been to rearrange the articles as supplements rather than substitution for the original text, had made no significant changes in the wording. Of the three propositions sent to the Senate we hear no more of the original fifth ("No state shall infringe . . ."), and it may be assumed that it was deleted by the upper chamber. From Madison's correspondence quoted above we know that what he had introduced as a substitute for the trial-by-jury clause of the original Constitution met with strong objections in the Senate. There is, on the other hand, no evidence of any change by the Senate in the provisions of the third proposition, the syllabus of procedural rights which Madison had taken from the recommendations of his own state, Virginia. That article remained unchanged (except for the Committee of Eleven's deletion of the requirement of confrontation by the accuser) until, following the joint conference, it appeared minus the exemption from its operation of the land and naval forces, and with the added proviso for an "impartial jury of the State and district wherein the crime shall have been committed, which district shall have been previously ascertained by law," words clearly intended to replace some of the language of the jury article so strenuously opposed by the Senate. Where, when, and by whom this addition was made does not appear from the available records. It is just as likely that this modification may originally have been suggested as a possible compromise in the conference committee, or that it was proposed upon the floor of the House, or agreed upon in informal discussion.

The available information thus permits only the following limited conclusion as to the immediate genesis of the Sixth Amendment: in its basic structure, compactness of arrangement, and enumeration of rights the amendment follows the recommendation of the ratifying convention of Virginia, which in turn was but an amplification of the corresponding section of the Bill of Rights drawn up by George Mason; the exact time and place, however, at which the vicinage provision was inserted, and by whose pen or suggestion, remains unknown until further historical data are uncovered.

Chapter III

Scope and Application of the Amendment

The Sixth Amendment, as proposed by Congress and ratified by the states,[1] enumerated certain features of procedure to which an accused should be entitled "in all criminal prosecutions." What these, the opening words of the amendment, could be taken to mean would determine, therefore, where and how far the rights guaranteed by the amendment could be invoked. Hence, before the substance of these rights is to be ascertained, it appears appropriate to inquire into the judicial gloss by which the words "in all criminal prosecutions" have been translated into concrete limitations on the scope and application of the amendment.

The Constitution contains references to criminal trials not only in the Sixth Amendment but also in the Judiciary Article[2] and in the Fifth Amendment.[3] Their terminology is sufficiently different to have invited comparison and contrast. Thus Frankfurter and Corcoran, in their pioneer study on "Petty Federal Offenses and the Constitutional Guarantee of Trial by Jury,"[4] examined at length the verbal discrepancy between the Third Article's use of "crimes" and the Sixth Amendment's term "criminal prosecutions." They concluded that no legal significance could be attached to this difference in wording.

On the other hand, a distinction has been recognized to exist between a "criminal case" under the Fifth Amendment, and a "criminal prosecution" under the Sixth. In a case in 1892,[5] involving the applicability of the Fifth Amendment's self-incrimination clause to grand jury proceedings, it was urged by the government that "criminal case" should be interpreted to mean the same as "criminal prosecution" in the Sixth Amendment. Under such an interpretation the proceedings before the grand jury would have been no part of the "case," and the accused therein not entitled to the constitutional protection against self-incrimination. The Supreme Court, speaking through Mr. Justice Blatchford, rejected this view. "The guarantees of the Sixth Amendment," the opinion stated,

are distinctly intended for the protection of a person who is accused and who is to be tried by a petit jury. A criminal prosecution under Article 6 of the amendments is much narrower than a "criminal case," under Article 5 of the amendments.[6]

Although both the Judiciary Article and the Sixth Amendment have reference to the place of jury trial in criminal proceedings, their wording in that respect is not identical. Article III, section 2, clause 3 of the original Constitution is couched in positive and mandatory language: "The trial of all crimes . . . *shall* be by jury." The Sixth Amendment, on the other hand, merely stipulates that "the accused . . . *shall enjoy the right*" to a trial by jury, etc.[7] In the absence of any definite information on the circumstances in which the amendment received its final form,[8] this difference and apparent inconsistency between two provisions relating to the same subject called for judicial clarification. The contention that the distinction was intentional and hence meaningful was advanced by government counsel in *Callan* v. *Wilson*.[9] "This marked change of phraseology," it was urged in that case, "could not have been adopted without an intention to convey in the amendment a sense different from that of the third article."[10] But this view was not shared by the Supreme Court, which replied through Mr. Justice Harlan: "We do not think that the amendment was intended to supplant that part of the third article which relates to trial by jury. There is no necessary conflict between them."[11] The opinion quoted from Story's *Commentaries* to the effect that the amendment "does but follow out of the established course of the common law in all trials for crimes,"[12] and concluded that it was but an enumeration of specific elements already implied in the jury clause of Article III.[13]

Justice Brewer apparently differed from Harlan, for in *Schick* v. *United States*[14] he considered the possibility that the clauses might be found to be conflicting. If that should be the case, he stated in a dictum, "The amendment must control, under the well-understood rule that the last expression of the will of the lawmaker prevails over an earlier one."[15]

As a lower court suggested only two years later, *Schick* v. *United States* did not, in itself, determine anything. It merely referred to a well-known rule of statutory interpretation to be applied "*if* there be any conflict,"[16] but at the same time left undisturbed the earlier declaration of the *Callan* case that "there is no necessary conflict."[17]

The language of *Callan* v. *Wilson* was again approvingly cited when the Supreme Court decided *Patton* v. *United States* in 1930. [18] Following closely the argument presented by counsel for the government,[19] Mr. Justice Sutherland declared that the Sixth Amendment,

which deals with trial by jury clearly in terms of privilege, although occurring later than [the provision] in respect of jury trials contained in the original Constitution, is not to be regarded as modifying or altering the earlier provision; and there is no reason for thinking such was within its purpose. The first ten amendments and the original Constitution were substantially contemporaneous and should be construed *in pari materia*.[20] So construed, the latter provision may fairly be regarded as reflecting the meaning of the former. In other words, the two provisions mean substantially the same thing.[21]

In this manner the plainly mandatory language of the original Constitution was construed to confer a right on the accused which he might freely waive. In effect, the Court thus followed the dictum of the *Schick* case, although it achieved that result inversely, by suggesting that the absence in contemporaneous literature and debates of any discussion of an intent to make the jury an inseparable and irremovable part of all criminal courts proved that such was not intended at all, but rather that it had been the Founders' desire to perpetuate an individual privilege, not a legal institution.[22] The only reason, therefore, why it was not necessary to assume that the language of the Constitution had been subjected to a modification by the amendment, was to be found in the allegation that the original wording had not been intended to mean what it said. The practical result was the same: the divergence of phraseology has been resolved by subordinating the language of Article III, section 2, clause 3, to that of the Sixth Amendment.

By this solution the Court confirmed the nature of the Sixth Amendment as a grant of rights. Against whom might this grant be asserted? The language of the amendment did not, by itself, supply an answer to this question. In common with the other articles of the Bill of Rights (except the First Amendment), it safeguarded rights of the individual but did not specify against whom such rights could be asserted. The landmark case of *Barron v. Baltimore*[23] interpreted the provisions of the entire Bill of Rights to be applicable against the federal government only and not against the states. Although in the specific instance the Court was asked to dispose only of the question of the availability of the due process clause of the Fifth Amendment as a protection against state action, the language of the opinion clearly embraced all clauses of the Bill of Rights, including, of course, those of the Sixth Amendment.

The Supreme Court confirmed this understanding of the decision when it was asked, more than thirty years later, in the case of *Twitchell* v. *Pennsylvania*,[24] to rule specifically upon the applicability of the Sixth Amendment to the states. "The scope and application of [the Fifth and Sixth] amendments," said Chief Justice Chase speaking for an unanimous Court, "are no longer subjects of discussion here. . . . The views [of *Barron* v. *Baltimore*] . . . apply to the Sixth as fully as to any other of the amendments."[25] The Supreme Court reaffirmed this opinion when it was asked to reverse, because it violated the Sixth Amendment, the sentence of an Iowa county court which had been imposed by the judge, without a jury, upon evidence in the form of affidavits. Dismissing the petition for a writ of error, the Court said, through Mr. Justice Miller: "The first eight articles of the amendments to the Constitution have reference to powers exercised by the government of the United States and not to those of the States."[26] More recently, the rule has been restated by Chief Justice Taft with an air of finality that appears to allow of no further doubt:

The Sixth Amendment to the Federal Constitution does not apply to the trial of criminal prosecutions by a State. It has been well settled for years that the first ten Amendments apply only to the procedure and trial of causes in the federal courts and are not limitations upon those in the state courts.[27]

Twitchell v. Pennsylvania was decided at the December term of 1868, only a few months after the ratification of the Fourteenth Amendment. However, the reports of the case do not indicate that any reference was made to the new amendment. Several years were to pass before the potentialities of this addendum to the Constitution began to be exploited. The first suggested extension of meaning, to include civil and personal rights through a liberal interpretation of the privileges and immunities clause, was rejected by the Court in the *Slaughter House Cases*,[28] when it held that these words did not include "the fundamental rights," with regard to which no change had been effected.[29] Yet the contention continued to be made that such had been intended, a suggestion which was forcefully presented by John Randolph Tucker in his argument before the Supreme Court on behalf of petitioners in *Spies v. Illinois*.[30] "I do not," he argued,

controvert the doctrine of this court since *Barron v. Baltimore;* but I maintain that all the declared privileges and immunities in these ten Amendments of a fundamental nature and of common law rights, not in terms applicable to Federal authority only, are privileges and immunities of citizens of the Unted States, which the Fourteenth Amendment forbids every State to abridge.

. . . A trial by an impartial jury is secured by the Fourteenth Amendment to these prisoners.[31]

The Court, without discussing the particular point, found that there was no federal question for their decision.[32] But on reiteration of the same contention in a later case the Court met the argument and declared unequivocally: "The rights protected against Federal action [by the Sixth Amendment] are not privileges and/ or immunities of United States citizenship."[33]

The Court was equally reluctant to include the procedural requirements of the Sixth Amendment in the Fourteenth Amendment's concept of "due process." The authoritative statement of this position was made by the Court in *Hurtado v. California*.[34] This case involved an indictment without grand jury of a person who was accused of murder. The case was brought to the Supreme Court of the United States, on the ground that the statute of California which authorized such a procedure deprived the accused of his life and liberty without due process of law and thus violated the Fourteenth Amendment. Mr. Justice Matthews answered this contention by a twofold argument: first, that due process was a changing concept which could not be attached to specific procedures, otherwise the progress of the law itself might be thwarted; secondly, that if the Fourteenth Amendment had been intended to secure the right to an indictment by grand jury as a prerequisite to trial in state courts, its framers would have enumerated this right in the same manner as had been done in the Fifth Amendment with regard to federal courts. "Due process of law in the latter," declared Mr. Justice Matthews,

refers to that law of the land which derives its authority from the legislative powers conferred upon Congress by the Constitution of the United States, exercised within the limits therein prescribed, and interpreted according to the principles of the common law. In the Fourteenth Amendment, by parity of reason, it refers to that law of the land in each State, which derives its authority from the inherent and reserved powers of the State, exerted within the limits of those fundamental principles of liberty and justice which lie at the base of all our civil and political institutions, and the greatest security for which resides in the right of the people to make their own laws, and alter them at their pleasure.[35]

The Court then quoted the language of Mr. Justice Bradley in *Missouri* v. *Lewis*,[36] an equal protection case from which the following dictum, lifted out of its context, was taken:

The Fourteenth Amendment does not profess to secure to all persons in the United States the benefit of the same laws and the same remedies. Great diversities in these respects may exist in two States separated only by an imaginary line. On one side there might be a right of trial by jury, and on the other side no such right. *Each state prescribes its own modes of judicial proceeding.*[37]

Mr. Justice Harlan, in his vigorous and eloquent dissent, pointed at the obvious conclusion to be drawn from these words. By expression and intimation this dictum placed the rights guaranteed by the Sixth Amendment beyond the pale of due process. Yet, so the dissenting justice maintained, these rights, "recognized at common law to be essential to personal security, jealously guarded by our national Constitution against violation by any tribunal or body exercising authority under the general government," ought properly to be considered the essence of due process.[38]

The procedural guarantees of the Sixth Amendment were, in Harlan's opinion, not only part and parcel of the notion of due process but also constituted privileges and immunities which the Fourteenth Amendment forbade the states to abridge.[39] The reasons for Justice Harlan's dissents in these and other cases touching on personal rights and procedural safeguards transcended the mere logic of law. "The principles stated in the first ten amendments were to him sacred elements of liberty, and he naturally opposed any decision that gave to the States a constitutional right to abridge those principles. He was not willing that the States individually should be left to determine whether their citizens had been deprived of any of the fundamental rights of fredom."[40]

But the Kentucky jurist remained a minority of one, and there was no voice of protest when, six years after his death, Justice Pitney declared that it was settled that trial by jury was not embraced in the rights secured by the Fourteenth Amendment.[41] However, in an earlier case the Court had already suggested in a dictum that some of the rights enumerated in the first eight amendments might also be protected against state action because by their nature they were included in the conception of due process of law.[42] In *Powell* v. *Alabama*[43] the Court announced that when an ignorant and indigent person is accused of a capital crime a state could not deny him counsel without violating those "fundamental principles of liberty and justice which lie at the base of all our civil and political institutions."[44] Today, a majority of the Court hold that no part of the Sixth Amendment applies to the states,[45] but in a number of decisions,[46] each predicated upon its special circumstances, the Court has found violation of the due process requirements of the Fourteenth Amendment on the part of state courts which had denied the defendant the assistance of counsel. As the result of these decisions it would seem that at least in capital cases the protection of the right to counsel may be invoked in state courts as well as in the federal courts.

None of the other provisions of the amendment have to date been held necessary to "due process"[47]—although it is difficult to conceive of due process of law without, for instance, confronting the accused with the prosecution witnesses. Generally, the application of the amendment has, therefore, been confined to the federal courts. This, however, has been true only with respect to federal courts located within a state, the District of Columbia, or in an incorporated Territory of the United States.

The Supreme Court has apparently always taken it for granted that the Sixth Amendment applied to those Territories which had been organized in the course of the nation's expansion to the Pacific shores.[48] There is no record of any published judicial opinion even suggesting that, not being within any State, the federal courts in these Territories might not be bound by the limitations of the Amendment. Yet, in the case of *Callan* v. *Wilson*,[49] that position was urged upon the Court with regard to the courts in the District of Columbia.

This case had originated in an intra-union dispute in the Washington local of the musicians' union of the Knights of Labor. The defendants were charged with conspiracy and were found guilty and sentenced by the Police Court, without a jury. The pertinent statute enabled that court to try "simple assaults and batteries and all other misdemeanors not punishable by imprisonment in the penitentiary; and . . . all offenses against the laws and ordinances of the District of Columbia in force therein."[50] Proceedings before the Police Court were to be without a jury, but it was provided that, on appeal, the Supreme Court of the District of Columbia would hear the case with the aid of a jury, "as though the case had originated therein."[51] The defendants claimed denial of their constitutional right to a trial by jury. The government contended that the Sixth Amendment was not intended to apply to the District of Columbia, as witness its express reference to a jury "of the State."

The Supreme Court rejected this interpretation in no uncertain terms. "There is nothing in the history of the Constitution," said Justice Harlan, "or of the original amendments to justify the assertion that the people of this District may be lawfully deprived . . . of the privilege of trial by jury in criminal cases."[52] This right could not be considered to have been preserved by the provision for a jury on appeal inasmuch as access to the appellate courts is not a matter of right but of judicial discretion. The Police Court's exercise of criminal jurisdiction without the aid of a jury was thus held to violate the Sixth Amendment, and the act authorizing this procedure was declared unconstitutional. For, said the Court, "we cannot think that the people of this District have, in that regard, less rights than those accorded to the people of the Territories of the United States."[53]

But the applicability of these constitutional provisions to areas under territorial government was itself soon to become the subject of legal disputes. As a result of the Spanish-American War, the United States came into possession of territories over which, because of their location, their economic and industrial status, and especially the character of their populations, it was deemed expedient to give to the Executive or to Congress a maximum of discretion with reference to the kind of government to be established. The question of how far the exercise of these discretionary powers was limited by the constitutional guarantees applicable within the states (and the then existing Territories), to what extent "the Constitution followed the flag," led to the celebrated *Insular Cases*[54] and Justice White's doctrine of incorporation. In the wake of these decisions the applicability of the Sixth Amendment in each of the outlying Territories was passed on by the Supreme Court of the United States.[55]

Chronologically, the first case was that concerning the new Territory of Hawaii.[56] Congress had annexed the islands forming this Territory by Joint Resolution of July 7, 1898.[57] This resolution provided, *inter alia*, that "the municipal legislation of the Hawaiian Islands, . . . not inconsistent with this resolution nor contrary to the Constitution of the United States . . ., shall remain in force until the Congress of the United States shall otherwise determine." Subsequent to the adoption of this resolution, but prior to the effective date of the Organic Act for Hawaii,[58] which by its terms made the Constitution in its entirety applicable to the Territory, one Mankichi was tried for manslaughter in a Hawaiian court and was found guilty by a majority verdict of nine of the twelve jurors. Under Hawaiian municipal law the verdict constituted a valid conviction. If, however, this provision of the law of Hawaii had been considered to be contrary to the Constitution of the United States, the defendant would, under the established interpretation of the Sixth Amendment, have been entitled to a jury trial as at common law, including the requirement that a verdict of guilty should be found by an unanimous jury only. Mankichi pressed this contention successfully in habeas corpus proceedings before the District Court but suffered a reversal when the Attorney General of Hawaii appealed the case to the Supreme Court of the United States.

No less than four opinions were delivered by the justices, with a bare majority of five denying Mankichi's claim. The opinion of Mr. Justice White, concurred in by Mr. Justice McKenna, disposed of the case by the application of the doctrine of incorporation.[59] The principal majority opinion, however, written by Mr. Justice Brown, proceeded primarily on an interpretation of the Joint Resolution of 1898. "There are many reasons," it was said there,

which induce us to hold that the act was not intended to interfere with the existing practice when such interference would result in imperiling the peace and good order of the islands. . . . Where the immediate application of the Constitution required no new legislation to take the place of that which the Constitution abolished, it may well be held to have taken immediate effect; but where the application of a procedure hitherto well known and acquiesced in, left nothing to take its place, without new legislation, the result might be so disastrous that we might well say that it could not have been within the contemplation of Congress.[60]

It is difficult to perceive what disaster might have befallen the Hawaiian islands if the trial jury, which had existed there long before the annexation, had been compelled to reach a unanimous verdict. Justice Brown suggested the consequences would be "that every criminal in the Hawaiian islands convicted of an infamous offense between August 12, 1898 [the effective date of the annexation resolution], and June 14, 1900, when the act organizing the territorial government took effect, must be set at large."[61] It is not clear why every convicted criminal would have received his freedom when obviously only those verdicts would have been open to attack which had not been rendered by a unanimous jury. That the number of convicts so liberated would have been so large as to bring about a disastrous calamity may well be doubted. The Hawaiian Commission, appointed by the same Joint Resolution which effected the annexation, reported in 1898 that the organization and procedure of Hawaii's judiciary was already "very similar to what is found in the United States,"[62] and apparently failed to conceive that adjustment of the existing practice might, as Justice Brown suggested in this case five years later, "result in imperiling the peace and good order of the islands."[63]

Nor is it apparent why it should have been necessary to subject the Joint Resolution to such strained construction. As Chief Justice Fuller said in his dissent: "By the specific language of this resolution no legislation which was contrary to the Constitution of the United States remained in force. The language is plain and unambiguous, and resort to construction or interpretation is absolutely uncalled for. To tamper with the words is to eliminate them."[64]

The majority opinion, however, asserted that it by no means intended to deprive the words "contrary to the Constitution of the United States" of all their meaning. Several constitutional provisions were enumerated, such as those with respect to treason, or confiscation of private property for public use without just compensation, or the due process clause of the Fifth Amendment, which clearly would override any Hawaiian law in contradiction to them. Indeed, declared Justice Brown, "most, if not all, the privileges and immunities contained in the bill of rights of the Constitution" should be presumed to have applied from the moment of annexation. But: trial by jury was not a right that was fundamental in nature, and hence was not to be considered to have been among the privileges acquired by the people of the new Territory by virtue of the annexation.[65]

Thus the Court not only interpreted the language of the Congress in a sense plainly contrary to the obvious meaning of its words but also read into the Constitution an entirely novel understanding of what hitherto had habitually been acclaimed as a basic right of citizens. This was indeed, as W. W. Willoughby has said, the enunciation of a new principle in American juris-prudence.[66]

Rising in righteous wrath, Justice Harlan called the new doctrine "most mischievous in every aspect."[67] But his words, echoing as they did the attachment which Story and his generation had held for the institution of jury trial, were like a voice from the past. None of the other justices joined in his dissent, and none then or since has championed the right to jury trial as did Harlan.[67a] The Court had given recognition, in Brown's words, to the steady decline which jury trial had taken in the affections of the people and the esteem of the profession during the closing decades of the nineteenth century.[68]

Justice Brown's announcement, that the right to trial by jury was not a fundamental one, was already considered a binding precedent when the next case in this group was argued before the Supreme Court, April 22, 1904.[69] The question presented for decision was whether the jury trial provisions of the Constitution applied in the Philippines. The Attorney General for the Philippine Islands and the Solicitor General of the United States both argued that *Hawaii v. Mankichi* had decided this issue, and the Court concurred and found the jury trial provisions not applicable to the Philippine Islands. Of the dissenters in the Hawaiian case Harlan alone remained adamant. He deplored this "obviously inconsistent" interpretation of the Constitution, which, he said, "plays havoc with the old-fashioned ideas of the Fathers."[70] Chief Justice Fuller, and Justices Brewer and Peckham, on the other hand, acquiesced in the result, merely noting in a brief concurring opinion by Peckham that they had joined the majority only because they considered themselves bound by the Court's ruling in *Hawaii v. Mankichi*.[71]

However, the question of jury trials in the Philippines was hardly on all fours with the question presented in the *Mankichi* case. In Hawaii, American institutions had been consciously imitated for nearly two generations; courts had operated by rules of Anglo-American law and the decisions of American tribunals were quoted and obeyed as precedents; juries as an institution were well known and widely used, the only divergence from the practice of the federal courts, the unanimity requirement, being one common also to several of the American states. The judicial system of the Philippines, however, was that of Spain. Juries were foreign to their procedure. The accused was tried before a bench of judges, who acted in effect as a board of inquiry and whose judgments were not final until passed in review before the *audiencia* or Supreme Court of the islands. Following American occupation of the islands, the President had instructed the Philippine Commission, charged with the administration of the new Territory, to assure the availability to the people of the Philippines of all guarantees of the Bill of Rights, excepting trial by jury. The reason for this reservation, as ascribed by the Supreme Court, would appear plausible: that it was "doubtless due to the fact that the civilized portion of the islands had a system of jurisprudence founded upon the civil law, and the uncivilized parts of the archipelago were wholly unfitted to exercise the right to trial by jury. . . ."[72]

Conditions in the Philippines would appear to have been sufficiently different from those existing in Hawaii to have enabled the Court to distinguish the two situations. Had it not been for the artificial and essentially unsatisfactory doctrine of incorporation, the distinguishing element could have been found in Article IX of the Treaty with Spain, which expressly provided that "the civil rights and political status of the native inhabitants of the territories hereby ceded to the United States shall be determined by the Congress."[73] In any case, the same result might well have been reached if *Hawaii* v. *Mankichi* had never been decided, or if it had been decided differently; and it would surely have been possible to pass on the question of jury trial in the Philippines without reaffirming the banishment of that institution from the ranks of the fundamental rights—if that had been desired.

The same arguments which applied to the Philippines obtained, of course, with equal validity in the case of Porto Rico, which had the same civil law background and had been acquired by the same treaty as the Philippines. It should not have been a matter of argument, therefore, what the status of jury trial would be in Porto Rico except for the Jones Act of 1917,[74] by which full citizenship was conferred on the Porto Ricans. The Supreme Court, however, found that the new status of the people of Porto Rico had no effect upon their right to a trial by jury. They could insist upon it only so far as their own territorial legislature had granted it to them. As for the Constitution of the United States, its application was to be determined by locality and not by the status of the people who lived in the locality.[75] Chief Justice Taft summarized the problems involved in introducing the jury in the islands acquired by the Treaty of Paris and applauded the wisdom of Congress in not "forcing a jury system on a Spanish and civil-law country until it desired it."[76] Following the precedents of *Hawaii v. Mankichi* and *Dorr v. United States*, the Sixth Amendment's guarantee of a trial by jury was held not to apply to Porto Rico.

The problem of jury trials in the Virgin Islands combined features of the Hawaiian case with aspects resembling the conditions of the former Spanish possessions. By the Organic Act for the islands[77] the Danish law was continued in force "in so far as compatible with the new sovereignty,"—a clause similar to that found in the resolution annexing Hawaii. Under Danish law, trial by jury was as unknown as it was under the Spanish law in Porto Rico and the Philippines. The government merely produced the record of a "police investigation" and on the basis of this record the case was tried by a bench consisting of one professional judge and four "lay judges." On a review of a murder trial, held according to this procedure, the Circuit Court of Appeals for the Third Circuit, applying the test of incorporation and the rule of *Hawaii v. Mankichi*, declared the islands to be an unincorporated Territory and hence covered only by those guarantees of a "fundamental" nature. The court evolved a division of constitutional rights into artificial or remedial rights, peculiar to the American judicial system, and natural or personal rights, interference with which the Constitution forbids. Of the rights preserved by the Sixth Amendment trial by jury fell into the first category, and hence was not assured to any inhabitant of the Virgin Islands. On the other hand, confrontation by witnesses was held to be one of the fundamental, natural, or personal rights which might not be infringed and which were to be considered to have been bestowed upon the new Territory by the Organic Act's proviso denying further validity to any local law not "compatible with the new sovereignty."[78]

The only one of the outlying Territories in which the Sixth Amendment was found to be fully applicable was Alaska.[79] The question arose under the Alaska Penal Code which provided for criminal trials by a jury of six.[80] The Supreme Court was asked to reverse a conviction rendered by such a jury, on the grounds that a six-man jury failed to satisfy the requirements of the Sixth Amendment.[81] The entire bench of the Supreme Court concurred in holding the six-man jury unconstitutional, but their reasoning displayed the same cleavages of opinion which had been noticeable in *Hawaii* v. *Mankichi*. Justice Brown placed his findings solely on interpretation of the treaty[82] by which Alaska had been acquired; Justice Harlan declared once again that all persons under the American flag were entitled to the benefits of all constitutional guarantees. The principal opinion was written by Mr. Justice White, who declared that Article 3 of the treaty of cession was "the equivalent . . . of the formula employed from the beginning to express the purpose to incorporate territory into the United States," and as an incorporated Territory Alaska was subject to all the limitations of the Constitution.[83]

One further geographic exception has been noted by the courts to the general rule that United States courts are limited by the provisions of the Sixth Amendment. This exception concerned American consular courts in foreign countries and hence is of only academic interest today. On a petition for habeas corpus the Supreme Court was asked to review the judgment of such a consular court, which, it was claimed, had proceeded in violation of the accused's constitutional rights.[84] However, such rights, the Court decided, could not be asserted by one tried outside the United States. "The Constitution can have no operation in another country."[85]

The case of the consular courts differed from those pertaining to the several Territories in that it declared—needlessly and erroneously, as one eminent authority has suggested[86]—that the Constitution in its entirety would not apply. In the series of cases with respect to Hawaii and the other non-contiguous Territories, aside from their more far-reaching implications, the right which, specifically, was held inapplicable was that to a trial by jury. The same decisions, however, suggested that "most, if not all of the privileges and immunities contained in the Bill of Rights of the Constitution were intended to apply"[87] to the new Territories, and in the Virgin Islands case[88] it was so held as to confrontation by witnesses. However, neither the language of that case nor any other considerations have so far placed any of the rights guaranteed by the Sixth Amendment, with a partial and ill-defined exception of the right to counsel, within the requirements of due process.[89]

The right to the assistance of counsel, which in some specific instances, particularly in capital cases, has been held to be necessary to due process of law under the Fourteenth Amendment, has become the most widely operative of the guarantees of the Sixth Amendment.[90] On the other hand, the right to a trial by jury, in terms of geographic application, is today the least of the guarantees: its protection cannot be invoked in proceedings in state courts nor in the federal courts in Porto Rico or the Virgin Islands, and in Hawaii and the Canal Zone it is applicable only by virtue and within the limits of statutory enactment.[91] Between these two extremes in scope, the right to counsel on one hand and the right to a jury trial on the other, the remaining rights secured by the amendment are apparently applicable in federal courts wherever located (with the historical exception of consular courts and presumably also excepting the courts in the Canal Zone[92]).

Wherever provisions of the Sixth Amendment have been held to apply, their protection would extend to aliens as freely as to citizens. The Supreme Court found occasion to announce this rule in connection with the contest over section 4 of the Geary Act of 1892.[93] This statute provided that whenever a Chinese should be found, by an administrative official, to be unlawfully in the country, such Chinese should, pending deportation, be imprisoned at hard labor for not exceeding one year. The Court referred to the earlier case of Yick Wo v. Hopkins[94] and, applying the reasoning of that case, declared all persons, citizen and alien alike, within the territory of the United States to be entitled to the protection guaranteed by the Fifth and Sixth Amendments.[95]

The protection of the amendment extends, however, only to "criminal prosecutions." Proceedings by which punishment is imposed upon an individual have been held to come within the scope of this provision only if they were in the nature of a criminal trial. Thus, proceedings to deport an alien are not controlled by these constitutional guarantees.[96]

The authority of Congress to prohibit aliens from coming within the United States and to regulate their coming includes authority to impose conditions upon the performance of which the continued liberty of the alien to reside within the bounds of this country may be made to depend,

and proceedings to enforce such regulations are not criminal prosecutions within the meaning of the Sixth Amendment.[97]

Neither can the guarantees of the amendment be invoked by an attorney in disbarment proceedings. Chief Justice Cranch of the Circuit Court of the District of Columbia had occasion to state this rule in the course of the proceedings to disbar Aaron Burr. The latter claimed that the Constitution entitled him to a trial by jury, but Cranch, in an elaborate opinion, held that disbarment proceedings did not fall within the purview of the constitutional guarantee of a trial by jury.[98]

The Supreme Court of the United States declined to intervene on Burr's behalf, and it was not until 1882 that the issue was again presented to the supreme bench. In this case a federal district judge had ordered a lawyer struck from the rolls of the bar because of his participation in a lynching.[99] The Court reviewed fully the English and American precedents and concluded that the constitutional provisions were not applicable because attorneys, as officers of the court, are subject to be disciplined by the court. Disbarment proceedings are civil, not criminal in nature. They do not adjudge penal liability, but suitability for public trust.

Proceedings leading to the extradition to foreign countries of their nationals wanted by them for crimes committed there do not fall within the term "criminal prosecutions" either. The decision to surrender fugitives from justice to the prosecuting authorities of their countries is an administrative determination, arising from treaty obligations, and not a judicial proceeding under the authority of the United States.[100]

With respect to probation hearings it was said that "too plainly to require discussion, the power to revoke probation, when it exists, like the power to grant probation, is entitled to be exercised without the assistance of a jury."[101]

Petitions for a writ of habeas corpus are not of such a nature as to call into play the guarantees of the Constitution. The exercise of judicial discretion in passing on the sufficiency of such petitions does not constitute a criminal prosecution. Not even the right to counsel can be claimed by such a petitioner: ". . . neither the language of the Sixth Amendment nor of the judicial gloss 'at every step of the proceedings' [Powell v. Alabama, 287 U.S. 45, 69 (1932)] requires the appointment of counsel to represent a prisoner in such a matter, pending before a judge in chambers, long after the trial has been completed and the appeal determined."[102]

The language of the Sixth Amendment has been interpreted to make its guarantees effective only in the course of criminal trials proper. No constitutional rights of the accused would be impaired if he were denied counsel in a preliminary examination,[103] or at any time prior to the return of the indictment by the grand jury.[104] The trial terminates with the pronouncement of sentence by the court, and the accused's constitutional rights end at this point. The Sixth Amendment does not secure the right to appeal and does not impose a constitutional duty on the court to furnish counsel to every convicted person desiring to appeal his case.[105] The "criminal prosecution" begins with the arraignment of the accused and ends when sentence has been pronounced on the convicted or a verdict of "Not guilty" has cleared the defendant of the charge.

Trials by courts-martial of persons under military or naval jurisdiction are not affected by the requirements of the Sixth Amendment. To be sure, that amendment does not by its terms stipulate the kind of exception made by the Fifth Amendment, which requires a grand jury indictment in all cases other than those "arising in the land or naval forces, or in the militia, when in actual service, in time of war or public danger." However, judicial interpreters have concluded that this saving clause was "doubtlessly" meant by the Framers to delimit the application of the Sixth Amendment in the same manner.[106]

This has generally been held to be true of all rights enumerated in the amendment.[107] Although the right to the assistance of counsel has in recent years acquired a pre-eminent place among the procedural guarantees, assertions that counsel had been denied in military justice proceedings have been held insufficient to warrant the issuance of writs of habeas corpus.[108]

The existence or nonexistence of a state of war has been held to have no bearing on the operation of the amendment. Persons under military or naval jurisdiction may not claim its protection in peacetime any more than in time of war.[109] On the other hand, "the mere existence of a state of war could not suspend or change the operation . . . of the guarantees and limitations of the . . . Sixth Amendment."[110] War, and all that pertains thereto, runs counter to the normal balance and gradual evolution which our municipal law presumes. The latter denies, therefore, as far as possible, any effect of war upon its validity,[111] and in turn endeavors to remain aloof from those issues which are peculiarly resultant from a state of war.

The common law did not consider offenses against the law of war triable by a jury in civil courts, and it has been authoritatively declared that no part of the Constitution could be taken as having repudiated that rule. Espionage and sabotage committed by enemies have thus been held properly within the competence of military commissions, and persons so accused have not been permitted to claim the protection offered by the Sixth Amendment.[112]

With reference to the offenses of municipal law, the concept of a "criminal prosecution" has required clarification in three instances: with respect to statutory penalties, in cases of criminal contempt, and concerning so-called petty offenses. Where a statute imposes specific penalties on violators, it has repeatedly been urged on the courts that a suit by the government to recover such penalties was a "criminal prosecution" entitling the defendant to the benefits of the constitutional guarantees available in such prosecutions. Thus in *United States* v. *Zucker*,[113] a proceeding under the Customs Administration Act of 1890,[114] the defendants objected to the admission in evidence of a deposition taken in Paris, France, on the grounds that such admission would constitute a denial of their constitutional right to be confronted with the witnesses against them. The Supreme Court disposed of this objection somewhat obliquely in a statement carefully limited to the question of confrontation of witnesses and avoiding any more direct definition of the nature of the proceedings:

A witness who proves facts entitling the plaintiff in a proceeding in a court of the United States, even if the plaintiff be the government, to a judgment for money only, and not to a judgment which directly involves the personal safety of the defendant, is not, within the meaning of the Sixth Amendment, a witness against an "accused" in a criminal prosecution; and his evidence may be brought before the jury in the form of a deposition.[115]

In effect this statement declared that an action to recover a penalty was not criminal, but civil in nature. The decision has been accepted as precedent for the proposition that, although a statutory penalty has been incurred by the commission of a public offense, the government may recover such a penalty by a civil action of debt, and in an action of this kind the constitutional limitations pertaining to criminal prosecutions will not apply.[116] Nor does withdrawal or suspension of a license, upon an administrative finding that the conditions of the license have not been observed, constitute a criminal prosecution within the meaning of the amendment.[117]

It is apparently also the prevailing view that proceedings for criminal contempt do not fall within the purview of the Sixth Amendment.[118] Although the courts have acknowledged that "the only substantial difference between . . . a [criminal contempt] proceeding . . . and a criminal prosecution by indictment or information is that in the latter the act complained of is the violation of a law and in the former the violation of a decree,"[119] the constitutional right to a trial by jury is not available to one charged with criminal contempt.[120] This denial of the privilege of jury trial has been explained on the ground that "to submit the question of disobedience to another tribunal, be it a jury or another court,[121] would operate to deprive the proceedings of half its efficiency."[122]

Recently the trend has been toward a general extension of criminal law principles to cover contempt punishment.[123] By Rule 42 of the Federal Rules of Criminal Procedure[124] the use of summary proceedings has been restricted to contempt arising from conduct seen or heard by the judge in court, and in all other cases of criminal contempt notice and time to prepare a defense are now required to be given. Under the title of due process, at least the provisions for a speedy and public trial, for compulsory process, for the assistance of counsel are apparently applicable in cases of criminal contempt.[125] It has been suggested that these developments "cast doubt upon the propriety" of a continued refusal of trial by jury in contempt cases, and that whatever reasons could be urged for securing a trial by jury to one accused of crime should be accepted as equally compelling in the case of criminal contempts not committed in the actual presence of the court.[126] However, it has only recently been reasserted by members of our highest court that "contempt proceedings are *sui generis,*" and that "they are not to be circumscribed by procedural formalities, or by traditional limitations of what are ordinarily called crimes, except insofar as due process of law and the other standards of decency and fairness in the administration of federal justice may require."[127] In view of the repeated declarations that the right to a trial by jury is not fundamental in nature,[128] a modification of the present rule denying the privilege of jury trial in criminal contempt cases does not appear imminent.

There still remains to be discussed one other category to which the Sixth Amendment has been held not to apply: such criminal offenses as have been classified as "petty." Frankfurter and Corcoran's exhaustive research[129] indicated clearly that summary proceedings for minor offenses had, in varying degrees, been known in all the colonies, and that it could be presumed that "the framers did not mean to provide for jury trial in criminal cases under the new government beyond the established practice in their various states."[130] In the absence of any guiding principles to be scanned from precedents or constitutional debates, and without a policy determined by the Congress, the task of defining this exempt category fell to the courts.

In *Schick* v. *United States,*[131] Justice Brewer announced that the criteria to be applied were "the nature of the offense and the amount of the punishment prescribed rather than . . . [the] place in the statutes." Accordingly the offense in question, a violation of the Oleomargarine Act, punishable by a maximum fine of fifty dollars, was held not to require a jury trial. Similarly, a refusal to testify before a military commission, punishable by a fine not exceeding five hundred dollars and/or six months' imprisonment, was declared to be a petty offense,[132] as was a violation of the Food and Drug Act for which the maximum penalty was $200.[133] But an offense against the excise laws, with a possible maximum sentence of $500 and two years' imprisonment,[134] and a violation of the prohibition laws, punishable by twelve months in prison and $1,000 in fines,[135] were held to entitle the accused to a trial by jury.

However, by a decision in 1930, the Supreme Court apparently discarded this test and announced that "whether a given offense is to be classed as a crime, so as to require a jury trial, or as a petty offense, triable summarily without a jury, depends primarily upon the nature of the offense."[136] The case involved a police court conviction for reckless driving, an offense which, the Court found, "is an act of such obvious depravity that to characterize it as a petty offense would be to shock the general moral sense."[137] What motives may have moved the Court to discard what, to all appearances, had been a workable test, will presumably remain an object of conjecture. The immediate effect of the new formula was to remove the only element of relative certainty and predictability, to infuse extra-legal notions of morality into problems of law, and apparently to reserve to the Supreme Court the final determination of the status, rights, and privileges of countless persons previously convicted and still to be convicted.

Intending to provide some guidance for the future, Congress thereupon amended the Criminal Code by writing into it a definition of petty offenses solely on the basis of the criterion which the Court had just rejected. By this proviso, enacted December 16, 1930,[138] "All offenses the penalty for which does not exceed confinement in a common jail, without hard labor for a period of six months, or a fine of not more than five hundred dollars, or both," were declared to be petty offenses.

The Supreme Court itself, in a later decision,[139] then reverted to its former position. Although the nature of the offense might make it appear to be petty, the severity of the punishment, the court announced, may make the offense "so serious as to be comparable with common law crimes, and thus to entitle the accused to the benefit of a jury trial prescribed by the Constitution."[140] But,—and this appears to be the present status of the law,—where the offense is not one of so grave a nature as to offend the moral sense of the community, and the punishment not so severe as to make it comparable to a common law crime, Congress may properly withhold the privilege of jury trial from persons accused of having committed petty offenses.[141]

Chapter IV

Trial by Jury

By the terms of the Sixth Amendment the defendant in a criminal trial is assured the right to a "speedy and public trial by an impartial jury." What interpretation has been placed upon these words by the courts, and what do they import today?

What constitutes a speedy trial is necessarily a relative matter. Indeed, one court has said that "speed in trying accused persons is not of itself a primal and separate consideration. Justice, both to the accused and to the public, is the prime consideration."[1] Thus the right to a speedy trial may not be asserted merely in order to forestall the ends of public justice. With this characterization the Supreme Court condemned, for instance, the efforts of a defendant who faced several criminal charges to obtain a "speedy" trial for one offense in an attempt to avoid prosecution for the others.[2]

Nor may a defendant claim denial of this right unless he himself had asked for a trial during the period of delay. A defendant cannot acquiesce in the postponement of his trial, and then, when the case is called, move that it be dismissed because he had not been given a speedy trial. The courts will assume that a speedy trial would have been granted had it been asked for, and the burden is on the complaining defendant to show that he had not acquiesced in the delay.[3]

The defendant's duty to ask for a speedy trial before he may allege denial of this right is not lifted or lessened because he may be confined in prison. A person confined in a penal institution or jail is not immune from, nor is he denied access to, the judicial process, and hence the fact of imprisonment does not by itself raise a presumption that a speedy trial had been denied or that the defendant could not have asked for one had he so desired.[4]

The relatively few cases on the right to a speedy trial are thus in agreement that this procedural element continues to be a privilege rather than a right, something that must be asked for, and which furthermore remains subordinate to the broader aims of public justice.

Although the federal court decisions on the right to a "public" trial are even fewer in number, they do not present the same kind of unanimity. It is, of course, plain that a public trial does not mean one which takes place "under the eyes of the movie camera,"[5] and equally clear that it precludes a trial held in complete secrecy,[6] but to what extent a trial court may exercise its discretion in limiting the audience and spectators is a question upon which the cases have differed.[7]

In 1912 the Circuit Court of Appeals for the Ninth Circuit declared that the preservation of order in the courtroom or the protection of public morals justified the exclusion of some or all of the spectators from a trial unless it was shown that the defendant was prejudiced thereby, or deprived of the presence, aid, or counsel, of any person whose presence might have been of advantage to him.[8] Thus, by this rule, a burden of proof analogous to that established with respect to speedy trials was imposed upon the defendant.

This position was not accepted by another Circuit Court of Appeals when it was presented with the same question.[9] This court observed that, by its very expression, a public trial implied that the public should be at liberty to attend. A status of relationship to the parties or of membership in a group or class such as the press could not be made an essential prerequisite to a person's attendance. For, indeed, a prospective spectator might be without any interest whatsoever in the cause being tried, and be desirous only of observing the administration of justice in action. Disorderly spectators could always be ejected, but a defendant should not be required to show that the exclusion of the public had operated to his disadvantage. "A violation of the constitutional right necessarily applies prejudice and more than that need not appear."[10]

The cases were capable of distinction on the basis of their facts; the latter one dealt with a train robbery, whereas the former cases involved statutory rape. However, their conflict as to the nature of the constitutional guarantee could not be rationalized on the grounds of factual differences. The doctrine of the *Reagan* case, which viewed a public trial as a privilege the abridgment of which could not be claimed without a showing of actual injury, was declared to be the "better" doctrine by some commentators.[11] Nevertheless, by a decision of the same tribunal which originally enunciated the rule, it has today apparently been disavowed, except possibly in application to a strictly identical set of facts.

This, the most recent decision with respect to public trial in federal courts, was *Tanksley v. United States*,[12] a rape case in which the trial judge, in reliance on the *Reagan* case, had excluded the public. The court of appeals, however, decided to treat as a dictum that portion of the opinion of *Reagan v. United States* which would place the burden on the defendant to show that denial of publicity had been prejudicial, and accepted the contrary view that the fact of a violation of the constitutional right carried a necessary implication of prejudice. "One of the main purposes of the admission of the public," the court declared, "is the reasonable possibility that persons unknown to the parties or their counsel, but having knowledge of the facts may be drawn to the trial," and presumably by their presence aid in the better dispensation of justice.

Thus in spite of the propinquity of the two requirements of speed and of publicity in the text of the Sixth Amendment their judicial construction has given them altogether unequal status. The right to a speedy trial must have been claimed before denial may be asserted. On the other hand, with the possible exception of statutory rape cases, publicity must now be granted, and denial of public trial will, without anything more, result in voidance of the proceedings.[13] One commentator has suggested that neither speed nor publicity today represents an advantage to the accused, that, indeed, most defendants would prefer a private and long-delayed trial, and that this explains the small number of cases in which these guarantees have been invoked.[14] This comment was made, however, before the *Tanksley* case was decided and, while it is probably borne out by extra-legal observations, would not appear to answer the obvious question of why these companion requirements should have received such divergent construction. This may perhaps be made more intelligible if the *Tanksley* case is considered in conjunction with the series of decisions in which the Supreme Court has extended its supervision over judicial proceedings through the due process clause. Read in that context, speed, once thought so vital when transportation beyond the seas threatened the accused in the American colonies and defendants were rarely permitted the assistance of proper legal advisers, is, indeed, not a primary consideration. Publicity, on the other hand, acquires increased significance in an era in which judicial and public attention increasingly focuses on the fairness of court procedures and equality in the dispensation of justice.

The Sixth Amendment entitles one accused of crime to be tried "by an impartial jury." The meaning of the phrase "trial by jury" within the context of the amendment was set out most clearly by Mr. Justice Sutherland, deciding *Patton* v. *United States*:[15]

... that it means a trial by jury as understood and applied at common law, and includes all the essential elements as they were recognized in this country and in England when the Constitution was adopted, is not open to question. Those elements were— (1) that the jury should consist of twelve men, neither more nor less; (2) that the trial should be in the presence and under the superintendence of a judge having power to instruct them [the jurors] as to the law and advise them in respect to facts; and (3) that the verdict should be unanimous.

In an earlier case, the insistence on a jury of twelve persons "neither more nor less" was based by Justice Harlan on the fact that "when Magna Charta declared that no freeman should be deprived of life, etc., 'but by the judgment of his peers or by the law of the land,' it referred to a trial by twelve jurors."[16] Since the recognition of the error in this historical interpretation of Magna Carta[17] the courts have usually referred to the common law as it existed in 1789, in order to maintain the proposition that the requirement of twelve jurors was constitutionally anchored.[18] It may be well to note that that requirement had, in fact, been the result of historical accident;[19] it has been frequently recommended that the number be reduced, and in England and in several of the states such a reduction has been carried out without injury to the system.[20]

It would seem to matter but little, in reality, whether the re-requirement of a twelve-man jury is traced back to 1215 or to 1789. In terms of socially desirable results it would be more important to determine whether the embodiment in the Constitution of such a procedural stipulation of the common law had the effect of an immutable codification; whether, as the late Chief Justice Stone asked, we are to be confined, in developing the law, to those devices which may be found in the "legal scrap heap of a century and a half ago";[21] or whether the incorporation in the Constitution of certain features of the common law served only to channel, not to impede, their growth.

Faced with the question whether the requirement of a twelve-man jury could be waived, the federal courts originally adopted a position of strict adherence to, and compliance with, the common law on the subject as it had existed at the time of the adoption of the Constitution. The presence of a full, twelve-man panel could not be dispensed with, not even with the consent of the parties.[22] The underlying reason, it was asserted, was that the Constitution had declared with finality by what mode criminal trials should proceed: "The court and the jury, not separately but together, constitute the appointed tribunal which alone, under the law, can try the question of crime . . . ."[23] In the early years of the twentieth century, however, the desire to prevent the frustration of justice by recourse to formal, technical requirements led to adjustments which, eventually, resulted in complete reversal of the Court's position.

The case of *Queean* v. *Oklahoma*[24] presented one of the earliest intimations of this shift. In the course of a trial for murder, and after the trial had been going on for some time, counsel for the government announced that he had just been informed of grounds for the disqualification of one juror. The defendant was asked by the court what action he desired to be taken and replied that he had nothing to say. Nevertheless, following his conviction, he claimed that he had been denied his constitutional right to a trial by a jury of twelve, and asserted—as, indeed, had been said in an earlier case[25]—that he could not effectively have waived that right. The Court easily disposed of the defendant's contention by reference to the procedural rule that an assignment of error might not be entertained on appeal if the question had not been saved by exception at the trial. Although the Court thus avoided the constitutional issue, in effect it had sanctioned a waiver of a full, twelve-man panel, even though that waiver had not been in express words.

Schick v. *United States*,[26] decided the following year, afforded the Court an opportunity to state explicitly that the constitutional guarantee of a trial by jury was in the nature of a privilege and not of a mandatory requirement. Although this case involved the waiver of the entire jury and not merely a part thereof, it represents a definite phase in the Court's shift from rigid adherence to the common law of the Framers' days to a flexible attitude of adjustment to modern needs. It is therefore properly discussed in this connection.

The *Schick* case and its companion case, *Broadwell* v. *United States*, arose under the Oleomargarine Act[27] and were argued and decided on the same days as *McCray* v. *United States*,[28] in which the constitutionality of the statute was affirmed. The only element of fact that distinguished the *Schick* and *Broadwell* cases from the *McCray* case was that in the former cases the parties had agreed in writing to waive a jury and to submit the issues to the court. Justice Harlan alone dissented from the Supreme Court opinion that the constitutional requirement of a jury did not apply to trials for petty offenses such as were here involved. The majority opinion found that the Sixth Amendment was, by its terms, the grant of a privilege, the acceptance and use of which could not be considered compulsory. "Is it possible," the Court asked,

that the accused cannot admit and be bound by the admission that a witness not present would testify to certain facts? Can it be that if he does not wish the assistance of counsel and waives it, the trial is invalid? It seems only necessary to ask these questions to answer them. When there is no constitutional or statutory mandate, and no public policy prohibiting, an accused may waive any privilege which he is given the right to enjoy.[29]

On the other hand, the jury clause of Article III, section 2, the Court found, was couched in such mandatory language as to allow of no waiver. The trial of crimes had to be by jury, which meant by twelve lawful jurors. Petty offenses, however, were not crimes within the meaning of this article, although this case still considered them covered by the Sixth Amendment.[30] In petty offense cases, therefore, a jury trial could be waived, while in the case of other criminal cases the mandatory language of Article III would bar any waiver or modification of the required jury of twelve.[31]

The shift in the Court's position became fully apparent with the decision in Patton v. United States[32] in 1930. The facts in this case, briefly, were that while the defendants were being tried in a federal court on an indictment charging a felony, one of the jurors became incapacitated; in this situation counsel for both the government and the defendants, with the personal assent of the defendants, stipulated that the trial should proceed with the remaining eleven jurors; defendants took the precaution of noting that they entered into this stipulation "if legally able to do so." The court approved the waiver and the trial proceeded with a jury of eleven. Subsequently, a verdict of guilty was returned and each of the defendants sentenced to prison. Appeal was then taken on the grounds that the defendants did not possess the power to waive any part of the jury in a trial for crime.

The Court enumerated, as its first step, the three elements of trial by jury, namely: trial by a panel of twelve, supervision by a judge, and unanimity of verdict; and it declared that the destruction of any one of these three elements would constitute a denial of the constitutional right to a trial by jury. Consequently an attempt to waive the presence of one of the required twelve jurors was tantamount to an effort to waive trial by jury altogether; "a constitutional jury means twelve men as though that number had been specifically named; and it follows that when reduced to eleven it ceases to be such a jury quite as effectively as though the number had been reduced to a single person."[33] There was, therefore, no distinction between waiving the presence of one member of the panel and waiving the entire panel, and the opinion proceeded to discuss and pass on the two problems as one.

The Court had no difficulty in declaring the earlier decision in *Thompson* v. *Utah*[34] distinguishable. That case had arisen under a statutory provision reducing the number of jurors to eight and the defendant's consent to such a departure from the constitutional jury's number of twelve was neither asked nor given. The question then presented had been whether elements of trial by jury could be modified by statute, and the answer had been in the negative. The Court in the *Patton* case indicated its approval of this position but declared that the comments of the earlier case with regard to the defendant's power to waive his right to a jury trial could only be considered as *obiter dicta*. Hence the issue of waiver still remained to be determined by the Court.[35]

It could be decided affirmatively only if it was possible to offset the mandatory language of Article III, section 2. The manner in which the Court succeeded in doing this has been related and criticized at another place in this study.[36] The Justices concluded that trial by jury, regardless of the phraseology of the Constitution, had never been looked upon as an integral part of the structure of the government but "uniformly was regarded as a valuable privilege bestowed upon the person accused of crime."[37]

In effect the Court subordinated the mandatory words of the Judiciary Article of the Constitution to the optional terminology of the Sixth Amendment. What had appeared to be an absolute jurisdictional requirement of the former was thus circumvented, and trial by jury was to be a privilege of the accused which he might forego at his election. "To deny his power to do so, is to convert a privilege into an imperative requirement."[38] No statutory authorization would be required for the court to accept a waiver of this privilege, and no grounds of public policy could be considered to stand in the way of such a waiver.[39]

The Court was, however, unwilling to allow the accused uncontrolled freedom to choose or reject the primary mode of procedure. Although a jury trial had been found to be a personal right of the defendant, he could decline it only with the concurrence of the prosecution and the approval of the court. "The maintenance of the jury," said Justice Sutherland near the end of his opinion, "as a fact-finding body in criminal cases is of such importance and has such a place in our traditions, that, before any waiver can become effective, the consent of government counsel and the sanction of the court must be had, in addition to the express and intelligent consent of the defendant."[40]

As a consequence of this language, federal courts have denied the defendant's privilege to waive the jury whenever the government prosecutor refused to join in a stipulation to that effect; the Supreme Court, by its disapproval of certiorari petitions from such decisions, has tacitly sanctioned this construction of its words.[41] As the law stands today, the accused may waive his right to a trial by jury in the most informal manner, even without the use of a written instrument, except where the statute prescribes it.[42] His waiver will be effective even though he has elected to be without counsel.[43] But he may not dispose of what has been declared to be his personal privilege if the court should withhold its assent or if his adversary, the prosecutor, should not see fit to concur. One might well ask, Of how much value is a privilege when its exercise may be foiled by the veto of the opposing side?

Indeed, by the test of the *Patton* case, trial by jury is either a personal privilege or a jurisdictional fact. If it be the former, it would seem that logic would compel the conclusion that the accused's freedom of action in this respect should not be limited by his prosecutor's desires; but if the latter be true and trial by jury is a jurisdictional fact, then it would appear necessary to limit the application of *Patton v. United States* to the facts of that case and to deny the defendant's right to waive a jury under any other circumstances.[44]

The difficulties are, however, more of a logical than of a practical nature. That the accused should be permitted to waive his right to a trial by jury has been more frequently recommended by students of criminal procedure than almost any other reform in that field.[45] Only the conceptual classification of jury trial as a personal right akin to freedom of speech or religion has prevented its being treated like any other procedural aspect of judicial business. Justice Brown's declaration in *Hawaii v. Mankichi*[46] that trial by jury was not fundamental to our system of government was symptomatic of the growing realization that procedural developments could no more be halted than the continuous evolution of the substantive law. The conflicting logic of *Patton v. United States* did not help to resolve the ambiguities inherent in such a shift of conceptual emphasis, but it served to illuminate the problem and to clarify the issues.

The specific point for decision in the *Patton* case had been the waiver of the requirement of a twelve-man panel. Although the Court's definition found this requirement to be but one of the three necessary elements of jury trial, it had treated it as tantamount to a waiver of the entire jury. Whenever the entire jury is waived there can, of course, be no further need for the other two requirements, unanimity and judicial superintendence. But what of these two elements of jury trial under any other condition? May they be waived, or are they jurisdictional requirements?

From the decision in the principal case it would appear to follow logically that any of the three elements of jury trial, not only the requirement of a twelve-man panel but also that of unanimity and that of superintendence by the court, would be susceptible of being waived by the defendant. Commentators have suggested that there was no reason why such a rule should not be put into effect with respect to the requirement of a unanimous verdict.[47] None of the federal courts have had occasion to pass on this point, but Rule 31 (a) of the new Federal Rules of Criminal Procedure, as approved by the Supreme Court,[48] rejected the suggestion. In view of the fact that the First Preliminary Draft of these rules had provided for majority verdicts on the stipulation of the parties with the approval of the court,[49] the reversion in the final form to the strict rule of the common law might be taken as expressive of the Supreme Court's attitude on the subject. The requirement of a unanimous verdict thus may not be waived.[50]

The third element of jury trial, the superintendence of the proceedings by a competent judge, presents a somewhat different problem. It would, of course, be absurd to expect the courts to permit the defendant to waive the court's control of the jury. Insistence on a logical extension of the rule of the *Patton* case so as to permit waiver of this requirement would defeat the purpose of judicial proceedings.

On the other hand, arguments can be advanced in favor of flexibility so as to allow substitutions for the judge, especially in long-protracted cases and for good cause, such as illness. Prior to the *Patton* case there had been no doubt that "in a criminal case trial by jury means trial by a tribunal of at least one judge and twelve jurors, all of whom must remain identical from the beginning to the end. It is not possible for either the government or the accused, or for both, to consent to a substitution of one judge for another judge . . . ."[51] Logically, there would be no reason why, by applying the rule of *Patton v. United States*, it should not be permissible for a defendant to waive the requirement that neither judge nor jurors should be changed in the course of a trial. The new Federal Rules of Criminal Procedure provide for alternate jurors who may be called to sit in addition to the regular jury and may replace any members of the regular panel in case of disability or disqualification.[52] In the case of judges, one Circuit Court of Appeals sanctioned substitution, with the agreement of prosecution and defense, after the arguments had been made to the jury but before the verdict had been returned.[53] The new Federal Rules, however, do not authorize any such substitution or waiver of the presence of the same judge throughout the trial. Only after verdict has been rendered may another judge step into a sick or incapacitated brother's place and at that stage, the trial technically being at an end, concurrence of the parties is no longer required.[54]

A trial is possible, of course, only where there are issues of fact to be determined. A plea of guilty operates as an admission of all facts as charged, and, as under the common law so under the Sixth Amendment, the court may proceed at once to pronounce judgment.[55] But where a plea of not guilty has left the issue of facts for the determination of the jury, the court may not direct the jury, without deliberation, to return a verdict of guilt. "There can, within the meaning of the Constitution, be no trial of a cause by a jury unless the jury deliberates upon and determines it."[56]

The jury trying the case must, by the terms of the amendment, be an "impartial" one. However, this constitutional requirement, while it embraces the right to challenge for cause, has been held not to include the granting of peremptory challenges to the accused.[57] These are given the parties by the common law or by Congress, and courts are not bound by state practice[58] or limited in the exercise of their discretion, provided only that the procedure employed should not be inconsistent with any settled principle of criminal law nor interfere with the selection of impartial juries.

What was to be understood by "an impartial jury" under the Sixth Amendment was first debated at the treason trial of Aaron Burr[59] when Luther Martin, speaking for the defense, insisted that this constitutional guarantee was the equivalent of a requirement that the jurors should be "perfectly indifferent and free from prejudice." In particular he urged that a juror should not be considered impartial who had formed an opinion as to the defendant's intent. Chief Justice Marshall, after dwelling briefly on the practical difficulties which the adoption of such a strict construction would produce, rejected Martin's contention in its sweeping nature. The Chief Justice distinguished light impressions, "which may fairly be supposed to yield to the testimony that may be offered, which may leave the mind open to a fair consideration of that testimony," from strong and deep impressions, "which will close the mind against the testimony that may be offered in opposition to them, which will combat that testimony, and resist its force." The latter, he declared, would constitute a sufficient objection to a juror, but with sound realism he recognized that to bar prospective jurors, because of casual opinions they may hold, would defeat the administration and ends of justice.

As a later Chief Justice, Waite, had occasion to observe, the theory of the law that a juror who has formed an opinion cannot be impartial is in evident conflict with the facts of life in a modern society. "In these days of newspapers and universal education it is not to be expected that in a case attracting public interest the jurors should not have heard about it."[60] The question of impartiality thus becomes a mixed one, of law and fact, which of necessity defies all efforts at clear classification. The reported decisions do not offer any concrete ratio decidendi except to affirm and corroborate the proposition that each situation requires appraisal on its own merits and to suggest that the challenged bias must bear some relation to the issues of the case in order to justify exclusion of a prospective juror for partiality.

In *Queen v. Hepburn*,[61] for instance, a civil case in which the plaintiff claimed to be held wrongfully as a slave, a prospective juror who, on *voir dire* examination, "avowed his detestation of slavery to be such that, in a doubtful case, he would find a verdict for the plaintiff," was held to have been properly excluded from the jury.

In a trial for polygamy, one who asserted a conscientious belief in the moral validity of polygamy was declared not to be sufficiently indifferent toward the issues of the case to serve as a juror.[62] Similarly, in a trial for a crime punishable with death, prospective jurors who, on *voir dire*, had stated that they had "conscientious scruples in regard to the infliction of the death penalty for crime" were held rightly to have been excused from serving.[63] On the other hand, in a trial for crimes which had resulted from party strife, the jurors' party affiliation was held to be irrelevant to the case.[64]

The answer to the question whether a government employee could be challenged for cause because of the government's interest in the case has not always been the same and continues to vex the Court. The issue had first been presented to the Supreme Court in 1909, in *Crawford v. United States*.[65] In that case the defendant had been charged with conspiracy to defraud on postal contracts. One of the veniremen was a druggist who for an annual compensation of $300 maintained a sub-post office in his store. Such a relationship to the government, the defendant argued, constituted employment by one of the litigants and disqualified this prospective juror from participation in the case. The Supreme Court of the United States, on appeal, accepted this position. The master-servant relationship, it was said by the Court, was one of the principal grounds for challenging prospective jurors at common law; the Sixth Amendment's guarantee of an impartial trial should be interpreted as embodying the common law criteria for challenging. In criminal cases, where, of course, the government always is one of the parties, its servants might properly be barred from the jury box.

It was to correct the results of this decision that Congress in 1935 extended by statute the category of persons eligible for jury service in the District of Columbia.[66] Included among those declared eligible for such duty were employees of the United States and of the District of Columbia, officers and enlisted men of the National Guard and of the reserve components of the services, notaries public, postmasters, recipients of pensions and gratuities from the United States or the District of Columbia, as well as those having contracts with either. It was as a test of the constitutionality of this act that the case of *United States* v. *Wood*[67] reached the Supreme Court.

The defendant in this case had been convicted in the police court of the District of Columbia on a charge of larceny from a private corporation. At the trial he attempted, but was denied the right, to challenge for cause three members of the panel because of their interest in the government. Of these, one was the recipient of a Civil War pension, one was employed in the Treasury Department, and the third worked at the navy yard. Counsel for the defendant urged that under the common law rule as restated in the *Crawford* case none of these fulfilled the requirement of impartiality.

The Court was able to draw on an exhaustive brief by the government which, based on elaborate historical research, disproved the existence of such a rule at common law. This array of evidence led the court to declare that

whatever the reason, it is manifest, to say the least, that there was no settled practice under the English law establishing an absolute disqualification of government employees to serve as jurors in criminal cases. And such a disqualification cannot, upon the grounds of such a practice, be treated as embedded in the Sixth Amendment . . . .[68]

Nor was there any showing that such a practice may have been in effect in the colonies or the states at the time of the Constitution's adoption. The *Crawford* case was not expressly overruled, but was held unacceptable as a determinative ruling.

However, even if it were assumed, as it had been in the Crawford case, that the eighteenth century common law excluded government servants from criminal juries, such a finding would not of necessity be conclusive. For, in the words of the opinion in the principal case, "whether a clause in the Constitution is to be restricted by a rule of the common law as it existed when the Constitution was adopted depends upon the terms or nature of the particular clause."[69] It may be noted that this conveniently flexible criterion for the application or modification of the old common law would still permit a return to strict construction in the future, although in the instant case the Court emphasized the progressive development allowed by the rule.

Reference was had to other modifications of common law rules which had been held not to have been precluded by the Sixth Amendment. Thus women had been admitted to jury service although such a practice was unknown when the Constitution was adopted.[70] Statutory reduction of the number of peremptory challenges allowed the accused by common law and earlier statutes had been held not to violate the Constitution.[71] The common law institution of the jury de medietate linguae— a jury consisting of one-half of aliens and one-half of citizens, to be convoked for the trial of alien defendants—had fallen into disuse since John Marshall had last allowed it in 1823.[72] Readjustments of procedure thus had been shown to be permissible and desirable where such changes promoted the spirit and purpose of the constitutional guarantees.[73]

As to the specific constitutional requirement invoked in this case, Chief Justice Hughes characterized it by the pithy observation that "impartiality is not a technical conception. It is a state of mind."[74] The Constitution had prescribed no tests by which to ascertain what mental attitude would be appropriately indifferent, nor should it be assumed that procedure was chained to any "ancient and artificial formula."[75]

The Court accepted the findings of the Congressional committees, which had recommended the passage of the act, to the

effect that continued disqualification of government employees
resulted in the exclusion from jury service of not only the major
but the most qualified portion of the population of the District
of Columbia.[76] The Court's examination of the legislative history
of the challenged statute resulted in the declaration that "the act
was passed to meet a public need and . . . no interference with
the actual impartiality of the jury was contemplated."[77]

"Why," the Court inquired rhetorically, "should it be assumed that a juror, merely because of employment by the Government, would be biased against the accused?"

In criminal prosecutions the Government is acting simply
as the instrument of the public in enforcing penal laws for the
protection of society. In that enforcement all citizens are interested. It is difficult to see why a governmental employee, merely
by virtue of his employment, is interested in that enforcement
either more or less than any good citizen is or should be.[78]

The mere fact of governmental employment was, therefore, not
to be viewed as constituting partiality in law, and the statute
authorizing the inclusion of government servants and similarly
situated persons in criminal jury panels was in contravention of
neither the letter nor the spirit of the Sixth Amendment.

At the time of the Wood decision a similar case was pending
in the Court of Appeals for the District of Columbia. That court,
following the Supreme Court's ruling, found nothing objectionable in the presence of four governmental employees on a jury
panel.[79]

The Circuit Court of Appeals for the Fifth Circuit found it
equally easy to follow the Wood precedent two years later in a
case which arose in the Panama Canal Zone. Several employees
of the German Hapag-Lloyd steamship line were tried on a charge
of having taken photographs of sensitive and restricted defense
installations in the Canal Zone. There was no dissent from the
court's ruling that jurors were not subject to peremptory challenge merely because they were employees or tenants of the
government.[80] It is perhaps not surprising that the court should

have been unwilling to foreclose or seriously limit the possibility of criminal jury trials in the Canal Zone—where of necessity most persons qualified for jury service would be in an employment or tenancy relationship to the government; but conversely there may be room for doubt whether defense workers, relatives of military personnel, and similarly situated persons living in a strategically highly vulnerable area would be able to sit in judgment on alleged spies and preserve an attitude of impartiality. The issue, it would seem, bears a distinct resemblance to the more recent problem of the propriety of the inclusion of public servants on criminal juries in the trial of alleged Communists.[81]

The only other recorded case before 1947 was without any such ramifications. Indeed, its facts recalled those of the *Crawford* case, for the challenged juror's relation to the government was once more that of a part-time assistant postmaster in a country-store post office in Arkansas. The rule of the *Wood* case plainly applied and the claim of a denial of constitutional rights was rejected.[82]

The appellate court reports reveal no further challenges of the presence of government employees on criminal juries until 1947. Then, in two narcotics cases, the same attorney[83] raised the issue and, in one instance, was able to bring it before the Supreme Court. In one case, nine of the jurors were government employees. The Court of Appeals rejected the challenge on the authority of *United States* v. *Wood* and the Supreme Court denied certiorari.[84] In the second litigation, a situation was brought about in which all jurors were government employees and irregularities in the selection of the panel were alleged. The Supreme Court agreed to hear this case.[85]

The accused in this case, Robert Frazier, had been apprehended with a large quantity of narcotics presumably misappropriated from United States Army stores. He was indicted under the Harrison Narcotics Act,[86] found guilty, and sentenced to five years in prison.[87]

At the trial, a total of twenty-five prospective jurors were examined. After one peremptory challenge by the prosecution and two excuses by the court, twenty-two remained. Of these, thirteen were employed by the government, while eleven were engaged in private occupations. The defense peremptorily challenged all eleven privately employed persons, plus one of the government employees. This left a jury composed entirely of government employees and the defense, having exhausted the number of peremptory challenges allowed by statute, now challenged the entire panel for cause. The court denied the challenge, and defendant assigned this ruling as error.[88]

The Supreme Court majority reached the not implausible conclusion that defense counsel had intentionally precipitated a situation in which none but government employees would sit on the jury. The manner in which he exercised his peremptory challenges, Mr. Justice Rutledge declared, was "a deliberate choice, not an uninformed one." Since he had thus indicated an arbitrary preference among prospective jurors, the Court declined to "join in repudiating the consequences of his own selection."[89]

The defense had further alleged that the panel from which the talesmen were taken had been improperly selected. Counsel had stated, and the government failed to deny, that it was common practice in the courts of the District of Columbia to inquire which veniremen did not desire to serve and permit those to step aside. Persons in steady private employment, it was alleged, would prefer thus to be excused rather than to incur the pecuniary loss which would result from the difference between meager jury fees and their regular incomes. This monetary consideration did not apply to government employees who do not receive any special emoluments for the performance of jury duty but are given leave with full pay while serving on a jury.[90]

The Court asserted, first, that this exception was raised too late and hence might not be considered; secondly, that counsel's statements, unsupported by proof, had no standing in court. The government, it was said, was under no necessity to deny such unsupported allegations.[91]

Similarly, the challenge for "actual bias" of two of the jurors employed by the department responsible for the enforcement of the Harrison Act (Treasury) was rejected as having come too late.[92]

The actual decision of the majority thus rests upon the narrowest technical grounds. Two of the objections were rejected as having been asserted too late, while in the case of the third one (first in the sequence of this discussion) estoppel was invoked to bar the claim. Since the decision was based on these grounds, the recourse to a "broader, non-technical basis of impartiality as a state of mind"[93] is of interest only as a series of dicta designed to answer the dissent. The substance of these elaborations by Justice Rutledge rests on references to the Wood case as establishing the proposition that governmental employment was not a factor of legal relevance in determining impartiality of a jury panel.

In contrast to Justice Rutledge's terse and technical opinion, Justice Jackson, speaking also for Frankfurter, Douglas, and Murphy, dissented with the felicitous flourishes of phrase which one has come to expect of him. He "reject[s] as spurious any view that government employment differs from all other employment in creating no psychological pressure of dependency or interest in gaining favor, which might tend to predetermine issues in the interest of the party which has complete mastery over the juror's ambition and position." With a minimum of circumlocution the Justice points to the loyalty program in the government service, the "Washington witch hunt," as a dramatic illustration of the pressures to which the servants of the state are exposed. He suggests that there are "grounds to assume . . . that the normal proportion of them are subject to that very human weakness, especially displayed in Washington, which leads men to '. . . crook the pregnant hinges of the knee where thrift may follow fawning.' "[94] The Wood case is "a weak crutch"[95] on which to lean.

There three government beneficiaries were held not to be subject
to individual challenge for cause because their common law disqualification had been removed by statute. "But to hold that one
or a few government employees may sit by chance is no precedent
for holding that they may fill all the chairs by a system of retiring
everyone else."[96]

It is also emphasized that the *Wood* case involved larceny
from a public corporation, a type of case which elsewhere might
be handled by the state courts, whereas the offense of which
Frazier was accused was the violation of a federal policy. At least
one of the jurors was employed (as a messenger) in the office
of the Secretary of the Treasury, whose responsibility the enforcement of this policy is.

The dissenting Justices concluded that "almost within a
stone's throw from where we sit, a system is in operation which
has produced and is likely again and again to produce what dis-
interested persons are likely to regard as a packed jury." They
would "reverse this insignificant conviction and end this system
before it builds up into a scandalous necessity for reversal of some
really significant conviction."[97]

The major premise of the dissent is the identification of the
government prosecuting criminal cases as one of the litigants,
analogous to the parties in a civil suit. Chief Justice Hughes had
answered that proposition in *United States* v. *Wood*, and many
of our state jurisdictions remind us by the style of their criminal
cases that the government prosecutes crime on behalf of the
people, not against them. The suggested distinction between
crimes of common law origin and governmental policies to which
criminal sanctions attach does not appear to offer any ready criteria for practical application. In what category would the Mann
Act fall, or the Federal Stolen Goods Act? Nor should we lose
sight of the fact that, both historically and in present practice,
criminal juries do not function in the same manner nor to the
same ends as their civil counterpart.

On the other hand, the Court's majority uses the *Wood* case as if conditions of federal employment were entirely static. In 1909, the year of the *Crawford* decision, less than half of the government's employees were removed from political influences through the coverage of the Civil Service System. By 1932, a few years before the *Wood* case, the proportion of civil service employees among government workers had risen to eighty per cent.[98] In the light of this evolution Chief Justice Hughes' observations in *United States* v. *Wood* appear realistic; they envisage the existence of a career service the members of which partake of all the rights and duties of citizenship without any restraint or limitation resulting from their employment status.

Realism, however, demands that we recognize not only the mutations which took place between 1909 and 1936, but also the developments since the later date. In the interim Congress has seen fit to impose affirmative curbs upon the political rights of government employees[99] and Presidential action created a system of elaborate investigation into the loyalty to the nation of the individuals on the government's payroll.[100] There is much evidence that the apprehensions and fears to which Justice Jackson alludes are fairly widespread among the employees of the federal government of today.[101] Certainly the minimum effect of these measures has been to stigmatize government employ as a condition in which the rights of citizenship may be subject to limitation.

In the light of this trend the procedural and technical defects of the District of Columbia jury system as revealed in the *Frazier* case appear of minor significance and their correction, within seven months of the Court's decision, disposes of them, at least for the present.[102]

It may well be said that the accomplishment of these procedural adjustments represents a partial vindication of the dissenters in the *Frazier* case. Yet hardly had the official report of that case seen print when the Court faced the very same issue in a setting of facts compelling attention to the fundamental problem of substantive justice versus procedural regularity.[103]

Eugene Dennis, secretary general of the Communist Party in the United States, had been a most recalcitrant and unco-operative witness before the House Un-American Activities Committee and as a result had been charged with, and was convicted of, having wilfully failed to respond to a subpoena issued by a Congressional committee. On appeal, he urged that the district court should have upheld his challenge of all jurors who were employees of the United States government. The Court of Appeals held that his rights had not been impaired by the admission to jury service of government employees who were otherwise qualified. "Blanket disqualification for jury service," it was said, "would operate as a bill of attainder on the many hundreds of thousands of federal employees throughout the nation," by denying them the right [sic] to serve on juries. United States v. Wood and the Court of Appeals' own decisions in the Higgins and Frazier cases were cited as precedents.[104]

The Supreme Court's grant of certiorari was limited to the sole question of the effect of some of the jurors' employee relationship to the government on the impartiality of the trial.[105] Counsel for the appellant, denying the applicability of the Wood and Frazier rule, urged that the involvement of a reputed Communist in a criminal trial made it impossible for an employee of the government, under present-day conditions, to be truly impartial. He was able to adduce in support of this contention a forceful dissenting opinion by Judge Edgerton of the Court of Appeals for the District of Columbia, delivered in Eisler v. United States only a short time after a differently constituted panel of the same court had decided the Dennis case.[106]

Eisler, like Dennis a well-known and avowed Communist, had been tried on a charge of having made false statements in applying to the State Department for certain travel documents. Like Dennis, he sought to have governmental employees excluded from the jury. The court's majority (Miller and Clark, JJ.) dis-

missed the matter with a curt reference to the *Dennis* case. Judge
Edgerton, however, perceived a point of distinction between the
controlling *Wood* and *Frazier* decisions and the situation of Eisler
—and hence, by implication, of Dennis: "Government employment," he suggested, "is not commonly known to be endangered
by sympathetic association with thieves and drug peddlers. It is
commonly known to be endangered by sympathetic association
with Communists. Government employees are therefore anxious,
. . . to avoid seeming to sympathize with Communists. Acquittal
sometimes indicates, and it is often thought to indicate, that the
jury sympathized with the accused. It is therefore prudent for
government employees to convict an alleged Communist and im-
prudent to acquit him. For government employees to acquit this
alleged Communist leader would have been particularly impru-
dent. Trial by jurors whose personal security will either actually
or apparently be promoted by conviction and endangered by
acquittal is not 'trial by an impartial jury,' is not the due process
of law."[107]

Yet these arguments were not persuasive to a majority of
Supreme Court Justices hearing the *Dennis* case. Only Justice
Frankfurter and Justice Black dissented as the Court refused to
look beyond the record of the case. There, Mr. Justice Minton
found, was "no disclosure . . . that these jurors did not bring to
bear . . . the sense of responsibility and the individual integrity by
which men judge men."[108] The arguments of Judge Edgerton,
echoed in Justice Black's dissent, are rather cavalierly dismissed
as "vague conjecture" which "does not convince that government
employees are so intimidated that they cringe before their government in fear of investigation and loss of employment if they
do their duties as jurors, which duty this same government imposes upon them."[109]

Having thus reasserted the *Wood* doctrine, Justice Minton
rejects the suggestion that Communists represent a special case
calling for an exemption from the general rule: ". . . one of an
unpopular minority group must be accorded that solicitude

which properly accompanies an accused person, [but] he is not entitled to unusual protection or exemption."[110] The same approach commends itself to Mr. Justice Jackson: "Courts should give a Communist every right and advantage that they give to any defendant. But it is inconceivable that being a Communist entitles a defendant to more."[111] Justice Jackson's acquiescence in the affirmance of the lower court decision hinges almost entirely upon this disinclination on his part to admit political affiliation of the defendant as a basis for distinction. His concurring opinion reasserts his disapproval of the *Frazier* decision ("weird and misguided"), but the rule he would establish would bar government employees from all criminal juries, not merely from those summoned to hear cases against Communists.

The two dissenters, Justices Frankfurter and Black, eschew such general disapprobations and appraise the case in essentially pragmatic terms. Frankfurter suggests that government employees might well be considered disqualified to determine guilt or innocence where the immediate security of the nation is concerned. The Justice's strong concern for the integrity of the judiciary is exemplified in his reasoning: "The powerful claim in behalf of our civilization represented by our system of criminal justice will be vindicated and strengthened if those who in the popular mind appear to threaten the very existence of the government are tried by citizens other than those in the immediate employ of the government at the seat of the government."[112]

Justice Black, who had joined the majority in the *Frazier* case, emphasizes the effect of the recent "loyalty" probes on the government employee and his capacity to judge impartially where Communists are involved.

The prevailing pattern of loyalty investigations and threatened purges makes it wholly unrealistic to expect government employees to enter the jury box with that quality of disinterestedness essential to complete impartiality. . . . To say that employees of the United States could meet objective tests of complete impartiality in cases like this is to disregard human nature. Probably at no period of the nation's history has the "loyalty" of government employees been subjected to such constant scrutiny by so many government agents and secret informers. And for the past few years press and radio have been crowded with charges by responsible officials and others that the writings, friendships or associations of some government employee have branded him "disloyal." Government employees have good reason to fear that an honest vote to acquit a Communist or anyone else accused of subversive beliefs, however flimsy the prosecutor's evidence, might be considered a "disloyal" act which could easily cost them their jobs.[113]

Exclusion of government employees from juries deliberating the fate of accused Communists would thus safeguard the prospective juror as much as the defendant.

In the six opinions delivered in these two cases, *Frazier v. United States* and *Dennis v. United States*, in their cumulative effect, the first fact which stands out is that only one member of the Court, Mr. Justice Jackson, would overturn the rule of the *Wood* case entirely and summarily exclude government employees from service on criminal juries.[114] Justices Black and Frankfurter, though customarily dividing on matters of procedural regularity where state courts are involved,[115] appear to share the same pragmatic approach to the problem of substantial fairness of procedure in the federal courts. Their motivation differs but their reasoning proceeds on parallel lines. To Frankfurter, it is the standing and reputation of the judicial system which requires insistence on a standard of impartiality that would forbid the seating of government employees in the trial of Communists. For Black, it is the self-respect of the juror which needs to be protected as much as the member of the despised minority who may be on trial. Both Justices seem content to let the rule of the *Wood* case stand; but Black would suspend its operation whenever the standing of the accused or the nature of the offense would make it difficult for a government employee, under pressure of loyalty tests, to be truly impartial; Frankfurter would dispense with the *Wood* rule where its application would result in adverse reflections being cast upon the judicial system, as in the *Frazier* case with its double standard of compensation for jurors, or in the *Dennis* case with its implications of anti-Communist phobia in government service.

It is suggested that neither the majority view of the two cases nor Mr. Justice Jackson's position as evidenced by his concurrence in the *Dennis* case offers a constructive solution to the dilemma. It can hardly be maintained that such conditions as revealed by the *Frazier* case conform to ideals of equal justice commonly held by the American people; as Mr. Justice Frankfurter suggests (recalling perhaps the first perjury trial a year earlier of his protégé Alger Hiss), "Inroads have been made on the secrecy of the jury room"—a factor which can hardly be overlooked in determining a government employee's suitability for jury service in "sensitive" cases. In the great majority of cases the arguments of Chief Justice Hughes will, of course, continue to apply: there is no special reason for excluding the employees of the government merely because the government prosecutes a criminal suit. But to apply this rule to *any* suit is to ignore differences, in the name of law, which to the non-lawyer are strikingly apparent.

Recent trials of individuals suspected of or known to possess Communist leanings or affiliations have, with one exception (the trial of the Communist leaders under the Smith Act, in the Southern District of New York), been based on grounds of a technical, non-political nature. Perjury, contempt, deportation have been used as judicial weapons in an essentially political conflict. To this writer there is a striking analogy between the case of the German spies in the Panama Canal Zone, discussed above, and the cases of Dennis, Eisler, and other Communists. The mere assertion of "impartiality in fact" can hardly becloud the relative improbability of an individual's being free of any apperceptive bias where occupational pressures and associations have been continuously exerted.

One may be permitted to extend this reasoning even further: considering the increasing number of persons associated with government in one way or another—and hence subject to loyalty investigations—; considering further the well-known fact that such investigations commonly draw inferences and implications from associations, hence placing the friends or relatives of government employees in a position not much different from that of the employee himself; and bearing in mind the still greater number of those who must reasonably anticipate that, for one reason or another, their loyalty may, at some future date, become subject to scrutiny—can it be expected that citizens, of whatever status, would be possessed of complete impartiality where the nature of the crime or the person of the accused conjures up real or apparent threats to the security of the nation?

The jury trial has been subject to attack from many quarters in recent years.[116] It has been equally vigorously defended. It is suggested here that the issue of government employees serving on criminal juries permits a revealing magnification of one of the limits of trial by jury. To discard all distinctions between employees of the government and other citizens in respect to jury service accorded with the political neutralization of government employment through civil service. It would seem equally sound to insist on differentiation in law where practice has established preferential positions, as was clearly the case in *Frazier v. United States*. If the loyalty program places government employees in a category by themselves, the law can hardly close its eyes to such distinctions. Similarly, if the ramifications of the testing of individual loyalties transcend the relationship of governmental employment, if the same disability which bars government employees from jury service in certain cases is of general application, it may indeed become desirable to recognize that there are some matters which are properly not susceptible to trial by jury.

While *United States v. Wood* and the more recent *Frazier* and *Dennis* cases demonstrate judicial reaction in one limited area to public policy and public needs, a similar interplay of pressure and accommodation had, a number of years sooner, become evident in the decisions of the courts with regard to the systematic exclusion of race or class groups from jury panels. The most notable cases in this category have been those dealing with discrimination against Negroes. The constitutional protection invoked in these cases has, however, customarily been the equal protection clause of the Fourteenth Amendment rather than the Sixth Amendment. Interpreting and applying the equal protection clause, the Supreme Court as long ago as 1880 announced that a Negro was entitled to be tried by a jury from which Negroes had not by law been systematically excluded because of their race;[117] but it has also held that the mere fact that the jury of the trial did not include any Negroes would not constitute a basis for reversal.[118] Not until the second Scottsboro case,[119] was it ruled that exclusion by habitual administrative practice constituted denial of equal protection as fully as did exclusion by force of law. Evidence to the effect that for a generation or longer no Negro had been called for jury service in a county where sufficient numbers of qualified citizens of the African race resided, was held to be adequate ground for a finding that discrimination had purposely been practiced.

These and related opinions all proceeded on equal protection grounds. Only on rare occasions has the Sixth Amendment's requirement of impartiality been invoked where it was claimed that exclusion of named groups operated to disfavor the accused. In *Ruthenberg v. United States*,[120] a Selective Draft Law case, the defendants, who were Socialists, alleged denial of their constitutional rights under the Sixth Amendment because the grand and trial juries were composed exclusively of members of other political parties and of property owners, a contention of which the court easily disposed, following the precedent established in the Negro case of *Virginia v. Rives*.[121]

In a more recent case,[122] the defendants claimed to have been denied their rights under the amendment because, they alleged, all the names of women placed in the box from which the jury

panel was drawn were taken from a list furnished the clerk of the
court by one civic organization (the Illinois League of Women
Voters), which list contained only those members of that organization who attended "jury classes whose lectures presented the
views of the prosecution." However, the defendants were unable
to prove this allegation and that part of their case failed. But
Justice Murphy, speaking for the Court,[123] took the opportunity
to make some general observations on jury trial. "Our notions of
what a proper jury is," he stated, "have developed in harmony
with our basic concepts of a democratic society and a representative government." These notions, the Justice found, required the
jury to be a body truly representative of the community. The
selection of jurors from the membership of any particular private
organizations, however high-principled and civic-minded, would
run counter to the traditional requirements of jury trial.[124] This
dictum, though in reply to a contention raised under the Sixth
Amendment, was couched essentially in terms of equal protection,
as had been all the cases on racial exclusion. Justice Murphy's
allusion to terms and standards of the Sixth Amendment was
little more than a gesture.

In a similar manner the Court in another connection per-
functorily used language resembling that of the Sixth Amendment, only to proceed to decision on grounds of discrimination
in violation of the requirements of equal protection. Here[125] partiality of the jury was alleged to have been due to the omission
from the jury panel of all wage earners in order to "relieve the
economically least secure from the financial burden which jury
service involves under existing circumstances."[126] In a decision
which Justice Frankfurter, in his dissent, branded as reminding
him of "burning the barn in order to roast the pig," the Court
held such discrimination to be fatal error, for, so it was stated,
"were we to sanction an exclusion of this nature we would en-
courage whatever desires those responsible for the selection of
jury panels may have to discriminate against persons of low economic and social status."[127]

The rule in this case, which involved a civil suit for damages in negligence, was subsequently followed in a criminal case[128] in which it was charged that women had been purposely omitted from the jury lists. In neither case was the Sixth Amendment mentioned in the opinion.

The problem of the so-called "blue ribbon" jury which has occupied—and divided—the Supreme Court twice in recent years[129] was similarly discussed and decided in terms of equal protection. It seems worthy of note, however, that the minority of the Court, speaking through Mr. Justice Murphy, here, as its spokesman had previously done in individual opinions, appears to consider it necessary that the jury, in order to retain its "democratic flavor," must not only be impartial but must represent a fair (if not a true) sampling of one's neighbors. It is certainly fundamental to the notion of an impartial jury as embodied in the Sixth Amendment that systematic exclusion of any group of persons from jury service should not be permitted to work prejudice against a defendant. Yet neither the Sixth Amendment nor the Equal Protection Clause should be assumed to stipulate affirmatively who must be on a jury. The requirement of impartiality is an effective weapon for the suppression of prejudicial partiality but, as John Marshall had wisely recognized in the early day of the republic and Charles Evans Hughes observed in our day, impartiality is not a condition which can be measured by technical standards. If Justice Murphy's statements are meant to imply that impartiality cannot be attained unless the defendant's social, economic, racial, or religious group is represented on the jury the workability of such a requirement must be doubted. It should be noted, however, that while dissenting opinions in the "blue ribbon" jury cases invite such speculations the dissenters would base their decision on the classification of defendants rather than jurors.

Striking again is the absence in these two recent cases of references to the specific language of the Sixth Amendment. It would seem that the Court increasingly prefers to decide on broader grounds those issues arising with regard to jury trials which by their nature constitute manifestations of the more far-reaching social or political problems of the nation. The specific procedural guarantees of the amendments lose in importance as procedural due process is increasingly used to effect Supreme Court supervision over the proceedings of trial courts.

Chapter V

Vicinage, Indictment, and Witnesses

In addition to reaffirming the pre-eminent place of the criminal jury, already assured by the provisions of the Judiciary Article of the original Constitution, the Sixth Amendment purported to guarantee to the accused several other procedural rights which at the time of its adoption had either most recently been won, or whose denial by British authority had stirred the sensibilities of the former colonists. Of the guarantees thus added, that of speed and publicity of proceedings was discussed in connection with the mode of trial in the preceding chapter; another, that of assistance of counsel, has acquired such recent prominence that separate discussion in a subsequent chapter appears justifiable. Of the remaining guarantees, one deals with the locality from which the jury is to be taken, one aims at certainty of the charge, while two others concern witnesses and the defendant's rights with regard to them.

Vicinage

The Sixth Amendment requires that the jury trying a person accused of crime be "of the State and district wherein the crime shall have been committed" and the district referred to must previously have been ascertained by law. It should be noted at once that, strictly speaking, this provision does not constitute a limitation on the venue; it does not regulate the place at which the trial must be held. Only in the Judiciary Article[1] does the Constitution purport to restrict the *venue* of criminal cases. The Sixth Amendment's provision here under discussion pertains only to the locality from which the jury is to be selected; in other words, it defines the outer limits of the *vicinage* from which the jury must be summoned.[2]

The absence of a vicinage provision was, as previously related,[3] one of the principal objections raised against the Judiciary Article when the proposed Constitution was being discussed in the state ratifying conventions. The specific extent of the vicinage was apparently a major subject of contention when the First Congress deliberated on the amendments to be proposed to the states.[4] Yet, if the debates in the state conventions can be taken as typical, those who clamored for more specific and more narrowly defined criteria of vicinage were frequently speaking in terms of venue, or at least they failed to distinguish clearly between vicinage and venue, between origin of the jury and location of the trial. This may have been due, as has been suggested, to the colonists' customary appeal to the right of vicinage when they wished to assert immunity from the English practice of removing prisoners for trial to England or to some other colony.[5] "Transportation beyond the Seas" was then denounced as a violation of the right to vicinage; this concept was emotionally associated with Magna Carta and hence likely to evoke far more instantaneous defensive reaction than could have been expected from the technically more accurate charge of arbitrary changes of venue.

But if there is evidence to support this assertion, that the issue of vicinage had been confused by the use made of the term in Revolutionary and pre-Revolutionary days, the difficulties created by such loose usage were merely additional to the very evident disparity of opinion with reference to the proper area of vicinage. The wording of the amendment represented a compromise between the localist tendencies of those who wished to restrict vicinage to the county and the Federalists who urged a minimum of restraint on the exercise of the judicial power of the national government. By tying the concept of vicinage to a system of judicial districts subject to Congressional determination, the First Congress passed the problem to its successors and left unsolved the conflict of opinions which had divided its members.

It is clear, however, that at the time of the adoption of the amendment its terms must have appeared as assuring the broader, rather than the narrower, definition of vicinage. For by the Judiciary Act of 1789, which had been passed by Congress one day prior to its final action in recommending the amendments to the states, the district boundaries coincided in all but two instances with those of the states.[6]

Yet subsequent developments have tended to reverse that result, so that today the constitutional limitation of the vicinage to judicial districts has become a serious impediment to the efficient administration of justice.[7] For it would be misleading to conclude that the increase in the number of districts from fifteen in 1789 to eighty-four in 1945 merely paralleled the growth of the territory to be covered by the districts. It is necessary to visualize this district system not in terms of area, but in terms of time space. At the beginning of the national government a traveler passed, in the five days required to go from New York to Boston,[8] through only four districts. At the same time a journey from Boston to Savannah took 22½ days[9] and to reach the distant points of the interior was a four to five weeks' trip from almost any point of the east coast.[10] By contrast, it is today possible to cross the country from coast to coast in less than one day's time. The country has grown in size, but in effect its most distant points are nearer to each other today than Boston was to New York in 1789. In terms of time and distance the present districts are therefore much smaller than those established by the apportionment of the Judiciary Act of 1789.

In addition it should also be remembered that within the districts the load of judicial business has grown ever larger. The federal criminal law alone has expanded from the thirty-three sections of the Crimes Act of 1790[11] to the 540 sections now constituting the substantive provisions of Title 18 of the United States Code, not to mention the numerous sections scattered through other parts of the Code which carry criminal sanctions.[12] Criminal cases before the federal courts have increased at such a rate that in 1945 the district courts alone heard 39,355 criminal cases, involving 46,160 defendants.[13]

The results of this pressure on the courts has been the establishment of smaller districts in place of older, larger ones. Thus judicial districts have become smaller not only in terms of time and distance, but also in geographic area. The web of narrowing boundary lines increasingly tends to fetter the administration of justice by the federal courts. For, as a consequence of the vicinage provisions of the Sixth Amendment, if an accused is found in any district, other than the one in which the alleged crime was committed, a jury of that district cannot try him there. Congress and the courts have endeavored—as will be shown below—to devise means whereby the ends of justice might be more readily approximated in such cases; but essentially we remain faced with the fact that vicinage is an anachronism unsuited to modern conditions and productive of neither better justice nor greater liberty.

That the jury be taken from the neighborhood was, of course, essential in the days when the jurors were still expected to bring to the determination of the case their own knowledge of the facts. But that need had ceased long before 1789. Jurors had become hearers of evidence in court and, indeed, previous knowledge and opinion of the case had become a principal cause for the rejection of jurors. Vicinage, revitalized, as was suggested above, as a political argument of the Revolution, as a legal concept appears to be at cross purposes with the ideal of impartiality. The inclusion of both impartiality and vicinage in the same amendment is indicative of the transitory stage of criminal procedure at that time, but need not be taken as attaching equal weight and significance to the two requirements. Indeed, the recent apparent willingness of the Supreme Court to depart from the former rigid interpretation of the procedural guarantees[14] would seem to permit the inference that efforts to circumvent or at least ease the burden of the constitutional vicinage provision would probably not meet with disapproval on the part of the highest court of the land.

Congressional action has already pointed the way. As judicial business increased, Congress, instead of continuing to divide existing districts into new ones, created subdivisions within districts, and called these sub-districts "divisions."[15] By this device it was obviously intended to alleviate the pressure on the courts by the creation of additional forums of original jurisdiction. There is no indication, however, that Congress, in setting up divisions of district courts, intended to restrict the vicinage to the divisions so created. And only in rare instances have courts interpreted an act subdividing a judicial district as a mandatory decision by Congress that "jurors must be drawn from the counties constituting the division for which the term is held at which they are required to serve."[16]

In the majority of the cases involving divisions as vicinage the objection raised was to the opposite effect, namely that the jury was unconstitutionally selected because its vicinage was too narrow. Thus, for instance, in *Ruthenberg v. United States*[17] it was contended that the plaintiffs in error had not been tried by a jury of the state and district, as required by the Sixth Amendment, because the jurors had been drawn not from the entire district but only from one portion thereof. The Supreme Court, however, pointed to the Judiciary Act of 1789,[18] as a contemporaneous construction of the amendment, and to the continuous legislative and judicial practice under that act and analogous provisions in later enactments, and rejected the contention as unsound.

The provision of the Judiciary Act referred to by the Court in this case was section 29,[19] which provided that jurors should be returned

from such parts of the district from time to time as the court shall direct, so as shall be most favorable to an impartial trial, and so as not to incur an unnecessary expense, or unduly to burden the citizens of the district with such services.

This language was retained in the Revised Statutes[20] and today may be found, unchanged, in Section 277 of the Judicial Code.[21]

As a lower court observed in 1891, "It cannot be possible that in framing the Sixth Amendment Congress intended thereby to secure a constitutional enactment requiring juries to be summoned from an entire State or district, and at the same time, by the provisions of the Judiciary Act, declared that the courts should have the power to direct the juries to be summoned from parts only of the district."[22] The compelling conclusion appears to be that the Sixth Amendment, by its vicinage provision, established the outer limits only of the area from which the jury must be selected. The amendment does not require that the jury be summoned from the entire district; it means only that the jury cannot be selected from without or beyond the district.[23]

It should be noted that these outer limits are twofold: they are the state, which is a relatively fixed and immutable area, and the district,—a concept which was purposely left flexible and open to readjustment. As was previously shown in this chapter, the original districts were virtually identical with the states then in the Union. Subsequent developments have resulted in a situation in which most states now contain two or more districts. But there is nothing in the Constitution, nor in the history of its adoption, that stipulates that districts must be smaller than states. By the successful use of the division of districts it has already been determined that the vicinage provision of the Sixth Amendment does not require that each district constitute the vicinage of one court and one court only. There are no constitutional reasons why Congress could not provide for as many district courts, sitting in divisions, as the pressure of judicial business may require, and still reduce the number of judicial districts by enlarging them to statewide or even larger extent.

The advantages to be gained from an enlargement in the size and reduction in the number of existing judicial districts would become particularly apparent with respect to the removal of persons apprehended in some district, other than the one where the crime was committed, to that district where alone a jury can be called for their trial.[24] While the transfer of offenders between districts of a state judiciary system commonly is a matter of course and the procedures of interstate rendition have greatly facilitated the return to a state of fugitives from its justice, removal proceedings between federal districts continue to be time-consuming[25] and hedged about with uncertainties of the law.

There is no constitutional requirement that a defendant whose removal is sought should be given a hearing in removal proceedings, or, indeed, that there be any formal proceedings at all.[26] The only statutory basis for removal proceedings has remained essentially unchanged since 1789.[27] The law merely states that

where any offender . . . is committed in a district other than that where the offense is to be tried, it shall be the duty of the judge of the district where such offender . . . is imprisoned, seasonably to issue, and of the marshal to execute, a warrant for his removal to the district where the trial is to be had.

In what manner the judge is to proceed, whether he must grant a hearing to the person to be removed and what the scope of the hearing shall be, and other matters had to be worked out by the courts, with the resultant vacillation in the rules that had to be expected.[28]

A step toward reform was taken by the promulgation of Rule 40 of the new Federal Rules of Criminal Procedure.[29] The Advisory Committee which authored the new rules recognized the existence of two distinct problems: on the one hand, there was an undeniable need of protection for the defendant against removal without probable cause to a distant point for trial;[30] on the other hand, as the Committee observed, "experience has shown that removal proceedings have at times been used for dilatory purposes and in attempting to frustrate prosecution by preventing or postponing transportation even as between adjoining districts and between places a few miles apart."[31] Accordingly, the new rules differentiate between cases of removal to a nearby district and cases in which removal is sought to some distant point for trial. The first group includes by definition all instances in which a person accused of crime is apprehended in another district of the same state, or if in another state, then less than one hundred miles from the place where the prosecution is pending. In these cases removal to the district of prosecution is now a matter of course. In all other cases, and they constitute the second group, formal removal proceedings are continued. Their extent depends on whether the demand for removal is based upon an indictment or upon an information or complaint. But regardless of the basis for the demand the accused must be heard, and evidence must permit the conclusion that sufficient ground has been shown to warrant the issuance of a removal order before the judge of the district of arrest may order the actual transfer of the accused to the place of prosecution.

Under the circumstances, Rule 40 must be considered a substantial and commendable advance in judicial administration.[32] The distinction between near and distant points of prosecution clearly effects a necessary adaptation of the rules of law to the conditions of life. But it should be remembered that the new rules are also subject to judicial interpretation and that their effectiveness cannot as yet be fully appraised.[32a] Whether this step alone will suffice, or whether it will be necessary to overhaul and redesignate the entire system of districts to the maximum degree of flexibility reconcilable with the express words of the Constitution, remains to be seen.

By comparison with this general objection to vicinage as an antiquated and obsolete notion of procedure, other problems which have been raised in connection with this provision have been relatively minor in nature. These have been primarily concerned with two questions: where, exactly, is the place of commission of a crime? and what effect does re-districting have on the right to a jury of the vicinage?

Defendants have repeatedly attacked the jurisdiction of trial courts, alleging that they could not have been guilty of any crime in the district of trial because they had not been physically present therein at the time of the alleged crime. The Supreme Court has, however, declared that such a requirement was neither the purpose nor the effect of the constitutional provision.

The right secured [said the Court in a leading case] is not the right to be tried in the district where the accused resides, or even in the district in which he is personally present at the time of committing the crime, but in the district "wherein the crime shall have been committed."[33]

In order to place the commission of a crime it is, of course, necessary to determine what specific act it is to which the penal sanction is to apply. Because federal crimes are of statutory origin,[34] the nature of any crime cognizable by a federal court depends on the terms of the statute defining it. This is, therefore, not a question of procedure but of substantive criminal law.[35] Thus, for instance, where the punishable offense was defined as causing lottery material to be delivered through the mail, the district to which such matter was sent was held to be the proper place of trial.[36] But where the offense charged was the depositing in the mails of prohibited matter, the accused could be tried in no district other than the one in which the objectionable matter was placed in the mails.[37] The Supreme Court found no constitutional objection to a statute which constituted interstate transportation in violation of its provisions as a continuous offense subject to prosecution in any state or district through which such transportation passed.[38] But where a statute made it unlawful to ship into a state or territory any denture not made in accordance with the laws of the place of destination, the Court's majority would, "if the enactment reasonably permits," construe it as authorizing trial of the sender at the place of dispatch, and of the recipient in the district of receipt.[39]

The special problem presented by conspiracy cases is also to be resolved in terms of substantive law criteria. Contrary to the old common law, the modern American rule requires an overt act before a conspiracy can be prosecuted as criminal. The crime of conspiracy has, therefore, not been committed until an overt act has taken place. That overt act is part of the crime and wherever it may have been consummated, whether the accused was physically or only constructively present, there it may also be punished.[40]

If the phrase "where the crime shall have been committed" must be interpreted in the light of the statutory definitions of the several crimes, the provision that the district "shall have been previously ascertained by law" must stand on its own terms. These have been interpreted not to preclude a change in the territorial limits of a district, provided the jury is summoned from a vicinage contained within the district as it was at the time of the commission of the crime.[41] Nor does this provision prevent trial of an accused in the district within which the crime was committed although the specific locality of the crime has subsequently been transferred to another district.[42] An Act of Congress provides that whenever a new district is established, or territory transferred among districts, prosecutions begun prior to such transfer shall be proceeded with as if no transfer had taken place; in other words, the court of the district of commission may exercise its jurisdiction pro hac vice over its original territory regardless of subsequent changes.[43] The requirement of the Sixth Amendment is complied with "if, before the crime was committed, the district in which it was committed was ascertained by law, and the trial is . . . by an impartial jury of any part of that district,"[44] though for all other purposes the members of the jury may have become inhabitants of a new or different district.

Certainty of Indictment

The Sixth Amendment's provision that "in all criminal prosecutions, the accused shall enjoy the right . . . to be informed of the nature and cause of the accusation" against him is substantially a re-declaration of the common law rule requiring the charge to be set out with precision and fullness, so that the defendant may be enabled to make his defense and avail himself of his conviction or acquittal in a subsequent prosecution for the same offense.[45]

This provision does not impose a constitutional duty on the government to furnish the accused with copies of the indictment unless he requests them.[46] Nor does omission of a recital in the record that the indictment has been read to the defendant constitute fatal error.[47] The requirement that persons accused of capital offenses must be furnished copies of the indictment and lists of prospective jurors and government witnesses two (in treason cases: three) days before the trial is statutory in nature.[48] The Constitution itself does not specify when or how the accused is to be informed of the charges against him. It merely assures him of the right to demand such information.

What will constitute sufficient information to satisfy the requirement must of course be determined with reference to the specific facts and circumstances in each case. As a general rule, however,

where the statute creating the offense sets forth fully, directly, and expressly all of the essential elements necessary to constitute the crime intended to be punished, it is sufficient if the indictment charges the offense in the words of the statute. But where the statute is in general terms and does not set out expressly and with certainty all of the elements necessary to constitute the offense, the indictment must descend to particulars and charge every constituent ingredient of which the crime is composed.[49]

A leading case exemplifying insufficiency of the indictment was *Cruikshank* v. *United States*,[50] a prosecution under the Enforcement Act of 1870.[51] That statute provided criminal penalties for persons found guilty of conspiring to "injure, oppress, threaten, or intimidate any citizen, with intent to prevent or hinder his free exercise and enjoyment of any right or privilege granted or secured to him by the constitution or laws of the United States." The indictment in the case charged a conspiracy with intent to hinder and prevent two named Negro citizens in the free exercise and enjoyment of "every, each, all, and singular the rights" granted them by the Constitution, etc. No particular right was specified as having been violated or threatened by the conspiracy.

The Court quoted as an elementary principle of criminal pleading that "where the definition of an offense . . . includes generic terms, it is not sufficient that the indictment shall charge the offense in the same generic terms as in the definition; but it must state the species,—it must descend to particulars."[52] The Court found the conclusion "irresistible" that the indictment failed to attain the certainty and precision necessary in order to inform the accused of the nature and cause of the charges against them.[53]

The allegation of insufficiency of the indictment is frequently made and is, indeed, a common feature of omnibus attacks on criminal judgments.[54] But the true test of the sufficiency of an indictment has been declared to be "not whether it could have been made more definite and certain, but whether it contains the elements of the offense intended to be charged,"[55] and no greater particularity of allegation is required than may be of service to the accused in understanding the charge and preparing his defense.

But while the defendant may insist on his right to be apprised of the crime charged against him with such reasonable certainty as to enable him to make his defense and, after judgment, protect himself against another prosecution for the same offense, this right is not considered infringed by the omission from the indictment of indecent and obscene matter, alleged as not proper to be spread upon the records of the court.[56] Where such omitted matter forms part of a book or publication the defendant must, if he so desires, be afforded an opportunity, before the trial opens, to ascertain which parts or passages will specifically be relied upon by the prosecution.[57] Where the objectionable matter was contained in a letter, which the indictment identified by time and place of mailing, and name and address of the recipient, this description was held to advise the accused sufficiently of the nature and cause of the accusation against him.[58] Under a recent decision, tacitly sanctioned by the Supreme Court's denial of certiorari, a charge of lascivious conduct is sufficient if it merely follows the general words of the statute, and the indictment will not fail for uncertainty because it omits particulars of acts of sexual perversion.[59] It would appear that this case, reasoned by analogy to the obscene literature cases, would present the limit to which this exception might be taken in the interest of public morality without denying the required minimum of certainty in the indictment.

This requirement of the Sixth Amendment is also frequently invoked in attacks on statutes as being too vague or uncertain. This would only be a matter of consistency where the indictment is drawn in the terms of the statute: if the statute falls short of the required standard of certainty an indictment that follows the statutory language must be similarly deficient.[60] By contrast, it does not follow that an indictment based on a vague statute must of necessity be defective. It would seem to be perfectly possible to make the indictment specific even though the statute may be too general in its terms.[61] The problems, are, however, sufficiently related to invite interchange of arguments and precedents. The courts have been most careful, however, to base their decisions in cases involving uncertainty of legislation entirely on due process, either under the Fifth[62] or under the Fourteenth Amendment.[63] The Sixth Amendment's applicability is to uncertainty in procedure, not legislation.

Confrontation by Witnesses

The right of the accused in a criminal prosecution to be confronted with the witnesses against him did not originate with the provision of the Sixth Amendment, but was a common law right which had gained recognition as a result of the abuses in the trial of Sir Walter Raleigh.[64] The inclusion of this right among the guarantees of the Sixth Amendment, in addition to the amendment's solicitude for speed and publicity, aimed at the prevention of such abuses in the future. Essentially, to insist on the defendant's right to face and to challenge his accuser's witnesses is but to secure him an opportunity equal to his opponent's. As it is stated, the right is unequivocal and such infrequent litigation as has arisen with respect thereto has involved its limits and exceptions rather than its substance.

The common law knew only one exception to the rule, that of dying declarations.[65] More recently, Congress has authorized the introduction in evidence at criminal trials of certain writings made in the course of ordinary business.[66] The Federal Rules of Criminal Procedure allow for such a modification of the common law in their Rule 26,[67] and the courts have apparently found nothing objectionable in this new exception. Indeed, as Judge Augustus N. Hand said, "[the courts] think that business records kept as a matter of ordinary routine are often likely to be more reliable than dying declarations."[68]

The guarantee is, of course, clearly violated by the introduction of evidence given by witnesses whom the accused has not had an opportunity to cross-examine. Thus where the government based its case on two affidavits but called only one of the makers to testify in open court, it was held such a "palpable infringement" of defendant's right under the Sixth Amendment as to void the judgment even though the objection had not been raised in the trial court.[69]

Similarly, a statute declaring that the record of conviction against a thief should constitute proof at the trial of the receiver of the goods that such goods had been stolen, was held to impair the defendant's right under this provision.[70] The Court stated the rule in the following words:

A fact which can be primarily established only by witnesses cannot be proved against an accused—charged with a different offense for which he may be convicted without reference to the principal offender—except by witnesses who confront him at the trial, upon whom he can look while being tried, whom he is entitled to cross-examine, and whose testimony he may impeach in every mode authorized by the established rules governing the trial or conduct of criminal cases.[71]

The accused has, however, no right to insist on confrontation by a witness whom he himself had induced to stay away. "If a witness is absent by his [the defendant's] own wrongful procurement, he cannot complain if competent evidence is admitted to supply the place of that which he has kept away."[72] This rule appears to be entirely in accord with every basic notion of justice; it would, of course, be a flagrant miscarriage of the constitutional intent to permit an accused to claim protection against the legitimate consequences of his own wrongful acts.

Where, however, the absence of the witness could not be attributed to any suggestion, procurement, or act of the accused, the defendant's constitutional right will stand in bar of any reading of testimony given by an absent witness prior to the trial, even though the defendant had been present at the time such testimony had originally been given.[73] Only where the witness had died since giving his earlier testimony has it been held admissible to read a transcript at a later trial.[74] As the Supreme Court stated in announcing this rule, "To say that a criminal, after having been convicted by the testimony of a certain witness, should go scot free simply because death had closed the mouth of that witness, would be carrying his constitutional protection to an unwarrantable extent."[75]

It has been suggested that, inasmuch as the judicial definition of "criminal prosecutions" would seem to deny this constitutional guarantee to persons accused of misdemeanors or petty offenses, it might be sound policy to extend its operation to this latter category through the due process clause of the Fifth (and Fourteenth) Amendment.[76] No case to that effect has, however, been found; and the holding in West v. Louisiana,[77] reiterated more recently in the dictum of the Palko case,[78] would appear to indicate that an opportunity to confront the prosecution witnesses is not among the requirements of due process of law as presently applied by the courts.

Compulsory Process

The defendant's right to present his own witnesses had not been one of the ancient elements of the common law. It had, indeed, long been the rule to deny the accused the opportunity to present evidence in rebuttal of the charge, a practice which according to Blackstone had been derived from the civil law.[79] The rather scanty evidence on that subject apparently satisfied Holdsworth, who, asserting that such unfair treatment could not be justified "by any reason in English law," found that the inquisitorial methods of the European continental system had furnished the example which the common law judges had "eagerly" adopted.[80] It would seem at least equally plausible to assume that, regardless of the existence of foreign prototypes, the denial of adequate means of defense was entirely in keeping with the stringent methods which the Crown, with popular approval, employed to suppress the flagrant lawlessness of the sixteenth and seventeenth centuries.[81]

Whatever the reasons and origin of the original common law rule, its reversal by statute[82] had been so recent that at the end of the eighteenth century, when the Constitution and the first ten amendments were written, it was considered necessary and desirable to perpetuate this recent procedural improvement by the constitutional guarantee of compulsory process for the defense witnesses.[83] In the same vein, the First Congress implemented this guarantee in the Federal Crimes Act of 1790. There it was provided—and this language has remained on the statute books, without change, to the present day—that:

> Every person who is indicted of treason or other capital crime . . . shall be allowed, in his defense, to make any proof that he can produce by lawful witnesses, and shall have the like process of the court to compel his witnesses to appear at his trial, as is usually granted to compel witnesses to appear on behalf of the prosecution.[84]

That the process to be issued under this provision of the Sixth Amendment would exempt no class of individuals was determined at an early date in *United States* v. *Cooper*,[85] a decision by Justice Chase on circuit. The defendant, on trial for a libel on the President, applied to the court for a letter to be addressed to several members of Congress, requesting their attendance as witnesses on his behalf. Chase, in the bluff manner which made him so many enemies, announced that he would not sign "any letter of the kind proposed"; the Constitution had given to every man, accused of crime, the right to compulsory process to secure the attendance of his witnesses; there was no reason why members of Congress should be exempted from the service of such process, and hence it was unnecessary to request them to appear when they could be ordered to do so.

The compulsory process to which the defendant is so entitled includes the issuance and the serving of process (subpoenas) on the defense witnesses, but there is no general obligation on the part of the government to pay the expenses of such witnesses.[86] Only where the prisoner can show that he lacks the funds with which to defray his witnesses' expenses does it become the court's duty to pay such expenses.[87]

Implicit in the defendant's right to have his witnesses heard in court is the requirement that he should be allowed sufficient time to secure their attendance; and although it is within the court's discretion to grant or deny continuances, it has been held that the exercise of such discretion must be guided by the aims of this provision.[88]

The almost insignificant number of cases which have arisen under this provision would appear to indicate that its observance in letter and spirit is general and its place among the essentials of fair procedure uncontested. In view of this apparent acceptance, one would be inclined to surmise that any violation of this right, where not specifically within the scope of the Sixth Amendment, would constitute a denial of due process of law. No occasion has as yet arisen for adjudication of this point, and however reasonable it would appear to consider compulsory process for the defendant's witnesses an essential part of due process,[89] the Supreme Court has not so far seen fit to include it in that concept.[90]

Chapter VI

The Right to Counsel

It was the late Justice Cardozo who said that "the great generalities of the Constitution have a content and significance that vary from age to age."[1] The constitutional guarantee of the assistance of counsel in criminal trials[2] offers a striking example in point. If the importance of a constitutional provision can be gauged from the frequency with which its protection is invoked or its application contested, then the right to counsel has attained significance only within the last two decades.[3] The infusion of meaning into this clause by judicial interpretation will be the principal subject matter of this chapter.[4]

The incorporation in the Sixth Amendment of the right to counsel affirmed the rejection by American practice of the English common law rule on the subject. At the time of the American Revolution the law of England permitted a prisoner to be heard by counsel in misdemeanor and treason cases only. In ordinary felony cases the participation of counsel was prohibited.[5] It is necessary to recall, however, that in England the criminal defendant as a rule was confronted not by a public prosecutor but by the injured or some other interested party. In the colonies, on the other hand, the early eighteenth century had seen the establishment of full-time government officials with the duty of prosecuting crime.[6] The English practice, which Blackstone had denounced as "not all of a piece with the rest of the humane treatment of prisoners by the English law,"[7] was therefore even more inequitable under colonial conditions, and consequently was rejected by the colonists.

At the time of the adoption of the Constitution, twelve of the original thirteen states had made this renunciation of the common law rule as to counsel part of their constitutional systems.[8] The Sixth Amendment reflected the same intent and purpose that these provisions of the state constitutions were aimed at. Their end, and that of the Sixth Amendment, was to do away with the rules which denied representation by counsel in criminal prosecutions.[9] Their wording was that of a grant of a privilege, a sense also conveyed by the Judiciary Act of 1789, which is contemporaneous with the Sixth Amendment. Section 35 of that act provided:

That in all the courts of the United States the parties may plead and manage their own causes personally or by the assistance of such counsel or attorneys at law as by the rules of the said courts respectively shall be permitted to manage and conduct cases therein.[10]

That the amendment intended to do no more than to abrogate the common law with respect to representation by counsel has also been implied from the fact that, in the Federal Crimes Act of 1790, Congress imposed a statutory duty on the courts in capital cases to assign counsel to represent the accused.[11] "Obviously, if the constitutional guarantee comprised a duty on the part of the trial judge to assign counsel to the defendant, the statutory provision would be superfluous. Moreover, the enactment of such a law would seem to lead to an inference that there was no legal obligation on the part of a judge to appoint, or any legal right on the part of a defendant to secure the designation of counsel by the court in any other case."[12]

That the constitutional guarantee did not comprise the right of a prisoner to have counsel assigned to him by the court if, for financial or other reasons, he was unable to retain counsel appears to have been generally understood.[13] The Sixth Amendment was said to be, in that respect, "the declaration of a right in the accused, but not of any liability on the part of the United States."[14]

Until 1938,[15] it was not considered that there existed any constitutional duty on the part of the court to appoint counsel for a defendant who lacked the means to secure the assistance of counsel at his own expense. In practice, some of the federal courts were more magnanimous than the Constitution and Congress and assigned counsel in grave, though non-capital, cases.[16] But that the right to counsel imposed an obligation on the courts to provide the accused with counsel, at the risk of forfeiting their jurisdiction over the case, was not taken to be the rule until the Supreme Court, in *Johnson v. Zerbst*,[17] placed that interpretation on the Sixth Amendment.

The record in that case disclosed that Johnson and Bridwell, two enlisted men of the United States Marine Corps on leave, had been arrested in Charleston, South Carolina, on a charge of passing and possessing counterfeit Federal Reserve notes. Upon arraignment, both pleaded not guilty, said that they had no lawyer, and—in response to an inquiry by the court—stated that they were ready for trial. Thereupon they were tried, convicted, and sentenced, all without the assistance of counsel. Subsequently they sought a writ of habeas corpus to obtain their release from the Federal Penitentiary in Atlanta. Both the District Court and the Circuit Court of Appeals denied the petition and the Supreme Court took the case on certiorari.

Justice Black's opinion decided three points. In the first place he announced, without referring to or disposing of the previously accepted meaning of the amendment, that "the Sixth Amendment withholds from federal courts, in all criminal proceedings, the power and authority to deprive an accused of his life or liberty unless he has or waives the assistance of counsel."[18] The reason for this rule was to be found in the "realistic recognition of the obvious truth that the average defendant does not have the professional legal skill to protect himself when brought before a tribunal with power to take his life or liberty, wherein the prosecution is presented by experienced and learned counsel," and in the fact that the ". . . right to be heard would be, in many cases, of little avail if it did not comprehend the right to be heard by counsel."[19]

Secondly, the Court emphatically declared that a waiver of this important constitutional right could not be lightly assumed.

"The determination of whether there has been an intelligent waiver of the right to counsel must depend, in each case, upon the particular facts and circumstances surrounding that case, including the background, experience, and conduct of the accused."[20] To determine whether or not there is an intelligent and competent waiver by the accused is the responsibility of the trial judge, "and it would be fitting and appropriate for that determination to appear upon the record."[21]

Thirdly, the Court put its stamp of approval on the use of habeas corpus to test the validity of judgments alleged to have been obtained in contravention of the right to counsel. Assistance of counsel or a competent waiver thereof, it was declared, were necessary elements to a court's jurisdiction. "If this requirement of the Sixth Amendment is not complied with, the court no longer has jurisdiction to proceed. The judgment of conviction pronounced by a court without jurisdiction is void, and one imprisoned thereunder may obtain release by habeas corpus."[22]

Each of the three elements of the decision not only presented a departure from established interpretation and practice but also opened the door for further and more extended judicial activity in this field. The availability of the writ of habeas corpus in cases of alleged denial of counsel led to the reopening of countless decisions made prior to *Johnson v. Zerbst*. In passing on the petitions presented, there arose the question to what extent the record of the trial court should be permitted to be impeached. When and how far should evidence be accepted in support of the petition? Along a different line, the qualification imposed on waiver of counsel, that it be competent and intelligent, raised any number of factual questions.

One important question which required determination was, What effect should be attributed to a plea of guilty? Was one who had pleaded guilty entitled to contest his conviction because he had not had counsel? A number of courts have answered that question by holding that "where an accused personally enters a plea of guilty to a crime whereof he stands charged, and does so understandingly, freely and voluntarily without asking the assistance of counsel, a waiver of the right to be represented by counsel may fairly be inferred."[23]

These holdings were based on the proposition that a plea of guilty constitutes an admission of all that is alleged in the indictment and is in effect a waiver of trial, and consequently of all the incidents of trial, including the assistance of counsel. On the other hand, it has also been said that an accused who admits the offense with which the indictment charges him, still faces a number of questions of law for which he is properly in need of counsel. This position which declines to infer a waiver of counsel from a plea of guilty, has been taken by the Court of Appeals for the District of Columbia[24] and by the Circuit Court of Appeals for the Ninth Circuit.[25]

The Supreme Court appears to incline toward the same position. To be sure, in 1942 it was said in a dictum that "it is not suggested that a layman cannot plead guilty unless he has the opinion of a lawyer on the questions of law that might arise if he did not admit his guilt."[26] In the more recent case of *Rice v. Olson*,[27] however, it was just as unequivocally stated that "a defendant who pleads guilty is entitled to the benefit of counsel, and a request for counsel is not necessary." The Court adduced neither reasons nor authorities for this statement, which is probably only a dictum; but it would appear that in line with *Johnson v. Zerbst* the Court would also hold that a plea of guilty does not imply a waiver of counsel.[28]

On the other hand, it will be recalled, *Johnson v. Zerbst* had not maintained that the accused might not waive his right to counsel. The stipulation was that where the accused waived counsel he had to do so intelligently and deliberately, or, as Justice Frankfurter phrased it in another case, the accused "may waive his Constitutional right to assistance of counsel if he knows what he is doing, and his choice is made with eyes open."[29] To deny the accused's right to waive counsel would, of course, be tantamount to saying that "a layman is to be precluded from defending

himself because the Constitution is said to make him helpless
without a lawyer's assistance on questions of law."[30] To allow
waiver of counsel is also in keeping with the interpretation placed
on other portions of the Sixth Amendment. Inasmuch as the
accused may waive trial by jury,[31] consistent interpretation leads
to the conclusion that he may also waive counsel. Indeed, it has
been held that, having intelligently waived the assistance of counsel, he may also waive trial by jury.[32]

What will constitute an intelligent, hence effective waiver
must be determined in the light of the circumstances of each case.
One who has had legal training and had previously represented
himself in court would appear to be able to be sufficiently aware
of his rights and his position to proceed alone if he so desired.[33]
On the other hand, the inability of one who is deaf and unable
to read lips to execute an intelligent waiver may well be presumed.[34] Other circumstances which have been held to raise a
presumption that the waiver of counsel was not of the required
competence include occasions where the accused allegedly was
insane,[35] or had been coerced,[36] or induced by false promises,[37] or
had been under the influence of drugs.[38] Whether a boy of seventeen could competently and intelligently waive his right to counsel was held to be a question of fact, in the determination of
which the defendant's age, though not conclusive, was entitled
to serious consideration.[39]

The most immediate problem resulting from *Johnson* v.
Zerbst was, however, with regard to decisions rendered prior to
the announcement of the new rule. In many of these cases the
trial court had taken no steps to ascertain the defendant's desire
to have or to waive counsel, or, if it had done so, there was no
mention of it in the record; for neither step had been considered
necessary prior to *Johnson* v. *Zerbst*. As a result of that case the
courts, particularly those near federal penal institutions, were
virtually swamped by habeas corpus petitions from federal prisoners alleging denial of counsel. The District Court for the Northern
District of California, for instance, received, between June 1,

1938, and April 1, 1941, 131 petitions for habeas corpus from prisoners in Alcatraz Penitentiary; 75 of those were based on the decision in *Johnson v. Zerbst*.[40]

The Circuit Court of Appeals for the Tenth Circuit, which includes Leavenworth, initially solved the problem by holding that a waiver of the right to counsel would normally be implied where the accused had appeared without counsel and had failed to request that counsel be assigned him.[41] The courts of the Fifth Circuit (Atlanta) attempted similarly to limit the application of *Johnson v. Zerbst*.[42]

Both in the Tenth Circuit and in the Ninth, which includes Alcatraz, it was the practice to dispose of applications for habeas corpus on *ex parte* affidavits and without the taking of testimony.[43] This procedure was ruled improper by the Supreme Court in *Walker v. Johnston*.[44] Under the holding of this decision the issue of any petition for habeas corpus, the allegations of which, if true, would overcome the presumption of regularity of the record, must be determined by the court[45] on the testimony of witnesses, not merely on pleadings and affidavits. The same decision also held that the right to counsel was not satisfied if the accused was not in fact informed of his right and, if he proceeded to trial without counsel, had not knowingly and intelligently waived his right.[46]

That the solicitude of the courts for the right of counsel would be meaningless unless the assistance secured is effective assistance seems plain on the face of it. In practice, what has been held to be required in order for the assistance of counsel to be effective is that counsel must be competent, that he must have reasonable time and opportunity to prepare his case, that he be present at all stages of the trial, and that his service be exclusively in the interest of one defendant.

"The Constitution," it has been said, "does not guarantee that counsel appointed for, or employed by, a defendant shall measure up to his notions of ability or competency."[47] The considerations which motivate strict construction of the requirement of competence have been very aptly summarized by the Court of Appeals for the District of Columbia:

Few trials are free from mistakes of counsel. How much these mistakes contributed to the result can never be measured. There are no tests by which it can be determined how many errors an attorney may make before his batting average becomes so low as to make his representation ineffective. . . . To allow a prisoner to try the issue of the effectiveness of his counsel under a liberal construction of this phrase [of the Sixth Amendment] is to give every convict the privilege of opening a Pandora's box of accusations . . . .[48]

The prevailing view, in keeping with this reasoning, is that where the defendant claims denial of his constitutional right to counsel on the ground that assigned counsel was incompetent, the burden is on the defendant to prove such incompetence.[49] Where the attorney appointed by the court was a "substantial and trustworthy" member of the bar, his competency is to be presumed.[50] Indeed, it has been held that admission to the bar creates in itself a presumption of competency which is not overcome or lessened by the fact of the youth and brief professional experience of counsel.[51]

One charged with crime is not deprived of his constitutional right to the effective assistance of counsel merely because the counsel assigned to him by the court, after an investigation of the facts, advised him to plead guilty to the charge.[52] Nor may incompetence be conclusively implied from such omissions by counsel as failure to point out a defect in the indictment, or failure to include a bill of exceptions on appeal.[53] On the other hand, failure of appointed counsel in a capital case to examine the transcript of prior testimony and to file an appeal brief on time, was held to establish incompetence of counsel which should not be held against the accused.[54] But a defendant could not claim denial of effective assistance of counsel because the attorney appointed by the court had been intoxicated at some time during the trial where this condition had not been apparent to, or called to the attention of, the trial judge and no request was made for another attorney.[55] The effect of the cases to date appears to be that, in order for assistance of counsel to be held ineffective for want of competence of the appointed counsel, the representation must be "so lacking in competence that it becomes the duty of the court or the prosecution to observe and to correct it."[56]

The second element necessary to insure "effective" assistance is that counsel should have adequate opportunity to prepare and present his case. Although the granting of continuances is within the discretion of the court,[57] the court should make allowance for counsel's need to acquaint himself with an unfamiliar situation.[58] Presumably the availability and accessibility of witnesses and evidence must also be taken into account.[59] On the other hand, it is plain that the effective assistance of counsel has been denied if the court interferes with and hinders counsel in presenting the case.[60]

It has been said that "in an ideal system, counsel should be present at all stages of a criminal proceeding."[61] However, the protection extended by the Sixth Amendment covers by its terms "criminal prosecutions" only. A preliminary hearing does not fall within the definition of a criminal prosecution, and hence an accused is not entitled to counsel at that stage.[62] The Supreme Court has declined to review a decision of the Circuit Court of Appeals for the Tenth Circuit to the effect that no constitutional right has been violated by the trial court's failure to assign counsel prior to the return of the indictment by the grand jury.[63]

At the end of the trial, the return of the verdict by the jury and the imposition of sentence upon a verdict of guilty have been held to be steps in the trial at which the defendant still needs, and is entitled to, the guiding hand of counsel.[64] There is no constitutional right, however, to the assistance of counsel on appeal.[65]

During trial, it does not appear to contravene constitutional requirements to make substitutions for counsel when the accused is not in fact prejudiced thereby. Thus the accused's right to the assistance of counsel was held not to have been violated where the court permitted appointed counsel to withdraw and failed to appoint new counsel for six days but no further step was taken in the proceedings until new counsel declared himself ready to proceed.[66]

The Supreme Court has held that an accused is deprived of effective assistance of counsel if the court requests one lawyer simultaneously to represent co-defendants whose interests may conflict.[67] This does not rule out, however, the possibility of the court's appointing one attorney to represent co-defendants when this will neither embarrass counsel nor prejudice the accused.[68] Both propositions are only the logical implementations of the basic tenet of the legal profession which condemns as unethical the simultaneous representation of clients with conflicting interests.[69]

The principles enunciated in *Johnson* v. *Zerbst* and subsequent cases with regard to the right to counsel in criminal trials before federal courts are also reflected in the new Federal Rules of Criminal Procedure.[70] Rule 44 requires that "if the defendant appears in court without counsel the court shall advise him of his right to counsel and assign counsel to represent him at every stage of the proceeding unless he elects to proceed without counsel or is able to obtain counsel."[71] In the prescribed form for Judgment and Commitment the new rules require the court to note if the defendant appeared by counsel, and, if such was not the case, the entry must indicate that the defendant was advised of his right, had been asked his desire, and thereupon, by express statement, had waived the assistance of counsel.[72]

On the other hand, there were two problems which had become acute as a result of the courts' new solicitude for the right of counsel and for which neither decisions nor judicial rule-making could provide the remedy. In one case Congress came to the assistance of the courts: the many instances in which the validity of a waiver of counsel was found to depend on the actual words passed between judges and defendants emphasized the need for competent and complete official reporting of the court proceedings. The situation which actually existed in that respect was described by Mr. Justice Roberts in an opinion delivered in 1942:

There is no law of the United States creating the position of official court stenographer and none requiring the stenographic report of any case, civil or criminal, and there is none providing for payment for the services of a stenographer in reporting judicial proceedings. The practice has been for the parties to agree that a designated person shall so report. The one selected must be paid by private arrangement with one or more of the parties to the litigation. . . . [The law] does not authorize the procurement of a transcript of the testimony nor the payment for services in reporting evidence taken at the trial nor for the obtaining of it by the Government in behalf of an indigent defendant.[73]

This situation was, of course, not novel. The increased attention given to procedural matters, including the right to counsel, merely accentuated the need. The Judicial Conference of the United States, at its September 1941 session, expressed its belief that the system of court reporting in the federal courts was inferior to that prevailing in most of the states and recommended the passage of legislation to provide for official salaried reporters.[74] After some delay the requested legislation was passed by the 78th Congress, and court reporting in the federal courts is now being carried on by official reporters.[75]

The second problem, which is equally incapable of solution by judicial action, still awaits remedy. The federal courts are still operating on the principle of assigning counsel from among the members of the bar, a practice which originated in the days when the bar in any locality was a small, closely knit group intimately known to the court. It must be noted that there is no law authorizing the payment of compensation to counsel assigned in the federal courts. In the old days the court's close contact with the bar avoided hardships which might result from a lawyer's being assigned to defend an accused without receiving compensation. But under modern conditions, with the vastly increased number of federal criminal cases, the concentration of judicial administration in highly urbanized centers, and the numerical growth and functional specialization of the legal profession, it would be unrealistic to assume that the system of assigning counsel can be operated without placing an inequitable burden on some members of the bar, particularly in jurisdictions with large criminal calendars,[76] or that indigent defendants are adequately represented where attorneys inexperienced in criminal practice are assigned as counsel.

Legal Aid Societies have provided a partial remedy, but their voluntary character imposes a limit upon their effectiveness.[77] In several of the states, on the other hand, a Public Defender has successfully been employed.[78] For the federal courts Attorney General Homer Cummings first suggested the provision of such an official.[79] Johnson v. Zerbst, so Attorney General Jackson found, "accentuated the desirability of providing public defenders in the Federal courts to supplant the present system, which at times," he declared, "operates in a somewhat haphazard fashion."[80] Bills to accomplish that purpose were introduced in the 76th Congress by Senator Ashurst and Representative Celler,[81] but neither these nor similar proposals for the District of Columbia courts[82] were reported out of committee. It is submitted, however, that to oppose the public prosecutor with a public official charged with defending those who are unable to employ counsel of their own will bring about a closer approximation of that balance of contesting forces which appears to be the ultimate desideratum of Anglo-American judicial administration. The judicial policy since Johnson v. Zerbst urgently calls for legislative implementation by the provision of public defenders in the federal courts.

Reference was made above to the fact that a number of states have provided for public defenders. In other states, where counsel is assigned from among the members of the bar, varying provisions have been made for their compensation from public funds. On the other hand, a few states do not require appointment of counsel for indigent defendants, except in capital cases.[83] The policies of the several states with regard to the right to counsel, as in other respects, are by no means uniform. The question arises whether the right to counsel as safeguarded against federal action by the Sixth Amendment, is so fundamental and so essential to fair judicial proceedings that, by virtue of the due process requirement of the Fourteenth Amendment, it will override the policy of a state.

The first case in which this problem was placed in bold relief was the first "Scottsboro Case,"[84] one of the *causes célèbres* of our day. The case, it will be recalled, involved the alleged rape of two white girls by the Negro defendants. The offense allegedly was committed in an open gondola car on a freight train going through Alabama, and it was near Scottsboro, Alabama, that the defendants were seized by a sheriff's posse. In order to protect the prisoners against the intense hostility of the community, militia assistance was called in. "Every step taken from the arrest and arraignment to the sentence was accompanied by the military." The defendants, who were ignorant and illiterate, came from other states and had neither friends nor relatives in Alabama. They were not asked if they had counsel or wished to have counsel appointed for them, and "such designation of counsel as was attempted was either so indefinite or so close upon the trial as to amount to a denial of effective and substantial aid in that regard." Each separate trial was completed in one day and all the defendants were sentenced to death.[85] The Supreme Court of Alabama affirmed, Chief Justice Anderson dissenting.[86]

The Supreme Court of the United States reviewed the record and found as a fact that the defendants had not had effective assistance of counsel. It noted that it was powerless to interfere with the state Supreme Court's holding that the denial of counsel infringed neither the constitution nor the laws of Alabama. But it reserved for its own decision the question "whether the denial of the assistance of counsel contravenes the due process clause of the Fourteenth Amendment to the federal Constitution."[87]

The principal obstacle to an affirmative reply to this question was the Court's opinion in *Hurtado v. California*.[88] There the Court, in denying that the requirement of indictment by grand jury was part of due process, had announced as a test that no part of the Constitution could be considered superfluous or redundant, and hence that due process could not be interpreted as containing any rights specifically guaranteed by the Constitution. "In the face of the reasoning of the Hurtado case [said the Court in Powell v. Alabama], if it stood alone, it would be difficult to justify the conclusion that the right to counsel, being . . . specifically granted by the Sixth Amendment, was also within the intendment of the due process clause."[89]

There had, however, been several decisions which established the fact that the Hurtado rule was not without exceptions, notably the cases involving freedom of speech and the press.[90] The Court in the instant case was, however, as yet unwilling to abandon entirely the position it had taken in Hurtado v. California and allowed only that there might exist more compelling considerations than had been laid down in that case. Was the right to counsel of such a nature that its denial would bring into play considerations more compelling than the logic of Hurtado v. California? The Court's answer is of sufficient importance in this context to warrant quoting in extenso:

The fact [said Justice Sutherland for the majority] that the right involved is of such a character that it cannot be denied without violating those "fundamental principles of liberty and justice which lie at the base of all our civil and political institutions" (Hebert v. Louisiana, 272 U.S. 312, 316), is obviously one of those compelling considerations which must prevail in determining whether it is embraced within the due process clause of the Fourteenth Amendment, although it be specifically dealt with in another part of the Federal Constitution. Evidently this court, in the later cases enumerated [Gitlow v. New York, Stromberg v. California, Near v. Minnesota] regarded the rights there under consideration as of this fundamental character. That some such distinction must be observed is foreshadowed in Twining v. New Jersey, 211 U.S. 78, 99, where Mr. Justice Moody, speaking for the court, said that ". . . it is possible that some of the personal rights safeguarded by the first eight Amendments against National action may also be safeguarded against state action, because a denial of them, would be a denial of due process of law. *Chicago, Burlington & Quincy R. Co. v. Chicago,* 166 U.S. 226. If this is so, it is not because those rights are enumerated in the first eight Amendments, but because they are of such a nature that they are included in the conception of due process of law." While the question has never been categorically determined by this court, a consideration of the nature of the right and a review of the expressions of this and other courts, makes it clear that the right to the aid of counsel is of this fundamental character.[91]

The Court elaborated on the fundamental nature of the right to counsel by reference to the basic elements of notice and hearing. Historically in this country a hearing included the right to be heard by counsel "when desired and provided by the party asserting the right."[92] The layman's general lack of legal knowledge renders him incapable, as a rule, adequately to prepare his defense. Hence, "if . . . a state or federal court were arbitrarily to refuse to hear a party by counsel, *employed by and appearing for him,* it reasonably may not be doubted that such a refusal would be a denial of a hearing, and therefore of due process in the constitutional sense."[93]

Note that up to this point the Court had addressed itself to the right of counsel in general; remember that at the time this opinion was handed down the right to counsel was not considered to entail a duty of the trial court to assign counsel for the defense. It embraced merely the right to appear through counsel of one's own choice and procurement. That, of course, was not the problem of the *Scottsboro* case. The point at issue was *not* whether the Sixth Amendment's guarantee of counsel—as then applied and understood—was included in the due process concept of the Fourteenth Amendment. The issue *might* have been whether the Sixth Amendment should not be construed so as to impose an affirmative duty on the courts to provide counsel where the defendant is incapable of securing such assistance. But the Court did not choose to examine into this aspect. It found that its problem was to determine whether, under the circumstances of the case, the trial court's failure to make an effective appointment of counsel constituted a denial of due process. The famous "rule of Powell v. Alabama" was carefully prefaced by an emphatic denial that anything more was intended than to decide the specific case. "Whether [it] would be so in other criminal prosecutions," said the Court, "or under other circumstances, we need not determine. All that it is necessary now to decide, as we do decide, is . . ." —and here follows the statement of the rule—

that in a capital case, where the defendant is unable to employ counsel, and is incapable adequately of making his own defense because of ignorance, feeblemindedness, illiteracy or the like, it is the duty of the court, whether requested or not, to assign counsel for him as a necessary requisite of due process of law; and that duty is not discharged by an assignment at such a time or under such circumstances as to preclude the giving of effective aid in the preparation and trial of the case.[94]

The ultimate *ratio decidendi*, therefore, was not that a provision of the Sixth Amendment was made applicable but that a right which was not at all embraced within the Sixth Amendment as it was then understood was declared, under the circumstances of the case, to have been necessary to due process of law. The Court did not undertake to modify what apparently had been the accepted interpretation of the "right to counsel" in the Sixth Amendment. However, without applying a new and different interpretation of that concept its application to state action through absorption into the due process clause of the Fourteenth Amendment could not serve to decide the issue of the *Scottsboro* case. Therefore, whatever the Court said with reference to the Sixth Amendment was really not essential or necessary to the decision of the case and, properly speaking, should have been entitled to no more weight than any other dictum.

But the Court's own language in subsequent cases not only reiterated its regard for the right of counsel as "fundamental" but also implied that *Powell v. Alabama* had placed the Sixth Amendment's provision with respect to counsel within the concept of due process under the Fourteenth Amendment. In *Grosjean v.*

American Press Co.,[95] for instance, the Court asserted that in the *Scottsboro* case it had concluded that "certain fundamental rights, safeguarded by the first eight amendments against federal action, were also safeguarded against state action by the due process of law clause of the Fourteenth Amendment, and among them the fundamental right of the accused to the aid of counsel in a criminal prosecution."[96] Now, if the Court in this case believed that the right to the aid of counsel was more than a privilege, that it involved a duty on the part of the court to appoint counsel where none could be provided by the defendant, then that was not a right then safeguarded against federal action by the Sixth Amendment. But if it was referring to the right of counsel as it was then interpreted under the Sixth Amendment, then it misstated the basis for its decision in *Powell* v. *Alabama*.

Similarly, in *Brown* v. *Mississippi*,[97] the Court used language which invited the inference that any denial by a state court of the aid of counsel would run counter to the requirements of due process of law, and cited *Powell* v. *Alabama* as authority for this proposition. In view of the Court's express limitation in the *Powell* case to the specific circumstances of the case, the sweeping character of the dictum in the *Brown* case can hardly be justified.

The same problem is presented by the much-quoted language of Mr. Justice Cardozo in *Palko* v. *Connecticut*.[98] The Court was here faced with the contention, made by the appellant, that "whatever would be a violation of the original bill of rights (Amendments I to VIII) if done by the federal government is now equally unlawful by force of the Fourteenth Amendment if done by a state,"[99] and rejected it as a general rule. On the other hand, the Court was equally unwilling to endorse unqualifiedly the rule of *Hurtado* v. *California*[100] that due process of law and the other guarantees of the Bill of Rights must be considered to be mutually exclusive. The Court enumerated specific rights which, as a result of earlier decisions, were not protected against state action by force of the Fourteenth Amendment. On the other hand, it listed those guarantees which "have been found to be implicit in the concept of ordered liberty, and thus, through the Fourteenth Amendment, become valid as against the states."[101] Among these was the right of one accused of crime to the benefit of counsel, *Powell* v. *Alabama* being cited as authority. A footnote identified this as the right which the Sixth Amendment protected against the federal government.[102]

It can only be repeated that this association of the rule of *Powell* v. *Alabama* with the Sixth Amendment cannot be maintained in the light of the actual decision of that case. And, indeed, in another place in *Palko* v. *Connecticut* Cardozo stated accurately that "the decision [in *Powell* v. *Alabama*] did not turn upon the fact that the benefit of counsel would have been guaranteed to the defendants by the provisions of the Sixth Amendment if they had been prosecuted in a federal court. The decision turned upon the fact that *in the particular situation* laid before us in the evidence the benefit of counsel was essential to *the substance of a fair hearing*."[103] If *Powell* v. *Alabama* was not decided under the Sixth Amendment—and Cardozo correctly states, as was also shown above, that it was not—it seems difficult to see how that case could be cited as authority for the proposition that any part of the Sixth Amendment has, "through the Fourteenth Amendment, become valid as against the states."

As has been suggested before, the Sixth Amendment, even if made applicable to prosecutions in state courts, *could not* have furnished a basis for the conclusion of the *Powell* case unless its right to counsel provision had been given a meaning different from the one which it had held since its adoption in the early days of the republic. Such a reinterpretation of the provision, however, did not occur until 1938, and that event, the decision in *Johnson* v. *Zerbst*,[104] is in itself proof of the fact that prior thereto —and hence also at the time of *Powell* v. *Alabama*—a duty to appoint counsel for any defendant had not been understood to exist under this amendment.

But if the Court's dicta were at all indicative of its temper one would have assumed that, once the Sixth Amendment had been interpreted so as to fit into the pattern which these dicta seemingly prepared, it would only be a matter of time and a suitable occasion before the Sixth Amendment's right to counsel and *Johnson v. Zerbst* would be declared to be part of due process. However, the majority of the Court has declined to conclude that such should be the rule, or, for that matter, that *Powell v. Alabama* and the dicta following it compelled such a conclusion.

A clarification of this position was initially avoided in *Avery v. Alabama*,[105] a decision which turned largely on the facts. The defendant alleged that he had been denied the right of counsel "in violation of the Fourteenth Amendment." The specific violation complained of was the refusal of the trial court to allow a continuance. It was contended that this deprived counsel of the opportunity to prepare the defense; but the Supreme Court found that under the circumstances such was not the case. It has been suggested that the feature which, probably more than any other, distinguished this case from *Powell v. Alabama* was that

in the latter, emotional and almost hysterical prejudices accompanied the trial through every stage, from the arrest to the sentencing; in the *Avery* case these elements seem to be totally absent. Both cases arose in the same state, and the bases for appeal are much the same; yet in the *Powell* case the defendants were negroes charged with the rape of a white woman, and in the *Avery* case the charge involved a murder of a white by a white.[106]

In effect the Court decided that the circumstances of the *Avery* case were not so extreme as to warrant application of the rule of *Powell v. Alabama*. Although there are some *obiter dicta* in the case to the effect that the Fourteenth Amendment requires the appointment of counsel, there are no indications in the opinion that the Court considered that the requirements of the Sixth Amendment as to counsel were part of the Fourteenth Amendment. On the contrary, the Court said,

in determining whether petitioner has been denied his constitutional right to the assistance of counsel, we must remember that the Fourteenth Amendment does not limit the power of the States to try and deal with crimes committed within their borders, and was not intended to bring to the test of a decision of this Court every ruling made in the course of a state trial. Consistently with the preservation of constitutional balance between state and federal sovereignty, this Court must respect and is reluctant to interfere with the states' determination of local policy.[107]

Not only did this language bespeak a reluctance on the part of the Court to make the amendment's provision as to counsel applicable to the states, but the result of this case served further to emphasize the unusual and exceptional circumstances under which alone an impairment of the effective assistance of counsel would be held to violate due process of law.

Smith v. O'Grady[108] merely presented a different set of exceptional circumstances, one of which happened to be that the defendant was without counsel. The unfairness of the proceedings, in which a plea of guilty was induced by fraudulent promises on the part of the prosecuting attorney, was only accentuated by the lack of counsel. The alleged violation of due process was in the denial of a fair trial, of which the aid of counsel is a part, but the Court did not intimate that denial of that part alone, in the absence of other prejudicial facts, would be considered a violation of due process of law.

In Betts v. Brady[109] the Court at last met and faced the issue squarely. Betts had been indicted for robbery in the Circuit Court of Carroll County, Maryland. He was financially unable to employ counsel and, at the time of arraignment, requested the court to appoint counsel for him. "The judge advised him that this would not be done, as it was not the practice in Carroll County to appoint counsel for indigent defendants, save in prosecutions for murder and rape."[110]

Following his conviction the defendant petitioned for a writ of habeas corpus. He contended that the decisions of the Supreme Court allowed the deduction that, "in every case, whatever the circumstances, one charged with crime, who is unable to obtain counsel, must be furnished counsel by the State."[111] Justice Roberts, speaking for the Court's majority, admitted that "expressions in the opinions of this court lend color to the argument,"[112] but stressed the fact that the question as presented had never been properly adjudicated by the Supreme Court. *Powell* v. *Alabama* had presented a set of unusual and exceptional circumstances, aggravated by the fact that the state of trial had declared as its legislative policy that indigent defendants prosecuted for the offense charged in that case must be provided with counsel.[113] *Avery* v. *Alabama* as well as *Smith* v. *O'Grady* had decided no more than the applicability of the rule of *Powell* v. *Alabama* to other factual situations.

The question which the Court had to decide was therefore a novel one: does due process of law demand that in every criminal case, whatever the circumstances, a state must furnish counsel to an indigent defendant? "Is the furnishing of counsel in all cases whatever dictated by natural, inherent and fundamental principles of fairness? The answer to the question may be found in the common understanding of those who have lived under the Anglo-American system of law."[114] That understanding, so the Justice found from an examination of the constitutions and statutes of the original states, was that

in the great majority of the States, it has been the considered judgment of the people, their representatives and their courts that appointment of counsel is not a fundamental right, essential to a fair trial. On the contrary, the matter has generally been deemed one of legislative policy. In the light of . . . [the historical] evidence [the Justice concluded], we are unable to say that the concept of due process incorporated in the Fourteenth Amendment obligates the States, whatever may be their own views, to furnish counsel in every such case.[115]

It is difficult to conceive of any more unequivocal statement than this unless it be the Court's direct reference to the Sixth Amendment: "The Sixth Amendment of the national Constitution applies *only* to trials in federal courts. The due process clause of the Fourteenth Amendment *does not incorporate*, as such, the specific guarantees found in the Sixth Amendment." Nor could

there be a more concise synopsis of the rule in *Powell* v. *Alabama*
and *Smith* v. *O'Grady* than this: "A denial by a State of rights or
privileges specifically embodied in that [the Sixth] and others
of the first eight amendments may, *in certain circumstances or in
connection with other elements*, operate, *in a given case*, to deprive a litigant of due process of law in violation of the Fourteenth."[116]

It is submitted that the language quoted in the last two paragraphs in no manner contradicts, or conflicts with, the decision
in *Powell* v. *Alabama*. It is inconsistent with the language of the
dicta in *Palko* v. *Connecticut* and other cases, but, as has been
argued above, these dicta failed to reflect correctly what had been
held in *Powell* v. *Alabama*. They had treated that case as if it had
established a constitutional norm, ignoring the emphasis in the
opinion on the unusual and abnormal circumstances of the trial.
In *Betts* v. *Brady*, on the other hand, the Court stated a rule, not
as a dictum or *arguendo*, but as a holding, and it set off clearly
the *Powell* case and similar situations as exceptions. This case did
not qualify *Powell* v. *Alabama*,[117] but it was the long-established
rule, restated in *Betts* v. *Brady*, which had been qualified in
Powell v. *Alabama*.

Justice Black's eloquent dissent, in which he was joined by
Douglas and Murphy, maintained that any practice by which a
man would find himself deprived of counsel merely because of
his poverty would "defeat the promise of our democratic society
to provide equal justice under law."[118] The dissent made a strong
plea for the inclusion of the requirement to furnish counsel to
indigent defendants in the concept of due process;[119] but, if that
should not be conceded, it was contended that the instant case
(and hence presumably all similar cases) should have been decided in the light of its particular circumstances.

Black alleged that the majority opinion established a view of
due process which would give the Court vast supervisory powers.
But it must be asked if this would not be equally likely if, as
Black had suggested, each and every case were to be decided only

in the light of its attending circumstances? It may, indeed, be assumed that any attempt to introduce such a practice would eventually be rejected as counter to basic notions of Anglo-American law. Our legal system hinges on certainty, that is on rules, and flexibility, which means leeway for exceptions. If one disregards, therefore, the possibility that the Court might adopt a policy of deciding each case against its particular setting, the choice appears to be between two rules, that embodied in the majority opinion and that championed by Justice Black. Whichever rule is selected, it could not be without exceptions; the line demarking the rule from the exception will be uncertain and fluid; in either case the "vast supervisory powers" of the Supreme Court will have to be called into play.

It is submitted that, if one regards a high esteem for local mores as a postulate of the federal system, the rule of *Betts* v. *Brady* is to be preferred. The state statutes listed by Justice Black in an appendix to his dissent appear to prove rather than disprove Justice Roberts' point in that they show that the states are not unanimous in providing counsel for indigent defendants, not even on a statutory basis. A sweeping inclusion of a mandatory counsel provision in the due process concept would thus clearly constitute an imposition of federal procedure on at least some of the states.

Justice Black would probably agree with the lower court which said that "due process, or the lack of it, is based upon substance and not form"; yet, judging from his dissent in *Betts* v. *Brady*, he would probably deny the same court's assertion that "the substance of due process might be denied although the accused is represented by a coterie of counsel, yet he may have it although unaccompanied by counsel."[120] Yet the proposition appears as reasonable as the argument the Justice built on "common and fundamental ideas of fairness and right."[121] Once it is granted that procedural due process is a matter of substance rather than form, it would actually appear to be more in keeping with its needs and purposes not to insist on the form except in the federal courts for which specific forms are prescribed.

Regardless of the form, the substance will be safeguarded, if and when necessary, within the framework of due process, which, in the words of the majority opinion, is "a concept less rigid and more fluid than those envisaged in other specific and particular provisions of the Bill of Rights."[122]

The cases decided since *Betts* v. *Brady* have not put aside the rule of that case. Mostly, they presented conditions of such a nature as to warrant findings of denial of due process. In *Williams* v. *Kaiser*,[123] a Missouri case, the defendant had been charged with robbery in the first degree by means of a deadly weapon, a capital offense under state law. The record did not show that the accused had counsel, or that he had waived the assistance of counsel, nor did it show that he had made a request for appointment of counsel. However, his petition for habeas corpus alleged that he had asked and been denied counsel. The Court referred to the important distinctions made by the law of Missouri between various degrees of robbery and larceny as involving technical elements ". . . which are a closed book to the layman."[124] It concluded that the technical complexity of the issue was such that the absence of counsel in this case constituted a denial of due process. Hence the Supreme Court of Missouri had erred in denying the petition for habeas corpus. The Supreme Court of the United States admitted the possibility that "the allegations of the petitioner may turn out to be wholly specious. But," said the Court, "they are sufficient to establish a *prima facie* case of deprivation of the constitutional right."[125] Justice Frankfurter dissented vigorously from this presumption that the word of a convicted prisoner is on the face of it more credible than the record of a court. "To assume disobedience [he declared] instead of obedience to the Law of the Land by the highest courts of the States is to engender friction between the federal and state judicial systems, to weaken the authority of the state courts and the administration of state laws by encouraging unmeritorious resorts to this Court, and wastefully to swell the dockets of this Court."[126]

In a companion case, *Tomkins v. Missouri*,[127] the analogy of *Powell v. Alabama* was applied to "one who was not represented by counsel, who did not waive his right to counsel and who was ignorant of his right to demand counsel,"[128] and who was on trial for a capital offense (murder) hedged about with a number of highly technical distinctions, defenses, and requirements under state law.

In *White v. Ragen*,[129] decided at the same term, the Court declared that the denial of effective assistance of counsel to one accused of serious crime and unable to defend himself voided the judgment as much as would perjured testimony. The Court spoke of a "constitutional right to a fair trial" which it said had been violated in *Powell v. Alabama*. The charge in *White v. Ragen* was a serious but not a capital offense; the record revealed unusual arbitrariness on the part of the trial judge, including refusal to allow counsel sufficient time for the preparation of the case.

In *Rice v. Olson*,[130] the petitioner, an ignorant Indian, alleged that he had not been advised of his right to, nor had he been furnished, counsel to defend him against a burglary charge. The Court noted that the principal defense which the petitioner might have invoked, lack of jurisdiction in a state court over crimes committed on an Indian reservation by Indians, was highly technical in nature, and that the case was therefore of sufficient complexity to require the assistance of counsel before the defendant could be assured of a fair trial. In *Carter v. Illinois*,[131] on the other hand, an affirmative recital in the record that the defendant had been advised of and had waived his right to counsel was not permitted to be impeached collaterally by habeas corpus.

Canizio v. New York[132] presented an unique factual situation in which a nineteen-year-old boy, on trial for robbery in the first degree, had appeared without counsel, had not been advised of his right to counsel nor indicated a desire to waive counsel, and none was appointed. Two days before sentence was imposed an

attorney appeared on the accused's behalf. Fourteen years later
the defendant, serving a long prison term, sought to have the
judgment voided because of the trial court's failure to provide
counsel. The Supreme Court, speaking through Mr. Justice Black,
concluded that the defendant had in fact enjoyed the assistance
of counsel, and denied his petition.[133]

In *De Meerleer v. Michigan*,[134] the petitioner, then seventeen
years of age, had been charged with the crime of murder and, on
the same day, was arraigned, tried, convicted of first degree murder
and sentenced to life imprisonment, the maximum penalty under
state law. He had no counsel, none was offered or assigned, nor
was he apprised of the consequences of his plea of guilty. An
unanimous Court held that the petitioner had been deprived of
"rights essential to a fair hearing under the Federal Constitution,"
and reversed the state Supreme Court's decision denying a motion
for a new trial.

An equally crass instance of palpable lack of due process was
the case of Tony Marino,[135] who, at the age of eighteen and after
only two years' residence in this country, still unable to speak
English, had been sentenced to life imprisonment on a charge
of murder. The record showed a waiver of jury trial and a plea of
guilty. The defendant alleged that he had done neither. He had
no counsel, nor was counsel appointed for him. All his contacts
with the court were through an interpreter who was the officer
who had arrested him. The Attorney General of the state admitted
these irregularities and conceded them to be a denial of due
process.[135a]

A mere enumeration of these cases—and the list is not entirely
complete—may leave one with the impression that the Court has
done everything but declare the right to counsel an absolute
essential element of due process of law. However, it is necessary
to bear in mind that, from *Williams v. Kaiser* through *Marino v.
Ragen* and beyond, the cases in which due process was found to
have been denied presented abnormal conditions which shocked
the Court's "fundamental ideas of fairness." The majority of the

Court has as yet not departed from the position that no part of the Sixth Amendment applies to proceedings in state courts by virtue of having been absorbed into the due process concept.

This rule, which by and large had been unquestioned in the years before *Powell* v. *Alabama*, and which *Betts* v. *Brady* confirmed, has been reaffirmed by the Court on several occasions.[136] *Foster* v. *Illinois* reflects clearly the contrast between what the law now *is* and what the Court's minority thinks the law *ought to be*. The case had its origin in 1935 when the petitioners pleaded guilty to a charge of burglary and larceny. The record recited that they were advised of their "rights of Trial" and of the consequences of their plea. The court sentenced both petitioners to prison terms. Eleven years later, the prisoners sought to be released on the ground that the record in their case failed to show "a compliance with the Fourteenth Amendment insofar as the Due Process Clause of the Amendment requires an accused to have the benefit of counsel."[137]

Justice Frankfurter's majority opinion restated the result of the recent decisions, stressing the distinction between the right of counsel under the Sixth Amendment and the effect which lack of counsel may have on due process of law:

The considerations that guide the disposition of this case have been canvassed here in a series of recent opinions. The "due process of law" which the Fourteenth Amendment exacts from the States is a conception of fundamental justice. See *Hebert* v. *Louisiana*, 272 U.S. 312, 316; *Palko* v. *Connecticut*, 302 U.S. 319, 325. It is not satisfied by merely procedural correctness, nor is it confined by any absolute rule such as that which the Sixth Amendment contains in securing to an accused "the Assistance of Counsel for his defence." By virtue of that provision, counsel must be furnished to an indigent defendant prosecuted in a federal court in every case, whatever the circumstances. See *Palko* v. *Connecticut, supra*, at 327; *Johnson* v. *Zerbst*, 304 U.S. 458; *Betts* v. *Brady*, 316 U.S. 455, 464-465. Prosecutions in State courts are not subject to this fixed requirement. So we have held upon fullest consideration. *Betts* v. *Brady, supra*. But process of law in order to be "due" does require that a State give a defendant ample opportunity to meet an accusation. And so, in the circumstances of a "particular situation," assignment of counsel may be "essential to the substance of a hearing" as part of the due process which the Fourteenth Amendment exacts from a State which imposes sentence, *Palko v. Connecticut, supra,* at 327.[138]

The record of trial in this case, so the majority found, revealed no miscarriage of justice nor any error which the assistance of counsel might have prevented. The claim, it was held, was in effect based merely on the omission in the record of an affirmative recital that the aid of counsel was offered by the court. This claim the Court rejected.[139]

The penultimate paragraph of the opinion of Justice Frankfurter offers a revealing insight into some of the considerations which presumably contributed to the majority's decision.

It is not for us to suggest [said Justice Frankfurter] that it might be desirable to offer to every accused who desires to plead guilty the opportunities for counsel and to enter with formality upon the record the deliberate disclaimer of his need for counsel because of a full appreciation of the meaning of a plea of guilty as expounded by responsible judges. Our duty does not go beyond safeguarding "rights essential to a fair hearing" by the States. After all, due process, "itself a historical product," *Jackman v. Rosenbaum Co.,* 260 U.S. 22, 31, is not to be turned into a destructive dogma in the administration of systems of criminal justice under which the States have lived not only before the Fourteenth Amendment but for the eighty years since its adoption. It does not militate against respect for the deeply rooted systems of criminal justice in the States that such an abrupt innovation as recognition of the constitutional claim here made implies, would furnish opportunities hitherto uncontemplated for opening wide the prison doors of the land.[140]

There were two dissenting opinions filed in which all four dissenting Justices joined. Justice Rutledge prefaced his dissent with an assertion of his belief that "the Sixth Amendment's guaranty of the right to counsel in criminal cases is applicable to such proceeding as this in state courts." Justice Black's dissenting opinion similarly charged that the majority had diluted and attentuated a constitutional right. *Betts* v. *Brady,* which the Court had followed, was "the kind of precedent that I had hoped this court would not perpetuate." The Court's fear that a different result would lead to an opening of the prison gates, could not even be considered relevant to a determination of rights under the Constitution.[141]

Justice Douglas expressed the same objections in different words in his dissent to *Bute* v. *Illinois.*[142] "I fail to see," was his comment on the prevailing rule, "why it is due process to deny an accused the benefit of counsel in a state court when by constitutional standards that benefit could not be withheld from him in a federal court."

The conflicting views of the majority and the minority in these cases are indicative not merely of disagreements with regard to one provision of the Constitution but of essential and basic differences in the approach to the entire document. Commentators have variously labeled the dichotomy of our highest Court as "judicial austerity v. activism,"[143] or as a clash between "selective naturalism," attributed to Justice Frankfurter, and "selective subjectivism," identified with Justice Black.[144] Whatever the name, the differences which divide the present Court not only go to the basis of our constitutional system but indeed involve fundamentally divergent conceptions of the judicial function. To analyze and evaluate this controversy would transcend the limits set for this study. For the purposes of this inquiry it must suffice to state the respective positions as they appear to pertain to its subject.

The purpose of this chapter has been stated to be the ascertainment of the meaning which judicial interpretation has placed upon the Sixth Amendment's guarantee of the right to counsel. The question was phrased with reference to this particular constitutional provision; it was not intended that the answer should encompass an interpretation of the meaning of due process of law. In this light it can only be concluded that the right to the assistance of counsel as guaranteed by the Sixth Amendment requires that one accused of crime in a federal court must either have counsel or intelligently waive counsel. The assistance of counsel must be effective, which means that counsel must be competent, he must have time to prepare his case, he must not be unduly interfered with in presenting the case, and he must be present at all stages of the trial. In all probability one who has pleaded guilty has the same right to counsel as one who elects to stand trial. A criminal defendant in a state court, on the other hand, is not protected by the Sixth Amendment but may be found to have been denied due process if the want of counsel deprives his trial of the essential element of fairness; but the majority of the present Court does not admit that a trial cannot be a fair one even though the accused is not represented by counsel, or has not deliberately chosen to be without counsel.

Chapter VII

Crime and the Ideal of a Fair Trial

"The history of the Constitution reveals a panoramic mixture of continuity and change."[1] The rigidity of the written document and the flexibility of its interpretation by the judges blend to provide the legal matrix for the satisfaction of the social needs of each generation. Constitutional language, which may have been full of meaning in one era, may be found to have little but historical significance for another. Conversely, clauses of the Constitution that have lain dormant for scores of years may under modern conditions be seen to possess new and unforeseen vitality. The Sixth Amendment, as the preceding chapters may have indicated, illustrates both tendencies. Framed to reaffirm the right to a trial by jury, its central provision assuring this right has steadily declined in scope and importance.[2] On the other hand, the right to counsel, a privilege of limited practical value for nearly 150 years, has had a sudden emergence to a significance plainly not contemplated by the Framers.[3] To state that the Sixth Amendment today has a content and meaning different from that which it held at the time of its adoption is to say no more than that the written language of the Constitution takes varying interpretations under changing conditions.

When the Constitution was adopted and the Bill of Rights, including the Sixth Amendment, was added thereto, the forcible severance of the ties with Britain was still of present memory. The grievances which led to the Revolution were still clearly recalled. The guarantees which were written into the Constitution were aimed at forestalling any renewal of the tyrannical abuses of which the colonists had complained. With respect to criminal trials the colonists' principal grievances had been the denial of trial by jury and the removal of accused persons for trial in England or at other points distant from their homes. In their state constitutions and declarations of rights the new states had given expression to the popular desire to be assured of the retention of the criminal jury and of the other recent procedural changes through which the potential arbitrariness of judicial magistrates might be held in check.

It is well to bear in mind that the particular features of the criminal trial for which such anxiety was shown were all of relatively recent origin or development. Less time had elapsed between the days of the Star Chamber and the American Revolution than separates the present generation from the Founding Fathers. Only a little over a century had passed since the jury had attained independence from court domination.[4] The accused's right to present his own witnesses under the same conditions as the prosecution[5] dated from the Glorious Revolution—an event no more remote in time from the Founders than the Civil War is from us today. The right to be represented by counsel was then, indeed, still being denied in England and the rejection of this rule in the Colonies was of the most recent date.[6]

The generation of Americans who, in the name of individual liberty, took their fate into their own hands, endeavored to perpetuate these newly gained safeguards of fairness to the accused by writing them into their Constitution. In Justice Frankfurter's phrase, "Procedural devices rooted in history were written into the Bill of Rights not as abstract rubrics in an elegant code but in order to assure fairness and justice before any person could be deprived of 'life, liberty or property.' "[7] In 1789, the guarantees written into the Sixth Amendment assured to the criminally accused those elements which had then been found to enhance the probability of a fair trial.

Yet as early a commentator as Justice Story realized already that insistence on forms of procedure could not be expected inevitably to produce judicial fairness. He observed that "unless the whole system [of the common law] is incorporated, and especially the law of evidence, a corrupt legislature, or a debased and servile people may render the whole little more than pageantry."[8] In any case, however, the procedural safeguards, which he called "appendages of the trial by jury," were "truly admirable."[9] And with regard to the jury trial itself Justice Story, echoing Blackstone, affirmed his belief that "so long . . . as this palladium remains sacred and inviolable the liberties of a free government cannot wholly fail."[10]

Writing a few decades later, Francis Lieber enumerated no less than twenty distinct advantages of the jury, which he eulogized as "a guarantee of liberty in giving the people a participation in the administration of justice," and "the best school of the citizen, both in teaching him his rights and to protect them, and of practically teaching him the necessity of law and government."[11]

In Lieber's catalog of liberties "a well-secured penal trial" was held to be "intimately connected with civil liberty," but it was also asserted as a fact that "a sound penal trial is invariably one of the last fruits of political civilization . . . it requires long experience to find the proper mean between a due protection of the individual and an equally due protection of society."[12]

Of special importance to Lieber was the element of publicity. He considered publicity and "orality" of all public business an important element of liberty, for he had concluded that "all governments hostile to liberty are hostile to publicity."[13] But oddly enough he asserted that "no law insures the publicity of the courts of justice, either in England or the United States,"[14] a seemingly flagrant oversight of the Sixth Amendment's guarantee of a public trial.[15] One may also question the desirability of what he called "orality" unless that term was intended to convey no more than that criminal cases should not be decided on written pleadings alone. Any interpretation of "orality" as opposed to written records of trials would, of course, reduce to naught the practical value of all procedural safeguards and it can hardly be assumed that Lieber intended such an understanding.

Lieber was in the main stream of nineteenth century thinking when men were most concerned with the individual, when the limitations upon governmental interference with individual liberty received pre-eminent emphasis. He was, however, as one of the above quotations from his writings indicates, not unaware of the needs of society when faced with crime. But in his day the problem of law enforcement had not yet assumed serious proportions. Industrialization had barely set in, the country's settlements were still largely rural, and the frontier offered a safety valve for those who felt the urge to revolt against social pressure. Sociologists and historians have chronicled the developments which so markedly changed these conditions.[16] "Within a generation," says Dean Pound, "there have been profound changes in the background of social control to which all its agencies must be adjusted. The points at which the claims and desires of each individual and those of his fellows conflict or overlap have increased enormously. Likewise new agencies of menace to the general security have developed in profusion."[17]

The early decades of the twentieth century saw an increase in criminality, lawlessness and, indeed, defiance of law that caused widespread alarm among citizenry and government. Increasingly the American people displayed concern over the problem of law enforcement.[18] Even the most casual observer could not fail to see that the machinery of enforcement was inadequate in the face of organized professional crime operating in disregard of, and actually utilizing the protection afforded by, state boundaries.[19] The guarantees which were intended to protect the innocent against magisterial tyranny had seemingly been turned into shields from behind which palpably guilty "public enemies" frustrated the ends of justice.[20] In the words of a Wisconsin judge, "since the days of Penn and Raleigh, these [constitutional guarantees] have grown from weakness into the strength of a veritable Old Man of the Sea, bestriding and strangling the society that labored to give them birth."[21]

It is not surprising, in this light, that the constitutional safeguards of criminal procedure, collected primarily in the Sixth Amendment, should recently have been subjected to question, atack, and reinterpretation. "Criminal law," to quote Dean Pound once more, "must safeguard the general security and the individual life against abuse of criminal procedure, while at the same time making that procedure as effective as possible for the securing of the whole scheme of social interests."[22] Our system of criminal law must serve two masters: ideally, it strives toward the goal of a fair trial; practical needs demand that it should secure strict enforcement of the law. The guarantees of the Sixth Amendment were intended to assure the former; modern conditions have evoked doubts lest law enforcement be defeated under the guise of safeguards intended for the furtherance of fairness in the criminal trial.[23]

Of all the safeguards found in the Sixth Amendment that which has most frequently been attacked and questioned has been the jury itself. It has been called "the great obstructing incubus of the administration of American law,"[24] "as preposterous and out of date as the sun dial of James I or the coach of Charles II,"[25] and "a paralyzing yoke,"[26] to quote but a few. Scholars and judges alike have attributed to the jury a large share of the responsibility for the apparent failure of law enforcement.[27] To a notable extent the criticisms and condemnations, which gathered momentum in the last quarter of the nineteenth century,[28] may be interpreted as reactions to the trend of the preceding century, when the jury had been exalted at the expense of the judge. The general desire of Revolutionary America to prevent the recurrence of judicial tyranny and the Blackstonian panegyrics of the jury had combined to conceal the essential necessity of judge-jury co-operation. Instead, the American jury was accorded a position not only of independence but of a supremacy entirely unknown to the English law. This was—and is—particularly true of juries in state courts, where not infrequently the jury are judges of the law as well as of the facts and not only find the verdict but determine the sentence.[29] But public sentiment is not apt to differentiate between jurisdictions. Critics of the jury system did not and do not, as a rule, exempt the juries in the federal courts from their charges.

Indeed, the most poignant objection to the trial jury would appear to apply regardless of jurisdiction or location:

Stated baldly, the use of the petty jury means that matters requiring adjudication, instead of being submitted to professional experts, trained in the performance of their duties and acting under a continuing responsibility, are handed over to a body of laymen, selected almost at random, regarding whose ability to perform the delicate function of weighing evidence free from sentimental and emotional influences nothing is known, and who perform their duties under no sense of continuing responsibility.[30]

Laymen may have possessed the necessary competence to judge facts in the days of leisurely, rural society; in the age of industrial, urban civilization the issues of many a case have acquired a technical complexity which few non-experts can master.[31] In addition, there has been an increasing tendency to grant wholesale exemptions from jury service, frequently to groups and professions actually most nearly qualified for such service.[32]

Last but not least, there has come about an increasing realization, no longer confined to the specialists, that the entire problem of crime could not and would not be solved by the methods of two hundred years ago. A widespread belief has arisen that the cure of crime should be therapy, not surgery. The criminal, who only a short while ago was viewed as one possessed by the devil, today is looked upon as a patient whom proper diagnosis can restore to health and social usefulness.[33] Twelve honest men, however good and true, temporarily called away from their means of livelihood, are not likely to accomplish a task which those who hold this view of crime believe proper for an expert physician or psychiatrist.

The judiciary's response to these trends has passed through two discernible stages. The criticism of the late nineteenth century, generated largely by the inadequacy of the jury under urban conditions, called for a revision of the association of trial by jury with the essentials of civil liberty. Story's eulogy of the jury was replaced by Brown's dry declaration that the right to a trial by jury was not fundamental in nature.[34] The renewed attacks on the jury system in the third decade of the twentieth century, stemming both from the clamor for more effective law enforcement and from the spread of changed concepts of crime, found their reflection in the judicial sanction of waivers of jury trial.[35] If, as has been asserted, we are witnessing the gradual obsolescence of the jury,[36] it may well be expected that the courts will adjust their position accordingly. That "the accused shall enjoy the right to a trial by jury," may, if the trend should continue, some day mean no more than that he may not be denied a jury if he asks for one.[37]

Assuming that this analysis is not in error and that there is a latent tendency to limit the jury system, which tendency is exemplified in the Supreme Court's inclination to relax the requirement of a trial by jury in criminal cases, what is the effect of this trend on the overall purpose of the Sixth Amendment? That purpose, as has been noted, was "to assure fairness and justice before any person could be deprived of 'life, liberty or property.' "[38] The practices and procedures which the amendment purported to safeguard were intended to foster the ideal of a fair trial as against its competing ideal, the efficiency of law enforcement. The jury, if the evidence here presented be accepted, has been found to operate to such disadvantage to the needs of law enforcement, and to contribute so little to the achievement of fair justice, that it may be dispensed with and "justice still be done."[39]

Has this debilitation of one of the intended guarantees of fairness resulted in greater weight and reliance being placed on the others? It is submitted that such has been the case. Not only has the right to counsel been given a new and far more stringent application,[40] but the few cases on the publicity of criminal trials also reveal an increasing tendency on the part of the courts to apply this guarantee with a minimum of exceptions or conditions attached.[41] It is suggested that vitalization of these guarantees in effect compensates for the decline of the jury. The less the jury is called on to act as a check on potential judicial arbitrariness, the more does it become important and necessary that the doors of the courtroom shall not be closed to the public and that the accused shall not face the court unassisted by counsel. The increased emphasis on publicity and counsel is therefore a correlative development to the decreasing importance of the jury; both modifications correspond to shifting public concepts of the relative value and place of law enforcement and individual security.

It may be said, therefore, that the Sixth Amendment has changed in content but not in intent. When placed in the Constitution its aim was to assure fairness in judicial proceedings through the guarantee of continued availability of certain procedural devices. This basic aim has not been affected by time or judicial decisions. Time merely has shown, and judicial decisions have manifested the realization, that among the devices so secured some have been found more useful than others, but the decline of one has been compensated for by the rise of others, leaving unchanged the aim and effect of the amendment, which, to repeat, is to secure fairness of proceedings, not specific unalterable forms.

But it will be asked, Why should not all or some of the elements of this amendment also be necessary to "due process of law"? We may put aside, for the moment, the formalistic logic of Hurtado v. California.[42] It is highly probable that when due process of law was written into the Fifth Amendment, it was considered "a general phrase designed to prevent general arbitrary action on the part of the government," and, "even though [the term] had been frequently used in the colonies and in England, no settled meaning was yet attached to it."[43] Hence nothing could be gained by resorting to the "intent of the Framers." The formulation of the Fourteenth Amendment has been subjected to rather careful scholarly scrutiny, but here, too, it has been suggested that "the better interpretation seems to be . . . that the members of Congress, with the exception of a very few first-rate constitutional lawyers in that body, really had no definite conception of what the phrase meant."[44]

A minority of the present Supreme Court, led by Mr. Justice Black, adhere to the view that the Fourteenth Amendment was intended to make the guarantees of the Bill of Rights applicable against the states.[45] The majority join their brethren in reading the freedoms of the First Amendment into the liberty concept of the Fourteenth.[46] But they do not concede that any part of the Sixth Amendment as such has been absorbed into due process.[47]

In effect, of course, this means no more than that the Court is divided over the desirability of insisting on compliance by the states with the specific requirements of the Sixth Amendment. Actually, the question which the Court is asked to decide is this: does the right to a trial by jury, the right to counsel, or any other right guaranteed by the Federal Bill of Rights obtain against state action? Can it actually be presumed that the justices in deciding such a question are asking themselves: is this particular right part of due process, because, if so, it will apply to the states? Or is it not more likely that their query would go to the fundamentals, namely, whether the application to the states of the particular right appears socially desirable? And if they so concluded it would follow therefrom that the right involved should be held to be part of due process. In other words, while the opinions proceed on arguments of due process and deduce therefrom whether or not a given guarantee applies to the states, it is suggested that the judicial minds decide first whether or not to extend the guarantee to the states and then expound their decision in terms of due process.

As has been noted before, the term "due process" carried no clearly defined meaning when it was placed in the Constitution. The Court has given it substance, but indeed a fragmentary and ever-changing substance, subservient to the ends of social and economic policies for which it furnishes the structure of support or the weapon of destruction as the Court sees fit. The question of why a given right should or should not be considered part of due process is therefore not fully answered by reference to a "concept of ordered liberty"[48]—a term which itself may be found difficult of definition—but must be viewed in terms of the ends which "due process" is made to serve.

If the original question is transposed into this context, the answer will be that a majority of the judges, weighing the advantages of the availability of specific procedures against the disadvantages of imposing these procedures on diverse jurisdictions, have concluded that the latter still outweigh the former. The Court will indeed assert its power, under the name of "due process," to curb excesses of arbitrariness and unfairness, but the majority does not consider that there is no other road to fairness in criminal trials than that prescribed for federal courts in the Sixth Amendment.

The problem which the Court here faces is, of course, by no means confined to the right of counsel or any other provision of the Sixth Amendment. Indeed, perhaps the sharpest division of the Court in matters of procedural due process occurred in a recent case involving the permissibility of comment on a defendant's failure or refusal to testify.[49] The issue is, however, customarily stated in terms of the relationship of the Fourteenth Amendment to the Bill of Rights. In determining the applicability of the guarantees of the first eight amendments to state action, the Court has employed, and its bare majority still does employ, an eclectic method which, however, under whatever label, fails to furnish more than pragmatic guidance. The Black-Douglas-Murphy-Rutledge position, particularly as it has been expounded in the 1946 and 1947 terms of the Court, urges as an alternative the unconditional extension of the Bill of Rights to the states. Few there will be who would take issue with the humanitarian motives and general aims of justice which the proponents of this constitutional interpretation advance. Yet the question must be asked whether the several specific clauses comprising the federal

Bill of Rights are, in fact, of equal signficance to our social order and enjoy equal recognition and respect as desirable methods of social control.

Is indictment by grand jury as essential to democratic government as freedom of thought and expression? It is hardly necessary to elaborate on the merits of the two concepts[50] in order to answer this question. And while it may be objected that this juxtaposition contrasts extreme cases on either end of the scale, these are not the only examples at hand. To be sure, the Sixth Amendment offers in its several parts and in their unequal and shifting emphases an illustration in point. Is it as pertinent to procedural fairness, and hence to the freedom of the person, that there be twelve men on the jury as that the defendant be allowed counsel? Are speed and publicity in fact equally important perquisites of a criminal trial?

These questions can hardly be answered without reference to the basic outline of one's concept of what a criminal trial ought to be, and, further still, what society should do about crime. Preceding paragraphs have suggested that agreement on these matters is less in our day than ever before. The reluctance of the Supreme Court majority to stipulate affirmatively standards of criminal procedure to be observed by the state courts may thus, to some extent, be founded in a recognition of the uncertain nature of some of the premises upon which present procedure is based.

Another source of hesitancy might possibly be spelled out from the Court's own history. For there, indeed, is recorded the attempt of the Court to delineate formal criteria for "due process" in legislation—and the almost immediate rejoinder, pointing an accusing finger at a formal rectitude behind which injustice in substance might find concealment.[51] It would not seem to be inconceivable that Justices who themselves had been instrumental in banishing the doctrines of substantive due process to the history books might hesitate to subscribe to a constitutional interpretation which could eventually lead them similarly to face the choice between formal correctness and substantive fairness, this time in judicial procedure.[52]

That is not to say that such reasoning from consequences is necessarily compelling. On the contrary, in terms of values in a society based upon and dedicated to individual liberty, neither these nor any other propositions could detract from the validity of many of the arguments of the present minority; indeed, they do not even strike at the core of the minority's position. The latter, on the other hand, has similarly preferred to remain on its own ground. There has, in fact, been hardly any true joining of the issues but rather more frequently an exposition and explication of alternative choices based upon the individual Justice's scheme of values, but limited by the confines of the constitutional document.

The verbal tools which comprise the workshop of our governmental order were fashioned for us five generations ago. Some, to be sure, have become dull with age; others have shown qualities of endurance and utility beyond the imagination, and sometimes beyond the intent, of their makers. Those in the latter category are commonly characterized by latitude of expression and breadth of conception; the former have tended to a specificity marked by the exigencies of their day. The Sixth Amendment, it can be argued, bears many of the earmarks of belonging among the specific remedies rather than the broad directives. Its affirmative language conceals but partially the negative intent of the framers; for this is not so much a prescription of what a criminal trial ought to be as it is a catalog of abuses to be suppressed: "Let us not be tried by arbitrary magistrates serving a tyrant king; let us not be 'transported beyond the seas' for trial; let there be no Star Chamber, no lingering in dungeons pending trial, no summary and unsubstantiated charges, no refusal to hear our witnesses and our counsel." All these, it was seen earlier, had been specific, oppressive abuses of which the colonists had complained. The incorporation in a constitution of prohibitions aimed particularly at contemporary evils may have, as indeed in this case it has had, the effect of concentrating attention of subsequent glossators upon the problem of articulating latter-day facts in words fashioned for a more limited end. The interpreters of constitutional language are then apt to conceal from themselves the more fundamental diversity of the issues.

The adjustment of individual and state interests in the control of crime presents today a challenge in terms hardly anticipated by the framers of the Sixth Amendment. The inadequacy of its provisions in such a perspective appears to be flagrant. (The analogy of the declining years of the pre-jury forms of trial seems tempting: Indeed, a parallel can be observed in the increasing substitution of the professional spokesman before the law to the introduction of the hired champion in trial by battle.) If our society should, as it well may, accept a reorientation of its attitude toward crime, it seems difficult to conceive any alternative except to discard, expressly or by circumvention, the specific terminology of the Sixth Amendment, and to base the adjustment of the competing ideals of individual safety and of community peace upon one of the broad directive clauses of the Constitution. Should the statesmanship of the judiciary fail to provide the formula which, unfettered by historical limitations, would facilitate development in this area, our society might be subjected to stresses and tensions which only the constituent power itself can resolve.

References

Preface

1. Roscoe Pound, *Criminal Justice in America* (New York: Henry Holt and Company, 1930), pp. 12-13.
2. David Fellman, "Some Consequences of Increased Federal Activity in Law Enforcement," *Journal of Criminal Law and Criminology*, XXXV (1944), 16-33; Martin Conboy, "Federal Criminal Law," in Alison Reppy, ed., *Law: A Century of Progress 1835-1935* (New York: New York University Press, 1937), I, 295-346; (Symposium) "Extending Federal Powers over Crime," *Law and Contemporary Problems*, I (1934), 399-508.
3. Lester B. Orfield, *Criminal Procedure from Arrest to Appeal* (New York: New York University Press, 1947).
4. Theodore W. Housel and Guy O. Walser, *Defending and Prosecuting Federal Criminal Cases* (2nd ed.; Buffalo, New York: Dennis & Co., Inc., 1946).

Chapter I

1. Sir William S. Holdsworth, *A History of English Law* (4th ed.; London: Methuen & Company, Ltd., 1936-38), II, 43-44. The most detailed treatment of the general subject of the evolution of English criminal law is by Sir James F. Stephen, *A History of the Criminal Law of England* (London: Macmillan and Company, 1883).
2. Holdsworth, *op. cit.*, II, 46.
3. Tacitus, *Germania*, c. 12: "Pars multae regi vel civitati, pars ipsi qui vindicatur vel propinquis eius exsolvitur."
4. Sir Frederick Pollock, "The King's Peace," in *Oxford Lectures and Other Discourses* (London and New York: The Macmillan Company, 1890), and authors cited *supra*, n. 1.
5. Holdsworth, *op. cit.*, II, 48.
6. *Ibid.*, II, 23, 49.
7. *Ibid.*, II, 198-199; III, 607; and by the same author, *Some Lessons from Our Legal History* (New York: The Macmillan Company, 1928), p. 81.
8. Hector B. Murdoch, "Jury Justice," *Juridical Review*, XX (1908), 59, 61.
9. *Ibid.*; and see generally Holdsworth and Stephen, works cited *supra*, n. 1.
10. William Stubbs, *Select Charters* (9th edition, Oxford: Clarendon Press, 1921), pp. 167-173.
11. Fourth Lateran Council, Canon 18. The text may be consulted in *University of Pennsylvania Translations and Reprints from the Original Sources of European History*, IV, no. 4, 16-17.
12. Published in *Die Entstehung der Schwurgerichte* (Berlin: Weidmannsche Buchhandlung, 1872).
13. See, e.g., Holdsworth, *op. cit. supra*, n. 1, I, 145-169; Sir Frederick Pollock and Frederick W. Maitland, *The History of English Law before the Time of Edward I* (Cambridge: University Press, 1895), I, 138-153; James B. Thayer, *Preliminary Treatise on Evidence* (Boston: Little, Brown & Company, 1898) chap. II-IV; Charles H. McIlwain, *The High Court of Parliament and Its Supremacy* (New Haven: Yale University Press, 1910), pp. 173-184; William F. Willoughby, *Principles of Judicial Administration* (Washington: Brookings Institution, 1929), p. 195; William S. Carpenter and Paul T. Stafford, *Readings in Early Legal Institutions* (New York: F. S. Crofts & Company, 1932), pp. 345-347; Edward M. Sait, *Political Institutions: A Preface* (New York: D. Appleton-Century Company, 1938), pp. 206-207; Charles T. Coleman, "Origin and Development of Trial by Jury," *Virginia Law Review*, VI (1919), 77; same article under other titles: *Canadian Law Review*, XL (1920), 732, and *American Law Review*, LIV (1920), 750; Murdoch, *op. cit. supra*, n. 8; J. E. R. Stephens, "The Growth of Trial by Jury in England," *Harvard Law Review*, X (1896), 150; Charles L. Wells, "The Origin of the Petty Jury," *Law Quarterly Review*, XXVII (1911), 347. The significance of sociological factors is stressed by Frederick A. Fullhardt, "Evolution of the Petit Jury," *Thought*, IX (1934), 46. The Norman background has been authoritatively treated by Charles H. Haskins, "The Early Norman Jury," *American Historical Review*, VIII (1903), 613, and *Norman Institutions* (Cambridge, Mass.: Harvard University Press, 1918), chap. VI.

William Forsyth, *History of Trial by Jury* (London: John W. Parker and Son, 1852) is most frequently quoted as an exposition of the older view. More recent accounts are by Maximus A. Lesser, *The Historical Development of the Jury System* (Rochester, New York: Lawyers Co-operative Publishing Company, 1894) and Robert von Moschzisker, *Trial by Jury* (Philadelphia: George T. Bisel Company, 1922, revised 1930). The most recent re-interpretation, which in part dissents from the majority view, is by Robert L. Henry, "The Story of the Criminal Jury," in Max Radin, ed., *Legal Essays in Honor of Orrin Kip McMurray* (Berkeley, California: University of California Press, 1935), pp. 135-163.

14. Frederic W. Maitland and Francis C. Montague, *A Sketch of English Legal History* (New York: G. P. Putnam's Sons, 1915), p. 46; McIlwain, *op. cit.,* pp. 173-174.

15. The practice had originated in the later Roman empire as a method of determining fiscal claims. Edward Jenks, *A Short History of English Law* (2d ed., rev.; London: Methuen & Company, Ltd., 1920), p. 47.

16. Carpenter and Stafford, *op. cit.,* p. 346; McIlwain, *op. cit.,* p. 181.

17. Maitland and Montague, *op. cit.,* pp. 53-54.

18. *Ibid.,* pp. 58-59; Pollock and Maitland, *op. cit.,* I, 131 ff.; Jenks, *op. cit.,* pp. 39-43.

19. *Op. cit.,* I, 252.

20. Sait, *op. cit.,* p. 215.

21. Fullhardt, *op. cit.,* p. 56. This method of coercing recalcitrant defendants to accept a trial by jury was not abolished until 1772 (12 Geo. III, c. 20).

22. *Op. cit.,* I, 264.

23. Holdsworth, *op. cit. supra* n. 1, I, 321-327.

24. Pollock and Maitland, *op. cit.,* II, 619-625.

25. "The steps by which the jury ceased to be witnesses and became judges of the evidence given by others, cannot now be traced without an amount of labor out of proportion to the value of the result . . ."—Sir James F. Stephen, *op. cit.,* I, 260.

26. Sait, *op. cit.,* p. 222.

27. Sir John Fortescue, *De Laudibus Legum Angliae* (ca. 1468), chaps. XXV and XXVI. The text may be found in Francis Gregor's translation in various editions, and in Stanley B. Crimes' translation in the *Cambridge Studies in Legal History* (1942). The Gregor translation of the chapters cited is reprinted in Carpenter and Stafford, *op. cit.,* pp. 347-351.

The emergence and increasing importance of trial by jury did not result in complete or immediate disappearance of the older modes of proof. In 1679, a defendant startled the court and the legal profession by asking for trial by ordeal. *Whitebread's Case,* 7 How. State Trials 383. As late as 1818, trial by battle was still acknowledged to be a part of the criminal law of England, *Ashford v. Thornton,* I Bar. & Ald. 405, a finding which was corrected the following year by statute, 59 Geo. III, c. 46. Trial by compurgation was invoked even more recently, *Rex v. Williams,* 2 B. & C. 538 (1824), and abolished only in 1833, 3 & 4 Wm. IV, c. 42, s. 13. Sir James F. Stephen, *op. cit.,* I, 244-246 and 253 n.

28. Sir Thomas Smith, *The Commonwealth of England* (1565), II, chap. 26.

29. 1 How. State Trials 869, 884.

30. 1 How. State Trials 1271, 1281.

31. *Rex v. Thomas,* 2 Bulst. 147 (1613).

32. *Whitebread's Case,* 7 How. State Trials 311, 359.

33. II, 283, quoted by Thayer, *op. cit.,* p. 161 n.

34. 7 Wm. III, c. 3, s. 1 (1695), as to treason; 1 Anne, c. 9, s. 3 (1701), as to felony trials.

35. Holdsworth, *History of English Law,* V, 196.

36. 7 Wm. III, c. 3 (1695).

37. Thomas M. Cooley, *Constitutional Limitations* (8th ed., by Walter Carrington; Boston: Little, Brown and Company, 1927), I, 698 n.

38. 6 & 7 Wm. IV, c. 114.

39. Holdsworth, *History of English Law,* III, 615 n.

40. *Ibid.,* V, 195-196; IX, 224.

41. In 1367: Y. B. 24 Ed. III. Hil. pl. 10, cited by Holdsworth, *History of English Law,* I, 318 n.

42. Holdsworth, *History of English Law,* I, 399.

43. Thayer, op. cit., p. 140.
44. Ibid., pp. 157-159.
45. Holdsworth, History of English Law, I, 318-319, 342-343; Thayer, op. cit., p. 155, where footnote 2 quotes the following court order from Welcden v. Elkington, Plowd. 516, 518 (1577-8): "And for that a certain box of preserved barberries, and sugar, called sugarcandy, and sweet roots, called liquorish [sic], were found with the aforesaid John Mucklow, one of the jurors aforesaid . . . therefore the same John Mucklow is committed to the prison . . . of the Fleet, until he shall have made a fine with the lady, the Queen, etc. . . ."
46. Maitland and Montague, op. cit., p. 133.
47. William Hudson, "A Treatise on the Court of Star Chamber," in Francis Hargrave, ed., Collectanea Juridica (London: E. and R. Brooke, 1791), II.
48. Thayer, op. cit., pp. 162-163.
49. Ibid., p. 166; Maitland and Montague, op. cit., p. 133.
50. Vaughan, 135 (1670); 6 How. State Trials 999; Thayer, op. cit., pp. 166-168; Maitland and Montague, op. cit., p. 134; Stephen, op. cit., I, 374-375.
51. Penn and Mead's Case, 6 How. State Trials 951 (1670). Cf. William I. Hull, William Penn: A Topical Biography (New York: Oxford University Press, 1937), pp. 185-190.
52. Maitland and Montague, op cit., p. 134.

Chapter II

1. Herbert S. Hadley, "The Reform of Criminal Procedure," Proceedings of the Academy of Political Science (1923), X, 396, 398.
2. He saved his life by denouncing one Kendall, who was tried and shot for allegedly planning a mutiny. Related by E. M. Wingfield in his "Discourse of Virginia," reproduced in Edward Arber, ed., Travels and Works of Captain John Smith (Edinburgh: J. Grant, 1910), p. lxxxvii.
3. Francis N. Thorpe, The Federal and State Constitutions, Colonial Charters, and Other Organic Laws of the States, Territories and Colonies Now or Heretofore forming the United States of America (Washington: Government Printing Office, 1909), I, 49-53.
4. Ibid., I, 53 ff.
5. Ibid., V, 3783, 3788.
6. See supra, chap. I.
7. Magna Carta, c. 39.
8. Joseph Story, Commentaries on the Constitution of the United States (3rd ed.; Boston: Little, Brown, and Company, 1858), II, 587-588, § 1779.
9. See supra, chap. I, and authorities cited there; cf. also William S. McKechnie, Magna Carta: A Commentary on the Great Charter of King John (2d ed.; Glasgow: James Maclehouse and Sons, 1914), especially pp. 134 ff.; Sir Paul Vinogradoff, "Magna Carta, C. 39," in Henry E. Malden, ed., Magna Carta Commemoration Essays (London: Royal Historical Society, 1917), p. 78; and Frederick M. Powicke, "Per Iudicium Parium vel Legem Terrae," Ibid., p. 96.
10. Cf. Max Radin, "The Myth of Magna Carta," Harvard Law Review, LX (1947), 1060-1091.
11. The jurists themselves limit this theory by allowing that the colonies "adopted only that portion [of the common law] which was applicable to their situation." Story, J., in Van Ness v. Packard, 2 Pet. (27 U.S.) 137, 143 (1829).
12. Paul S. Reinsch, "The English Common Law in the Early American Colonies," Bulletin of the University of Wisconsin, II (1899), reprinted in John H. Wigmore, Ernst Freund, and William E. Mikell, eds., Select Essays in Anglo-American Legal History (Boston: Little, Brown and Company, 1907), I, 367-415 (references are to the reprint in the Essays). Cf. also Arthur P. Scott, Criminal Justice in Virginia (Chicago: University of Chicago Press, 1930, pp. 3-38; and Max Radin, "The Rivalry of Common-Law and Civil Law Ideas in the American Colonies," in Alison Reppy, ed., Law: A Century of Progress 1835-1935 (New York: New York University Press, 1937), II, 404-431.
13. Charles Warren, A History of the American Bar (Boston: Little, Brown and Company, 1911), 1-208.
14. (Alexander Hamilton), The Federalist, No. LXXXIII.

15. *Op. cit.*, p. 378.

16. John Gorham Palfrey, *History of New England* (Boston: Little, Brown and Company, 1858-64), I, 240, cited by Thomas M. Cooley, *Constitutional Limitations* (8th ed.; Boston: Little, Brown and Company, 1927), I, 660 n., and by Harlan, J., dissenting in *Maxwell* v. *Dow*, 176 U.S. 581, 609 (1900).

17. Cited in *Commonwealth* v. *Rowe*, 257 Mass. 172, 153 N.E. 537 (1926).

18. *Op. cit.*, p. 378.

19. *Ibid.*, p. 378, citing *Massachusetts Colonial Records.*

20. *Ibid.*, p. 386, citing *Connecticut Records.*

21. *Ibid.*, p. 386, citing *Massachusetts Historical Society Collections*, ser. II, vol. IV, p. 320.

22. *Ibid.*, p. 389, citing *Rhode Island Colonial Records.*

23. Harold D. Hazeltine, "The Influence of Magna Carta on American Constitutional Development," *Columbia Law Review*, XVII (1917), 1, 12; also in Henry E. Malden, ed., *op. cit. supra*, n. 9. The charter never received the royal assent but the colonists always claimed that it was operative as a protection of their constitutional liberties. Warren, *op. cit.*, p. 91.

24. Reinsch, *op. cit.*, p. 393, citing Berthold Fernow, ed., *Documents Relative to the Colonial History of New York* (Albany, N.Y.: Weed, Parsons and Company, 1853-87), V, 267 ff.

25. Thorpe, *op. cit.*, V, 2551.

26. Chapter XXIII: "That in all publick courts of justice for tryals ot causes, civil or criminal, any person or persons, inhabitants of the said Province may freely come into, and attend the said courts, and hear and be present, at all or any such tryals as shall be there had or passed, that justice may not be done in a corner nor in any covert manner, being intended and resolved, by the help of the Lord, and by these our Concessions and Fundamentals, that all and every person and persons inhabiting the said province shall, as far as in us lies, be free from oppression and slavery." *Ibid.*, p. 2551.

27. Reinsch, *op. cit.*, p. 395, citing Aaron Leming and Jacob Spicer, *The Grants, Concessions, and Original Constitutions of the Province of New Jersey* (Philadelphia: W. Bradford, 1758 [?]), p. 396.

28. Chapter XIX; Thorpe, *op. cit.*, pp. 2580-2581.

29. Chapter V; *ibid.*, p. 3060.

30. Chapter VIII; *loc. cit.*

31. Chapter VI; *loc. cit.*

32. Article XIX of the Frame of Government of 1682; *ibid.*, p. 3058; Article XVII of the Frame of Government of 1683; *ibid.*, p. 3067.

33. Reinsch, *op. cit.*, p. 398, citing *Pennsylvania Archives*, VII, 725-730, *et al.*

34. *Ibid.*, pp. 407-08, citing Francis L. Hawks, *History of North Carolina* (Fayetteville, N.C.: E. J. Hale and Sons, 1857-8), I, 182, and II, 122 and 128.

35. Framed by John Locke and amended by the Earl of Shaftesbury (Anthony Ashley Cooper). Thorpe, *op. cit.*, V, 2772.

36. Article 27; *ibid.*, p. 2775.

37. Article 68; *ibid.*, p. 2780.

38. Article 69; *ibid.*, p. 2781.

39. Article 70; *ibid.*, p. 2781.

40. Reinsch, *op. cit.*, p. 409, citing David Ramsay, *History of the Revolution of South Carolina, from a British Province to an Independent State* (Trenton, N.J.: Isaac Collins, 1785), I, 120; Simeon Baldwin, *The American Judiciary* (New York: The Century Company, 1905), p. 11; Herbert L. Osgood, *The American Colonies in the Seventeenth Century* (New York: The Macmillan Company, 1904), II, 297, 300.

41. Oliver P. Chitwood, *Justice in Colonial Virginia* (Baltimore: The Johns Hopkins Press, 1905); George L. Chumbley, *Colonial Justice in Virginia* (Richmond, Va.: The Dietz Press, 1938); Arthur P. Scott, *Criminal Justice in Colonial Virginia* (Chicago: University of Chicago Press, 1930).

42. The reference is to the elective House of Burgesses. The appointive Council was *ipso facto* also part of the General Court. It has been said that "before 1683 the assembly showed a strong tendency to subordinate all courts to itself, even the general court being no exception. In fact the house of burgesses attempted to make itself the supreme court of the colony." Elmer I. Miller, *The Legislature of the Province of Vir-*

ginia (New York: Columbia University Press, 1907), p. 168. This opinion, however, is not shared by Chitwood, op. cit., p. 19, who does not believe that usurpation of judicial powers was intended by the legislature.

43. Chumbley, op. cit., pp. 6-7, quoting from *Journals of the House of Burgesses 1619-1658/9* (H. R. McIlwaine, ed., Richmond, Va.: The Colonial Press, E. Waddey Company, 1915), p. 12.

44. William W. Hening, comp., *The Statutes at Large . . . of Virginia* (Richmond, Va.: Samuel Pleasants, 1809), I, 67-69.

45. Case of Dr. John Pott, *ibid.*, I, 145; Case of William Matthewes, *ibid.*, I, 146.

46. Chumbley, op. cit., p. 67; Scott, op. cit., pp. 87-88.

47. Hening, op. cit., IV, 403; cf. Scott, op. cit., p. 89.

48. Warren, op. cit., pp. 1-208, passim.

49. *Ibid.*, and see Reinsch, op. cit., passim. "In Delaware, no professionally trained judge held office before the Revolution." *Ibid.*, p. 396, citing Ignatius C. Grubb, *The Colonial and State Judiciary of Delaware* (Wilmington, Del.: The Historical Society of Delaware, 1897), p. 9.

50. Cf. Warren, op. cit., passim, for names and professional background of prominent lawyers of the period.

51. See *supra*, chap. I.

52. Pennsylvania Charter of Privileges (1701), Article V; Thorpe, op. cit., V, 3079.

53. Pendleton Howard, *Criminal Justice in England* (New York: The Macmillan Company, 1931), p. 5. The office of county prosecuting officer was apparently first established in Connecticut in 1704. *Ibid.*, p. 5 n., citing Herman G. James, *Local Government in the United States* (New York: D. Appleton and Company, 1921), p. 144. In Virginia, Lieutenant Governor Spotswood appointed the first King's Attorneys in 1711; Hening, op. cit., IV, 539. See also National Commission on Law Observance and Enforcement, *Report on Prosecution* (Washington: Government Printing Office, 1931), pp. 6-7.

54. Declaration of Rights of the Continental Congress (1774), Article 5; reprinted in Charles C. Tansill, ed., *Documents Illustrative of the Formation of the Union of the American States* (House Document No. 398, 69th Congress, 1st session, Washington: Government Printing Office, 1927), p. 3.

55. ". . . Acts of pretended Legislation: . . . For depriving us in many cases, of the benefits of Trial by Jury; For transporting us beyond Seas to be tried for pretended offences; . . . Thorpe, op. cit., I, 5.

56. Articles III, XVIII, and XIX; *ibid.*, III, 1686, 1688.

57. Articles VII and IX; *ibid.*, V, 2787.

58. *Ibid.*, V, 2587-2588.

59. *Ibid.*, VI, 3248.

60. Articles XXXIV and LXI; *ibid.*, II, 783, 785.

61. Articles XXIV and XLI; *ibid.*, V, 2635, 2637.

62. *Ibid.*, VII, 3812.

63. Massachusetts: Articles XII and XIII; *ibid.*, III, 1888; New Hampshire: Articles XV, XVI, and XVII; *ibid.*, IV, 2455.

64. Max Farrand, ed., *The Records of the Federal Convention of 1787* (revised edition in four volumes, New Haven: Yale University Press, 1937), III, 616.

65. *Ibid.*, III, 626.

66. *Ibid.*, III, 600.

67. *Ibid.*, II, 187. For proceedings in committee, see *ibid.*, II, 144 and 173.

68. James Madison on the floor of the convention; *ibid.*, II, 438. The motion is recorded in the Journal of the convention for August 28, 1787, *ibid.*, II, 434.

69. *Ibid.*, II, 576, 601.

70. Nelson B. Lasson, *The History and Development of the Fourth Amendment to the United States Constitution* (Baltimore: The Johns Hopkins Press, 1937), pp. 83 ff., gives a detailed and amply documented account of the emergence of the demand for a Bill of Rights and of the principal arguments for and against it. The essential sequence of developments is familiar to students of history and of the Constitution and its restatement in this context may be dispensed with.

71. Patrick Henry in the Virginia convention, June 20, 1788. Jonathan Elliot, ed., *The Debates in the Several State Conventions on the Adoption of the Federal Constitu-*

tion . . . (Philadelphia: J. B. Lippincott Company, 1835), III, 540. Cf. also Grayson's remarks in the same vein, *ibid.*, III, 568; Bloodworth and Spencer in the North Carolina convention, *ibid.*, IV, 151, 154; Luther Martin's "Genuine Information," *ibid.*, II, 381.

72. *Ibid.*, III, 541.

73. *Ibid.*, III, 545-546.

74. *Ibid.*, III, 568-569.

75. *Ibid.*, II, 109-111. See also the debates of the North Carolina convention, particularly speeches of McDowall, Bloodworth, and Spencer, *ibid.*, IV, 144, 150, 151, 154.

76. *Ibid.*, III, 558.

77. *Ibid.*, III, 537.

78. *Ibid.*, II, 112; III, 546.

79. Gore in the Massachusetts convention, *ibid.*, II, 112; and see *ibid.*, III, 558, and IV, 150-152.

80. Maclaine in the North Carolina convention, *ibid.*, IV, 175.

81. George Washington, First Inaugural Address, in James D. Richardson, ed., *Messages and Papers of the Presidents* (Washington: Government Printing Office, 1896), I, 45.

82. Davis, J., in *Ex parte Milligan*, 4 Wall. (71 U.S.) 2, 120 (1866).

83. James Madison to George Eve, January 2, 1789. In Gaillard Hunt, ed., *Writings of James Madison* (New York: G. P. Putnam's Sons, 1904), V, 320. See also letter to George Washington, *ibid.*, V, 318-321; and William W. Henry, *Patrick Henry* (New York: Charles Scribner's Sons, 1891), II, 44.

84. See the list in Herman V. Ames, *The Proposed Amendments to the Constitution of the United States During the First Century of Its History* (published as Volume II of the Annual Report of the American Historical Association for the Year 1896; Washington: Government Printing Office, 1897), pp. 307-310.

85. Elliot, *op. cit.*, II, 550.

86. *Ibid.*, I, 328.

87. *Ibid.*, III, 657.

88. *Ibid.*, IV, 243.

89. "[The Amendments] are restrained to points on which least difficulty was apprehended. Nothing of a controvertible nature ought to be hazarded by those who are sincere in wishing for the approbation of 2/3 of each House, and 3/4 of the State Legislatures." James Madison to Edmund Pendleton, June 21, 1789; *Documentary History of the Constitution of the United States*, V, 179. See also Madison's letter to Edmund Randolph, August 21, 1789, *ibid.*, V, 191-192.

90. *Annals of Congress*, 1st Congress, 1st session, cols. 451-453. Cf. Felix Frankfurter and Thomas G. Corcoran, "Petty Federal Offenses and the Constitutional Guarantee of a Trial by Jury," *Harvard Law Review*, XXXIX (1926), 917, 968 ff.

91. *Annals of Congress*, 1st Congress, 1st session, cols. 451-453.

92. *Loc. cit.*

93. As the ninth of a number of clauses to be inserted in Article I, section 9, between clause 3 and 4. *Ibid.*, cols. 452-453.

94. *Loc. cit.*

95. See also Charles Warren, "New Light on the History of the Federal Judiciary Act of 1789," *Harvard Law Review*, XXXVII (1923), 49, 111 ff., and Henry Von Hasseln, "The Work of the First Congress in 1789," unpublished Master's Thesis, University of Virginia, 1946.

96. *Annals of Congress*, 1st Congress, 1st session, cols. 783-784.

97. A further modification by the committee was the elimination of the requirement that the accused be confronted with his accuser. *Ibid.*, cols. 784-789.

98. *Loc. cit.*

99. *Ibid.*, col. 796.

100. *Ibid.*, cols. 794, 808.

101. *Ibid.*, cols. 808-809.

102. *Ibid.*, cols. 73-80.

103. Edgar S. Maclay, ed., *Journal of William Maclay* (New York: D. Appleton and Company, 1890), pp. 144-151.

104. *Annals of Congress*, 1st Congress, 1st session, col. 923.

105. *Writings*, V, 420-421; *Documentary History of the Constitution*, V, 205-206.
106. *Annals of Congress*, 1st Congress, 1st session, col. 923.
107. *Writings*, V, 424; *Documentary History of the Constitution*, V, 210-211.
108. *Annals of Congress*, 1st Congress, 1st session, col. 948.

Chapter III

1. Rhode Island was the ninth state to ratify, thereby completing the constitutional procedure for the adoption of the amendments. Cf. the acts of ratification of the several states in *Documentary History of the United States* (Washington: Department of State, 1894-1905), II, 325-390.
2. Section 2, clause 3: "The trial of all Crimes, except in Cases of Impeachment, shall be by Jury; and such Trial shall be held in the State where the said Crimes shall have been committed; but when not committed within any State, the Trial shall be at such Place or Places as the Congress may by Law have directed."
3. Amendment V: "No person . . . shall be compelled in any criminal case to be a witness against himself . . . ."
4. *Harvard Law Review*, XXXIX (1926), 917, 968 ff.
5. *Counselman* v. *Hitchcock*, 142 U.S. 547 (1892). (All citations of cases are to the official reports only. Alternate citations may be found in the Table of Cases.)
6. *Ibid.*, 563.
7. Italics supplied.
8. See *supra*, chap. II.
9. 127 U.S. 540 (1888).
10. Assistant Attorney General Maury before the Supreme Court of the United States, *ibid.*, 546.
11. *Ibid.*, 549.
12. Joseph Story, *Commentaries on the Constitution of the United States* (3rd ed.; Boston: Little, Brown and Company, 1858), II, 596, § 1791.
13. 127 U.S. 540, 549.
14. 195 U.S. 65 (1904).
15. *Ibid.*, 68.
16. *Loc. cit.*, italics supplied.
17. See *Dickinson* v. *United States*, 159 Fed. 801, 810-811 (C.C.A., 1st Cir., 1908), certiorari dismissed 213 U.S. 92.
18. 281 U.S. 276, 298.
19. *Ibid.*, 280.
20. Statutes *in pari materia*, i.e., upon the same subject matter, are to be construed together. William E. Baldwin, ed., *Bouvier's Law Dictionary* (Century ed.; Cleveland: Banks-Baldwin Law Publishing Company, 1940), p. 530.
21. 281 U.S. 276, 298.
22. *Ibid.*, 297.
23. 7 Pet. (32 U.S.) 243 (1833).
24. 7 Wall. (74 U.S.) 321 (1868).
25. *Ibid.*, 325, 327.
26. *Eilenbecker* v. *Plymouth County*, 134 U.S. 31, 34 (1890); approved and followed in *Lloyd* v. *Dollison*, 194 U.S. 445 (1904), *Ughbanks* v. *Armstrong*, 208 U.S. 481 (1908), and numerous lower court decisions.
27. *Gaines* v. *Washington*, 277 U.S. 81, 85 (1928).
28. 16 Wall. (84 U.S.) 36 (1873).
29. But cf. the evidence presented by Horace Flack, *The Adoption of the Fourteenth Amendment* (Baltimore: The Johns Hopkins Press, 1908), to the effect that the very opposite had been intended by the authors of the amendment, who desired to make all ordinary rights of citizens attributes of national citizenship and thus subject to control and protection by the federal government.
30. 123 U.S. 131 (1877).
31. *Ibid.*, 151-153. The same point was made by Roger A. Pryor, also of counsel for petitioners, *ibid.*, 156.
32. *Ibid.*, 170. Cf. William H. Dunbar, "The Anarchists' Case Before the Supreme Court of the United States," *Harvard Law Review*, I (1888), 307-326.

33. *Maxwell v. Dow*, 176 U.S. 581, 595 (1900); and see also: *in re Sawyer*, 124 U.S. 200, 219 (1888); *Brooks v. Missouri*, 124 U.S. 394, 397 (1888); *Brown v. New Jersey*, 175 U.S. 172, 174 (1899); *West v. Louisiana*, 194 U.S. 258, 263 (1904); *Howard v. Kentucky*, 200 U.S. 164, 172 (1906); *Hawkins v. Bleakly*, 243 U.S. 210, 216 (1917).
34. 110 U.S. 516 (1884).
35. *Ibid.*, 535.
36. 101 U.S. 22 (1879).
37. *Ibid.*, 31, italics supplied.
38. 110 U.S. 516, 558. Cf. Floyd B. Clark, *The Constitutional Doctrines of Justice Harlan* (Baltimore: The Johns Hopkins Press, 1915), pp. 59-65.
39. Dissenting in *Maxwell v. Dow*, supra, 606.
40. Clark, *op. cit.*, pp. 175-176.
41. *Hawkins v. Bleakly*, 243 U.S. 210, 216 (1917).
42. *Twining v. New Jersey*, 211 U.S. 78, 99 (1908). Immunity from self-incrimination was held not to be of such a nature as to be required under due process of law.
43. 287 U.S. 45 (1932).
44. *Ibid.*, 67, quoting from *Hebert v. Louisiana*, 272 U.S. 312, 316 (1926).
45. *Betts v. Brady*, 316 U.S. 455 (1942), *Foster v. Illinois*, 332 U.S. 134 (1947).
46. Discussed *infra*, chap. VI, pp. 121-135.
47. Except in criminal contempt cases; see *infra*, pp. 56-57.
48. *United States v. Dawson*, 15 How. (56 U.S.) 467, 489 (1853; Indian Territory); *Reynolds v. United States*, 98 U.S. 145, 154 (1878; Utah); *Lovato v. New Mexico*, 242 U.S. 199 (1916; New Mexico).
49. 127 U.S. 540 (1888).
50. Act of June 17, 1870, c. 133, s. 1, 16 Stat. 154.
51. *Ibid.*, s. 3.
52. 127 U.S. 540, 550.
53. *Loc. cit.* Cf. *Capitol Traction Company v. Hof*, 174 U.S. 1, 5 (1899): "It is beyond doubt, at the present day, that the provisions of the Constitution of the United States securing the right of trial by jury, whether in civil or criminal cases, are applicable to the District of Columbia."
54. *De Lima v. Bidwell*, 182 U.S. 1 (1901); *Dooley v. United States*, 182 U.S. 222 (1901); *Downes v. Bidwell*, 182 U.S. 244 (1901).
55. See James W. Garner, "The Right of Jury Trial in the Dependencies," *American Law Review*, XL (1906), 340.
56. *Hawaii v. Mankichi*, 190 U.S. 197 (1903). See Emlin McClain, "The Hawaiian Case," *Harvard Law Review*, XVII (1904), 386-399.
57. 30 Stat. 750.
58. Act of April 30, 1900, 31 Stat. 141, effective June 14, 1900.
59. 190 U.S. 197, 219-221.
60. *Ibid.*, 214, 215.
61. *Ibid.*, 216.
62. Senate Document No. 16, 55th Congress, 3rd session, p. 162.
63. 190 U.S. 197, 214.
64. *Ibid.*, 223.
65. *Ibid.*, 217-218.
66. Westel W. Willoughby, *The Constitutional Law of the United States* (2d ed.; New York: Baker, Voorhis and Company, 1929), I, 497.
67. 190 U.S. 197, 246.
67a. Justice Murphy most nearly approached him in our day.
68. See *infra*, chap. VII.
69. *Dorr v. United States*, 195 U.S. 138 (1904).
70. *Ibid.*, 155, 156.
71. *Ibid.*, 153-154.
72. *Ibid.*, 145.
73. 30 Stat. 1754, 1759.
74. Act of March 2, 1917, c. 145, 39 Stat. 951.
75. *Balzac v. Porto Rico*, 258 U.S. 298, 309 (1922); noted in *Harvard Law Review*, XXXVI (1922), 105.
76. 258 U.S. 298, 310.

77. Act of March 3, 1917, c. 171, 39 Stat. 1132.

78. *Soto* v. *United States*, 273 Fed. 628 (C.C.A., 3rd Cir., 1921); *Francis* v. *Virgin Islands*, 11 Fed. (2d) 860, (C.C.A., 3rd Cir., 1926), certiorari denied 273 U.S. 693.

79. The Panama Canal Act, Act of August 24, 1912, c. 390, s. 8, 37 Stat. 562, 565, United States Code (1940), Title 48, sec. 1377, provides that "a jury shall be had in all criminal cases . . . upon the demand of either party." But the Canal Zone is not an incorporated territory and its inhabitants enjoy the guarantees of the United States Constitution only to the extent that Congress has seen fit to extend such protection. *McConaughey* v. *Morrow*, 3 C.Z. 377, 381 (1922).

80. 31 Stat. 321, 359.

81. *Rassmussen* v. *United States*, 197 U.S. 516 (1905).

82. 15 Stat. 539, 542.

83. 197 U.S. 516, 522. Cf. George W. Spicer, *The Constitutional Status and Government of Alaska* (Baltimore: The Johns Hopkins Press, 1927), pp. 24-36.

84. *In re Ross*, 140 U.S. 453 (1891).

85. *Ibid.*, 464.

86. "There was no necessity for the court to declare that the American Constitution had no operative force outside the United States. Such an assertion was, in fact, both unfortunate and incorrect." Westel W. Willoughby, *The Fundamental Concepts of Public Law* (New York: The Macmillan Company, 1931), p. 399.

87. *Hawaii* v. *Mankichi*, supra, 217-218.

88. *Soto* v. *United States*, supra.

89. Cf. *Palko* v. *Connecticut*, 302 U.S. 319, 325 (1937); but see *Betts* v. *Brady*, infra, chap. VI. And note exceptions in criminal contempt cases, infra, this chapter.

90. See infra, chap. VI.

91. Act of April 30, 1900, c. 399, s. 83, 31 Stat. 157, United States Code (1940). Title 48, sec. 635; and Act of August 24, 1912, supra, note 79.

92. Cf. note 79, supra.

93. Act of May 5, 1892, c. 60, 27 Stat. 25.

94. 118 U.S. 356 (1886).

95. *Wong Wing* v. *United States*, 163 U.S. 228 (1886). The statute was declared unconstitutional because "it is not consistent with the theory of our government that the legislature should, after having defined an offense as an infamous crime, find the fact of guilt and adjudge the punishment by one of its own agents." *Ibid.*, 237. The availability to aliens in this country of the guarantees of the Sixth Amendment has most recently been confirmed in the case of the Australian-born labor leader, Harry Bridges. *Bridges* v. *Wixon*, 144 Fed. (2d) 927 (C.C.A., 10th Cir., 1944, reversed on other grounds 326 U.S. 135. Nor is such relief denied to enemy aliens in time of war. *Von Moltke* v. *Gillies*, 332 U.S. 708 (1948).

96. *United States ex rel. Turner* v. *Williams*, 194 U.S. 279 (1904).

97. *Zakonaite* v. *Wolf*, 226 U.S. 272 (1912). See also *Bugajewitz* v. *Adams*, 228 U.S. 585 (1913), opinion of Holmes, J., and *Choy Gum* v. *Backus*, 223 Fed. 487 (C.C.A., 9th Cir., 1915), certiorari denied 239 U.S. 649.

98. *Ex parte Burr*, Fed. Cas. No. 2,186, 4 Fed. Cas. 791 (1823). Mandamus denied in same cause, 9 Wheat. (22 U.S.) 529.

99. *Ex parte Wall*, 107 U.S. 265 (1882). The case was complicated by the fact that, due to local conditions, there was no proof of the attorney's participation in the lynching other than the disbarring judge's personal knowledge. See Field's dissent, *ibid.*, 290-317.

100. *Ex parte La Mantia*, 206 Fed. 330 (D.C., S.D.N.Y., 1912). Cf. John B. Moore, *A Treatise on Extradition and Interstate Rendition* (Boston: The Boston Book Company, 1891), I, 549 ff.

101. *Riggs* v. *United States*, 14 Fed. (2d) 5, 10 (C.C.A., 4th Cir., 1926); *Strickland* v. *United States*, 114 Fed. (2d) 556 (C.C.A., 4th Cir., 1940).

102. *Hodge* v. *Huff*, 140 Fed. (2d) 686, 689 (App. D.C., 1944), certiorari denied 322 U.S. 733. See also: *Brown* v. *Johnston*, 91 Fed. (2d) 370 (C.C.A., 9th Cir., 1936), certiorari denied 302 U.S. 728; *Burgess* v. *King*, 130 Fed. (2d) 761 (C.C.A., 8th Cir., 1942); *Dorsey* v. *Gill*, 148 Fed. (2d) 857 (App. D.C., 1945), certiorari denied 325 U.S. 890.

103. *Burall* v. *Johnston*, 146 Fed. (2d) 230 (C.C.A., 9th Cir., 1944), certiorari denied 325 U.S. 887. But see *United States ex rel. Mertner* v. *Hiatt*, 33 F. Supp. 545

(D.C., M.D.Pa., 1940), and cf. Rule 5 (b) and (c), *Federal Rules of Criminal Procedure*, 327 U.S. 821, 835-836 (1946).

104. *Gilmore v. United States*, 129 Fed. (2d) 199 (C.C.A., 10th Cir., 1942), certiorari denied 317 U.S. 631.

105. *Lovvorn v. Johnston*, 118 Fed. (2d) 704 (C.C.A., 9th Cir., 1941), certiorari denied 314 U.S. 607; *Gargano v. United States*, 137 Fed. (2d) 944 (C.C.A., 9th Cir., 1943); *Nivens v. United States*, 139 Fed. (2) 226 (C.C.A., 5th Cir., 1943), certiorari denied 321 U.S. 787, rehearing denied 321 U.S. 804, 322 U.S. 769.

106. *Ex parte Milligan*, 4 Wall. (71 U.S.) 2, 123 (1866); *Kahn v. Anderson*, 255 U.S. 1 (1921); *In re Waidman*, 42 Fed. (2d) 239 (D.C., D. Maine, S.D., 1930).

107. Cf. the broad language in *Ex parte Quirin*, 317 U.S. 1, at 40 (1942).

108. *United States ex rel. Innis v. Crystal*, 131 Fed. (2d) 576 (C.C.A., 2d Cir., 1943), certiorari denied 319 U.S. 755; *Ex parte Benton*, 63 F. Supp. 808 (D.C., N.D. Cal., 1945). But see *Shapiro v. United States*, 69 F. Supp. 205 (Ct. Cl., 1947, where the sentence of a court-martial was declared void because the accused had been denied his rights under the Fifth and Sixth Amendments; noted in *Virginia Law Review*, XXXIII (1947), 505-507.

109. *Kahn v. Anderson*, supra; *In re Waidman*, supra.

110. *United States v. L. Cohen Grocery Company*, 255 U.S. 81, 88 (1921); *Ex parte Milligan*, supra, 121-127.

111. Cf. *Duncan v. Kahanamoku*, 327 U.S. 304 (1946).

112. *Ex parte Quirin*, supra, 38-44; *United States ex rel. Wessels v. McDonald*, 265 Fed. 754 (D.C., E.D.N.Y., 1920), appeal dismissed 256 U.S. 705.

113. 161 U.S. 475 (1896).

114. Act of June 10, 1890, c. 407, 26 Stat. 131.

115. 161 U.S. 475, 481.

116. *Hepner v. United States*, 213 U.S. 103, 111 (1909); *Oceanic Steam Navigation Company v. Stranahan*, 214 U.S. 320 (1909); *International Mercantile Marine Company v. Stranahan*, 214 U.S. 344 (1909); *Southern Pacific Company v. United States*, 171 Fed. 364 (C.C.A., 9th Cir., 1909).

117. *Farmers' Livestock Commission Company v. United States*, 54 Fed. (2d) 375 (D.C., E.D., Ill., 1931; Packers and Stockyards Act).

118. *Myers v. United States*, 264 U.S. 95, 104 (1924).

119. *Michaelson v. United States*, 266 U.S. 42, 67 (1924).

120. *In re Debs*, 158 U.S. 564, 594 (1895). That this rule was "of immemorial usage" has been conclusively disproved by Sir John C. Fox, *The History of Contempt of Court* (Oxford: Clarendon Press, 1927), 4-15; see also Felix Frankfurter and James M. Landis, "Power of Congress over Procedure in 'Inferior' Federal Courts—A Study in Separation of Powers," *Harvard Law Review*, XXXVII (1924), 1010, 1042-1058, and Justice Rutledge's dissenting opinion in *United States v. United Mine Workers*, 330 U.S. 258, at 366 n. (1947).

121. But judgments for criminal contempt are reviewable on appeal. *Nye v. United States*, 313 U.S. 33 (1941); *Wilson v. Byron Jackson Company*, 93 Fed. (2d) 577 (C.C.A., 9th Cir., 1937).

122. *In re Debs*, supra, 595.

123. (Comment) "Civil and Criminal Contempt in the Federal Courts," *Yale Law Journal*, LVII (1947), 83, 95-98.

124. 327 U.S. 821, 865-866 (1946).

125. *Cooke v. United States*, 267 U.S. 517, 537 (1925); see *United States v. United Mine Workers*, supra, 365 n. (dissenting opinion).

126. (Comment), *Yale Law Journal*, op. cit., pp. 97-98.

127. Frankfurter, J., dissenting in *Penfield Company v. Securities and Exchange Commission*, 330 U.S. 585, 609 (1947).

128. See *Palko v. Connecticut*, 302 U.S. 319, 324 (1937), and cases cited there.

129. "Petty Federal Offenses and the Constitutional Guarantee of a Trial by Jury," *Harvard Law Review*, XXXIX (1926), 917-1019.

130. Ibid., p. 969.

131. 195 U.S. 65, 68 (1904).

132. *United States v. Praeger*, 149 Fed. 474 (D.C., W.D. Tenn., 1907).

133. *Frank v. United States*, 192 Fed. 864 (C.C.A., 6th Cir, 1911).

134. Low v. United States, 169 Fed. 86 (C.C.A., 6th Cir., 1909).
135. Coates v. United States, 290 Fed. 134 (C.C.A., 4th Cir., 1923).
136. District of Columbia v. Colts, 282 U.S. 63 (1930). Discussions of the case may be found in: Columbia Law Review, XXXI (1931), 325-326; Harvard Law Review, XLIV (1931), 465; University of Pennsylvania Law Review, LXXIX (1931), 640-642; Yale Law Journal, XL (1931), 1303-1309.
137. 282 U.S. 63, 73.
138. 46 Stat. 1029, United States Code (1940), Title 18, § 541.
139. District of Columbia v. Clawans, 300 U.S. 617 (1937). Criticized in Michigan Law Review, XXXV (1937), 1377-1380.
140. 300 U.S. 617, 625.
141. Smith v. United States, 128 Fed. (2d) 990 (C.C.A., 5th Cir., 1942); Latiolais v. United States, 129 Fed. (2d) 323 (C.C.A., 5th Cir., 1942).

Chapter IV

1. Frankel v. Woodrough, 7 Fed. (2d) 796, 798 (C.C.A., 8th Cir., 1925).
2. Beavers v. Haubert, 198 U.S. 77 (1905).
3. Phillips v. United States, 201 Fed. 259 (C.C.A., 8th Cir., 1912); Worthington v. United States, 1 Fed. (2d) 154 (C.C.A., 7th Cir., 1924), certiorari denied 266 U.S. 626; Daniels v. United States, 17 Fed. (2d) 339 (C.C.A., 9th Cir., 1927), certiorari denied sub nomine Appell v. United States, 274 U.S. 744; Poffenbarger v. United States, 20 Fed. (2d) 42 (C.C.A., 8th Cir., 1927); O'Brien v. United States, 25 Fed. (2d) 90 (C.C.A., 7th Cir., 1928); Pietch v. United States, 110 Fed. (2d) 817 (C.C.A., 10th Cir., 1940), certiorari denied 310 U.S. 648; Collins v. United States, 157 Fed. (2d) 409 (C.C.A., 9th Cir., 1946).
4. Frankel v. Woodrough, supra; United States ex rel. Whitaker v. Henning, 15 Fed. (2d) 760 (C.C.A., 9th Cir., 1926); United States ex rel Coleman v. Cox, 47 Fed. (2d) 988 (C.C.A., 5th Cir., 1931); Bayless v. United States, 147 Fed. (2d) 169 (C.C.A., 8th Cir., 1945), reversed on other grounds 150 Fed. (2d) 236.
5. Edward S. Corwin, The Constitution and What It Means Today (9th ed., Princeton, New Jersey: Princeton University Press, 1947), p. 176.
6. Henry Rottschaefer, Handbook of American Constitutional Law (St. Paul, Minnesota: West Publishing Company, 1939), p. 793.
7. Gaines v. Washington, 277 U.S. 81, 85 (1928).
8. Reagan v. United States, 202 Fed. 488 (C.C.A., 9th Cir., 1912); followed in Callahan v. United States, 240 Fed. 683 (C.C.A., 9th Cir., 1917).
9. Davis v. United States, 247 Fed. 394 (C.C.A., 8th Cir., 1917).
10. Ibid., 398.
11. Rottschaefer, op. cit., p. 793; Max Radin, "The Right to a Public Trial," Temple Law Quarterly, VI (1932), 381, 389.
12. 145 Fed. (2d) 58 (C.C.A., 9th Cir., 1944). Noted in Boston University Law Review, XXV (1945), 145-147. Accord: United States v. Kobli, 172 Fed. (2d) 919 (C.C.A., 3rd Cir., 1949).
13. The right of the court to order disorderly spectators out of the courtroom does not appear to be affected by the Tanksley case. It may be worthy of note that in England today the only exception to the requirement of a public trial is on the occasion of young witnesses testifying in cases involving moral charges. Lester B. Orfield, Criminal Procedure from Arrest to Appeal (New York: New York University Press, 1947), p. 353, citing Archbold, Criminal Pleading, Evidence, and Practice (30th ed., 1938), pp. 198, 209.
14. Herbert S. Hadley, "The Reform of Criminal Procedure," Proceedings of the Academy of Political Science, X (1923), 396, 400.
15. 281 U.S. 276, at 288 (1930).
16. Thompson v. Utah, 170 U.S. 343, 349 (1898).
17. Supra, p. 15.
18. Maxwell v. Dow, 176 U.S. 581, 586 (1900); Patton v. United States, supra, 296-297.
19. William F. Willoughby, Principles of Judicial Administration (Washington: Brookings Institution, 1929), p. 503.
20. Ibid., pp. 504-505; Orfield, op. cit., pp. 396-397.
21. Dissenting in Dimick v. Scheidt, 293 U.S. 474, 495 (1934).

22. *Thompson* v. *Utah*, 170 U.S. 343, 353 (1898; dictum); *Dickinson* v. *United States*, 159 Fed. 801 (C.C.A., 1st Cir., 1908), certiorari denied 213 U.S. 92; *Low* v. *United States*, 169 Fed. 86 (C.C.A., 6th Cir., 1909); *Coates* v. *United States*, 290 Fed. 134 (C.C.A., 4th Cir., 1923); and see note in *Massachusetts Law Quarterly*, IX (1924), 61.

23. Harlan, J., dissenting in *Schick* v. *United States*, 195 U.S. 65, at 82 (1904).

24. 190 U.S. 548 (1903).

25. *Thompson* v. *Utah*, *supra*.

26. 195 U.S. 65 (1904).

27. Act of August 2, 1886, 24 Stat. 209, as amended by Act of May 9, 1902, 32 Stat. 193.

28. 195 U.S. 27 (1904).

29. 195 U.S. 65, 72.

30. Cf. *supra*, pp. 57-59.

31. Cf. *Freeman* v. *United States*, 227 Fed. 732 (C.C.A., 2d Cir., 1915).

32. 281 U.S. 276. Noted in *Columbia Law Review*, XXX (1930), 1063-1064; *Harvard Law Review*, XLIV (1930), 124-125; *Michigan Law Review*, XXVIII (1930), 1054. Mr. Justice Sutherland's reasoning was accepted by only three of his colleagues: Chief Justice Hughes, recently appointed, had taken no part in the case; Sanford died before the decision was announced; Holmes, Brandeis, and Stone, while concurring in the result, apparently declined to follow Sutherland's reasoning. Their own position was not made a matter of record.

33. 281 U.S. 276, 292.

34. 170 U.S. 343 (1898).

35. 281 U.S. 276, 293.

36. See *supra*, pp. 36-38.

37. 281 U.S. 276, 296. The Court illustrated this statement with quotations from Blackstone and Story, referring to jury trial as a privilege. Cf. Erwin H. Griswold, "The Historical Development of Waiver of Jury Trial in Criminal Cases," *Virginia Law Review*, XX (1934), 655-669, citing evidence of colonial practice of waiver of jury trial in seven of the original states.

38. 281 U.S. 276, 298.

39. *Ibid.*, 299-301, 308. See the criticism of this and other phases of the opinion by J. A. C. Grant, "Waiver of Jury Trial in Felony Cases," *California Law Review*, XX (1932), 132, 151 ff., reprinted in *Selected Essays on Constitutional Law*, II, 1301, 1321 ff.

40. 281 U.S. 276, 312.

41. *United States* v. *Dubrin*, 93 Fed. (2d) 499 (C.C.A., 2d Cir., 1937), certiorari denied 303 U.S. 646, noted in *Georgetown Law Journal*, XXVI (1938), 762-764; *Rees* v. *United States*, 95 Fed. (2d) 784 (C.C.A., 4th Cir., 1938); *Irvin* v. *Zerbst*, 97 Fed. (2d) 257 (C.C.A., 5th Cir., 1938), certiorari denied 305 U.S. 597; *C.I.T. Corporation* v. *United States*, 150 Fed. (2d) 85 (C.C.A., 9th Cir., 1945).

42. *Jabczynski* v. *United States*, 53 Fed. (2d) 1014 (C.C.A., 7th Cir., 1931), certiorari denied 285 U.S. 546.

43. *Adams* v. *United States* ex rel. *McCann*, 317 U.S. 269 (1942).

44. Cf. dissent by Murphy, J., *ibid.*, 286.

45. National Commission on Law Observance and Enforcement, *Report on Prosecution* (Washington: Government Printing Office, 1931), p. 127; same, *Report on Criminal Procedure* (Washington: Government Printing Office, 1931), pp. 28, 47; Raymond Moley, ed., *Missouri Crime Survey* (New York: The Macmillan Company, 1926), p. 366; John H. Wigmore, ed., *The Illinois Crime Survey* (Chicago: Illinois Association for Criminal Justice, 1929), p. 219; Judicial Council of the State of New York, *Annual Reports*, II (1936), 30, 95-101; III (1937), 44, 105; IV (1938), 18; V (1939), 37, 151-178; VI (1940), 53; VII (1941), 53; VIII (1942), 59-60; IX (1943), 59; X (1944), 56-57; XI (1945), 45; XII (1946), 54. See Orfield, *op. cit.*, pp. 391-392.

46. 190 U.S. 197 (1903); *supra*, pp. 44-47.

47. Rottschaefer, *op. cit.*, p. 789; (note) *Michigan Law Review*, XL (1941), 113, 114.

48. 327 U.S. 821, 854 (1946).

49. *Preliminary Draft of Federal Rules of Criminal Procedure* (Washington: Government Printing Office, 1943), Rule 29 (a); Orfield, *op. cit.*, p. 483.

164 (pp. 70-79) REFERENCES

50. *American Publishing Company* v. *Fisher*, 166 U.S. 464 (1897), and *Springville* v. *Thomas*, 166 U.S. 707 (1897), although decided under the Seventh Amendment, are authority for the continued validity of the common law requirement of unanimity.

51. *Freeman* v. *United States*, 227 Fed. 732 (C.C.A., 2d Cir., 1915).

52. 327 U.S. 821, 851, Rule 24 (c).

53. *Simons* v. *United States*, 119 Fed. (2d) 539 (C.C.A., 9th Cir., 1941); see comment in *Nebraska Law Review*, XXI (1942), 171-174.

54. 327 U.S. 821, 851, Rule 25.

55. *West* v. *Gammon*, 98 Fed. 426 (C.C.A., 6th Cir., 1899).

56. *United States* v. *Taylor*, 11 Fed. 470 (Cir. Ct., D. Kansas, 1882). The specific nature of the judge-jury relationship is not controlled by the Sixth Amendment or any other constitutional provisions and is thus beyond the frame of reference of this inquiry. See, however, *Sparf and Hansen* v. *United States*, 156 U.S. 1 (1895), *United States* v. *Battiste*, by Story, J., Fed. Cas. No. 14,545 (1835); Leon Green, *Judge and Jury*, (Kansas City, Missouri: Vernon Law Book Company, 1930); James B. Thayer, *Preliminary Treatise on Evidence*, vol. 2 (Boston: Little, Brown & Company, 1898), ch. V, "Law and Fact in Jury Trials."

57. *Stilson* v. *United States*, 250 U.S. 583 (1919); *Philbrook* v. *United States*, 117 Fed. (2d) 632 (C.C.A., 8th Cir., 1940), certiorari denied 313 U.S. 577.

58. *Paschen* v. *United States*, 70 Fed. (2d) 491 (C.C.A., 7th Cir., 1934).

59. *United States* v. *Burr*, Fed. Cas. No. 14,692g and 14,693 (Cir. Ct., D. Va., 1807).

60. *Reynolds* v. *United States*, 98 U.S. 145, 155 (1878).

61. 7 Cranch (11 U.S.) 290 (1813), opinion by Marshall, C. J.

62. *Reynolds* v. *United States*, supra, 147, 157.

63. *Logan* v. *United States*, 144 U.S. 263, 298 (1892).

64. *Connors* v. *United States*, 158 U.S. 408 (1895).

65. 212 U.S. 183.

66. Act of August 22, 1935, c. 605, 49 Stat. 682.

67. 299 U.S. 123 (1936); noted in *Brooklyn Law Review*, VI (1937), 388, and *Journal of Criminal Law and Criminology*, XXVII (1937), 914.

68. 299 U.S. 123, 138.

69. *Ibid.*, 142.

70. *Tynan* v. *United States*, 297 Fed. 177 (C.C.A., 9th Cir., 1924), certiorari denied 266 U.S. 604; *Hoxie* v. *United States*, 15 Fed. (2d) 762 (C.C.A., 9th Cir., 1926).

71. *Stilson* v. *United States*, 250 U.S. 583 (1919).

72. *United States* v. *Cartacho*, Fed. Cas. No. 14,738 Cir. Ct., D. Va., 1823).

73. *United States* v. *Wood*, 299 U.S. 123, 145 (1936).

74. *Loc. cit.*

75. *Ibid.*, 146.

76. *Ibid.*, 148; House Report No. 1,421 and Senate Report No. 1,297, 74th Congress, 1st session.

77. 299 U.S. 123, 148.

78. *Ibid.*, 149.

79. *Great Atlantic & Pacific Tea Co.* v. *District of Columbia*, 89 Fed. (2d) 502 (1937).

80. *Schackow* v. *Government of the Canal Zone*, 108 Fed. (2d) 625 (1939).

81. *Infra*, p.

82. *Baker* v. *Hudspeth*, 129 Fed. (2d) 779 (C.C.A., 10th Cir., 1942).

83. The reports fail to indicate any connection between the cases.

84. *Higgins* v. *United States*, 160 Fed. (2d) 222 (1947), certiorari denied 331 U.S. 822.

85. *Frazier* v. *United States*, certiorari granted 333 U.S. 873.

86. Act of December 17, 1914, 38 Stat. 785 as amended; 26 United States Code (1940), § 2553.

87. *Washington Post*, April 23, 1948.

88. *Frazier* v. *United States*, 335 U.S. 497, 500-501 (1948), and notes thereat.

89. *Ibid.*, 506-507.

90. *Ibid.*, 503, 516-517 (dissent).

91. *Ibid.*, 503.

92. *Ibid.*, 513-514.

93. *Ibid.*, 514.

94. *Ibid.*, 515.

95. *Ibid.*, 519.

96. *Ibid.*

97. *Ibid.* Like all argument from consequences, this statement seems to leave many questions unanswered.

98. United States Civil Service Commission, *History of the Federal Civil Service, 1789 to the Present* (Washington: Government Printing Office, 1941), pp. 73, 119.

99. Hatch Act, 53 Stat. 1147 and 54 Stat. 767, constitutionality upheld in *United Public Workers v. Mitchell*, 330 U.S. 75 (1947). The case is severely criticized by Francis D. Wormuth, "The Hatch Act Cases," *Western Political Quarterly*, I (1948), 165. The literature on the Hatch Act is too voluminous to list.

100. Executive Order No. 9835, 12 *Federal Register* 1935 (1947). The background and operation of the program are the subject of a series of articles in the *Yale Law Journal*, LVIII (1948-49).

101. Cf. Bert Andrews, *Washington Witch Hunt* (1948), for a Pulitzer prize-winning account by an experienced journalistic observer; and see Robert E. Cushman's pamphlet *New Threats to American Freedoms* (1948), p. 6, for a succinct statement of the problem by a prominent political scientist.

102. The practice of permitting veniremen to withdraw if they did not desire to serve was discontinued even before the Supreme Court considered the case. *Washington Post*, April 23, 1948. The disinclination of persons not in government employ to serve on juries may have been reduced by the passage of S. 1042, 81st Congress, which raised the per diem compensation of jurors to seven dollars. 63 *Stat.* 411 (1949), 28 *United States Code* (1950), § 1871.

103. *Dennis v. United States*, certiorari granted 337 U.S. 954 (1949); decided 339 U.S. 162 (1950).

104. *Dennis v. United States*, 171 Fed. (2d) 986 (App. D.C., 1948).

105. 337 U.S. 954 (1949).

106. 176 Fed. (2d) 21 (App. D.C., 1949), certiorari denied 337 U.S. 958 (1949).

107. *Ibid.* at 25.

108. *Dennis v. United States*, 339 U.S. 162, 172.

109. *Ibid.*

110. *Ibid.*, 168.

111. *Ibid.*, 174.

112. *Ibid.*, 185.

113. *Ibid.*, 178-180.

114. Mr. Douglas' convalescence following a hunting accident prevented his participation in the *Dennis* case. Past performance permits the speculation that had he been present he would have joined with Mr. Justice Black, rather than Justice Jackson.

115. Cf. their sharp exchange in *Adamson v. California*, 332 U.S. 46 (1947).

116. See *infra*, pp. 143-147.

117. *Strauder v. West Virginia*, 100 U.S. 303 (1880). See also *Carter v. Texas*, 177 U.S. 442 (1898).

118. *Virginia v. Rives*, 100 U.S. 313 (1880).

119. *Norris v. Alabama*, 294 U.S. 587 (1935). Cf. *Patton v. Mississippi*, 332 U.S. 463 (1947). A full survey of the cases may be found in Bernard S. Jefferson, "Race Discrimination in Jury Service," *Boston University Law Review*, XIX (1939), 413-447.

120. 245 U.S. 480 (1918).

121. *Supra*, n. 118.

122. *Glasser v. United States*, 315 U.S. 60 (1942).

123. Justice Frankfurter wrote a dissenting opinion in which he was joined by Chief Justice Stone. Justice Jackson did not sit in the case.

124. 315 U.S. 60, 85, 86.

125. *Thiel v. Southern Pacific Company*, 328 U.S. 217 (1946).

126. *Ibid.*, 227.

127. *Ibid.*, 223-224.

128. *Ballard v. United States*, 329 U.S. 187 (1946).

129. *Fay v. New York*, 332 U.S. 261 (1947); *Moore v. New York*, 333 U.S. 565 (1948).

Chapter V

1. Art. III, Sec. 2, cl. 3: ". . . and such trial *shall be held* in the State where the said crime shall have been committed; . . ." Italics added.

2. William W. Blume, "The Place of Trial of Criminal Cases: Constitutional Vicinage and Venue," *Michigan Law Review*, XLIII (1944), 59, 60.

3. *Supra*, pp. 31-33.

4. Cf. Madison's letters to Pendleton, quoted *supra*, chap. II.

5. Blume, *op. cit.*, p. 65.

6. Massachusetts and Virginia were each divided into two districts. Act of September 24, 1789, 1 Stat. 73. Cf. Blume, *op. cit.*, p. 66, and Charles Warren, "New Light on the History of the Federal Judiciary Act," *Harvard Law Review*, XXXVII (1923), 57, 106.

7. Alexander Holtzoff, "Removal of Defendants in Federal Criminal Procedure," *California Law Review*, XXXIII (1945), 230.

8. Seymour Dunbar, *A History of Travel in America* (Indianapolis: The Bobbs-Merrill Company, 1915), I, 177.

9. *Ibid.*, I, 329.

10. Charles O. Paullin and John K. Wright, *Atlas of the Historical Geography of the United States* (Washington: Carnegie Institution, 1932), Plate 138A, "Rates of Travel, 1800."

11. Act of April 11, 1790, c. 9, 1 Stat. 112.

12. Cf. David Fellman, "Some Consequences of Increased Federal Activity in Law Enforcement," *Journal of Criminal Law and Criminology*, XXXV (1944), 16-17. See also Martin Conboy, "Federal Criminal Law," in Alison Reppy, ed., *Law: A Century of Progress 1835-1935* (New York: New York University Press, 1937), I, 295-346.

13. Administrative Office of the United States Courts, *Annual Report of the Director for 1945* (Washington: Government Printing Office, 1946), p. 25.

14. Cf. *Patton v. United States*, 281 U.S. 276 (1930), *United States v. Wood*, 299 U.S. 123 (1936), discussed *supra*, chap. IV.

15. The first judicial divisions within districts were established in Iowa, by Act of Congress of May 3, 1849, c. 124, 9 Stat. 411, but this method of subdividing districts was not used again until 1878 when judicial divisions were set up for Ohio (Act of June 8, 1878, c. 169, s. 4, 20 Stat. 102), Michigan (Act of June 19, 1878, c. 326, 20 Stat. 175), and Tennessee (Act of June 20, 1878, c. 359, 20 Stat. 235). Since then the majority of judicial districts have been organized into divisions.

16. Quoted from *United States v. Wan Lee*, 44 Fed. 707 (D.C., D. Wash., N.D., 1890).

17. 245 U.S. 480, 482 (1918).

18. Act of September 24, 1789, c. 20, 1 Stat. 73.

19. *Ibid.*, 88.

20. Section 802.

21. United States Code (1940), Title 28, § 413.

22. *United States v. Ayres*, 46 Fed. 651 (D.C., D. South Dakota, 1891, by Shiras, J.)

23. *Seadlund v. United States*, 97 Fed. (2d) 742 (C.C.A., 7th Cir., 1938).

24. The subject of "Removal of Defendants in Federal Criminal Procedure" was lucidly dealt with by Judge Alexander Holtzoff in his article under that title in *California Law Review*, XXXII (1945), 230-247, on which the following paragraphs are largely based.

25. Note, for instance, the dilatory tactics of B. I. Salinger, Jr., who by continued obstruction to removal proceedings protracted his trial on fraud charges from 1921 to 1926: *Salinger v. Loisel*, 265 U.S. 244 (1924), *Salinger v. United States*, 272 U.S. 542 (1926), and lower court decisions there cited.

26. *Hughes v. Gault*, 271 U.S. 142 (1926); *United States ex rel. Kassin v. Mulligan*, 295 U.S. 396 (1935), 400; Holtzoff, *op. cit.*, p. 230.

27. Sec. 33 of the Judiciary Act, September 24, 1789, c. 20, 1 Stat. 73, 91, essentially reenacted as § 1014, Revised Statutes, and subsequently as § 591 of Title 18, United States Code (1940).

28. See *Beavers v. Henkel*, 194 U.S. 73 (1904); *Tinsley v. Treat*, 205 U.S. 20 (1907); *Henry v. Henkel*, 235 U.S. 219 (1914); *Rodman v. Pothier*, 264 U.S. 399 (1924); *Morse v. United States*, 267 U.S. 80 (1925); *Hughes v. Gault*, *supra*; *Fetters v. United*

States ex rel. Cunningham, 283 U.S. 638 (1931); United States ex rel. Kassin v. Mulligan, supra.

29. 327 U.S. 821, 860-863 (1946).

30. Cf. Justice Holmes' eloquent indictment of this practice in his dissent in *Hyde v. United States,* 225 U.S. 347, 386 (1912).

31. *Notes to the Rules of Criminal Procedure for the District Courts of the United States* (Washington: Government Printing Office, 1945), p. 33.

32. Holtzoff, *op. cit.,* p. 247; Wendell Berge, "The Proposed Federal Rules of Criminal Procedure," *Michigan Law Review,* XLII (1943), 353, 374.

32a. The cautious note here injected has already been justified. Rule 20 of the new federal rules was designed to expedite proceedings where a defendant wished to plead guilty by allowing him to waive the requirement of vicinage. Shortly after this study was completed, the district court for the district of Oregon declared the rule unconstitutional. *United States v. Bink,* 74 F. Supp. 603 (1947).

33. *In re Palliser,* 136 U.S. 257, 265 (1890).

34. Except treason. Constitution, Art III, sec. 3.

35. See Armistead M. Dobie, "Venue in Criminal Cases in the United States District Courts," *Virginia Law Review,* XII (1926), 287, 288-289.

36. *Horner v. United States,* 143 U.S. 207 (1892).

37. *United States v. Conrad,* 59 Fed. 458 (Cir. Ct., D. W.Va. 1894).

38. *Armour Packing Company v. United States,* 209 U.S. 56 (1908).

39. *United States v. Johnson,* 323 U.S. 273 (1944).

40. *Hyde v. United States,* 225 U.S. 347 (1912); *Brown v. Ellett,* 225 U.S. 392 (1912). Note Holmes' dissents in these cases.

41. *United States v. Peuschel,* 116 Fed. 642 (D.C., S.D. Calif., N.D., 1902); *Quinlan v. United States,* 22 Fed. (2d) 95 (C.C.A., 5th Cir., 1927), certiorari denied 276 U.S. 627.

42. *Lewis v. United States,* 279 U.S. 63 (1929).

43. Section 59 of the Judicial Code, United States Code (1940), Title 28, § 121.

44. *Quinlan v. United States, supra.*

45. Sir William Blackstone, *Commentaries on the Law of England* (Cooley's second edition; Chicago: Callahan and Company, 1873), IV, 305-307.

46. *United States v. Van Duzee,* 140 U.S. 169 (1891).

47. *Johnson v. United States,* 225 U.S. 405 (1912).

48. Act of April 20, 1790, c. 9, sec. 29, 1 Stat. 112, 118, Revised Statutes, s. 1033, United States Code (1940), Title 18, § 562.

49. *United States v. Crummer,* 151 Fed. (2d) 958 (C.C.A., 10th Cir., 1945), certiorari denied 327 U.S. 785.

50. 92 U.S. 542 (1875).

51. Act of May 30, 1870, 16 Stat. 140.

52. 92 U.S. 542, 558, quoting Archbold, *Pleading and Evidence,* I, 291.

53. See also *Boykin v. United States,* 11 Fed. (2d) 484 (C.C.A., 5th Cir., 1926).

54. For an example of such a "manifestly frivolous" contention see *Hendricks v. United States,* 223 U.S. 178 (1912).

55. *Hagner v. United States,* 285 U.S. 427, 431 (1932).

56. *Rosen v. United States,* 161 U.S. 29 (1896); *Bartell v. United States,* 227 U.S. 427 (1913); *United States v. Bennett,* Fed. Cas. No. 14,571 (Cir. Ct., S.D., N.Y., 1879); *Skelley v. United States,* 37 Fed. (2d) 503 (C.C.A., 10th Cir., 1930); *Koa Gora v. Hawaii,* 152 Fed. (2d) 933 (C.C.A., 9th Cir., 1946), certiorari denied 328 U.S. 862.

57. *Rosen v. United States, supra.*

58. *Bartell v. United States, supra.*

59. *Koa Gora v. Hawaii, supra.*

60. *United States v. L. Cohen Grocery Company,* 255 U.S. 81 (1921), is the leading instance in which this twofold attack was successfully used.

61. Ralph W. Aigler, "Legislation in Vague or General Terms," *Michigan Law Review,* XXI (1923), 831, 850.

62. E.g., *Gorin v. United States,* 312 U.S. 19 (1941) (Espionage Act of 1917).

63. See: *Lanzetta v. New Jersey,* 306 U.S. 451 (1939), (New Jersey's "Gangster" Law).

64. Herbert S. Hadley, "The Reform of Criminal Procedure," *Proceedings of the Academy of Political Science*, X (1923), 396, 400; cf. Sir Harry L. Stephens, "The Trial of Sir Walter Raleigh," *Transactions of the Royal Historical Society*, Fourth Series, II (1919), 172-187.

65. Henry Rottschaefer, *Handbook of American Constitutional Law* (St. Paul, Minnesota: West Publishing Company, 1939), p. 796.

66. Act of June 20, 1936, c. 640, 49 Stat. 1561, United States Code (1940), Title 28, § 695.

67. ". . . The admissibility of evidence . . . shall be governed, *except when an act of Congress or these rules otherwise provide,* by the principles of the common law . . ." 327 U.S. 821, 852 (1946). (Italics supplied).

68. *United States v. Leathers*, 135 Fed. (2d) 507 (C.C.A., 2d Cir., 1943).

69. *United States v. Douglas*, 155 Fed. (2d) 894 (C.C.A., 7th Cir., 1946).

70. *Kirby v. United States*, 174 U.S. 47 (1899), holding unconstitutional the last portion of Section 2 of the Act of March 3, 1875, c. 144, 18 Stat. 579.

71. 174 U.S. 47, 55.

72. *Reynolds v. United States*, 98 U.S. 145, 158 (1878).

73. *Motes v. United States*, 178 U.S. 458 (1900).

74. *Mattox v. United States*, 156 U.S. 237 (1895).

75. *Ibid.*, 243.

76. Rottschaefer, *op. cit.*, p. 797.

77. 194 U.S. 258 (1904).

78. *Palko v. Connecticut*, 302 U.S. 319, 324 (1937).

79. *Op. cit.*, IV, 359.

80. Sir William Holdsworth, *A History of English Law* (London: Methuen and Company, Ltd., 1924-1938), V, 192-193.

81. Cf. Holdsworth's statement to this effect, in connection with the denial of counsel, *ibid.*, V, 196.

82. 7 Wm. III, c. 3, s. 1 (1695), and 1 Anne, c. 9, s. 3 (1701); see *supra*, p. 9.

83. Joseph Story, *Commentaries on the Constitution of the United States* (3rd ed.; Boston: Little, Brown and Company, 1858), II, 597-598, § 1792.

84. Act of April 30, 1790, c. 9, s. 29, 1 Stat. 112, 118, Revised Statutes, § 1034, United States Code (1940), Title 18, § 563.

85. 4 Dall. (4 U.S.) 341 (Cir. Ct., D. Pa., 1800).

86. *Casebeer v. Hudspeth*, 121 Fed. (2d) 1914 (C.C.A., 10th Cir., 1941), certiorari denied 316 U.S. 683, rehearing denied 317 U.S. 704; *Neufield v. United States*, 110 Fed. (2d) 375 (App. D.C., 1940), certiorari denied 315 U.S. 798; *Wallace v. Hunter*, 149 Fed. (2d) 59 (C.C.A., 10th Cir., 1945).

87. *United States v. Kenneally*, Fed. Cas. No. 15,522 (D.Ct., N.D. Ill., 1870).

88. *Paoni v. United States*, 281 Fed. 801 (C.C.A., 3d Cir., 1922).

89. Rottschaefer, *op. cit.*, p. 797.

90. *Palko v. Connecticut, supra,* 324.

Chapter VI

1. Benjamin N. Cardozo, *The Nature of the Judicial Process* (New Haven: Yale University Press, 1921), p. 17; also in Margaret E. Hall, ed., *Selected Writings of Benjamin Nathan Cardozo* (New York: Fallon Law Book Company, 1947), p. 111.

2. "In all criminal prosecutions, the accused shall enjoy the right . . . to have the Assistance of Counsel for his defence." Amendment VI.

3. *Powell v. Alabama*, 287 U.S. 45, decided in 1932, and *Johnson v. Zerbst*, 304 U.S. 458, decided in 1938.

4. Alexander Holtzoff, "The Right of Counsel under the Sixth Amendment," *New York University Law Quarterly Review*, XX (1944), 1-22, is the best brief summary of the evolution of this provision and has been relied on heavily in the preparation of this chapter. (Justice Burton's majority opinion in *Bute v. Illinois, infra,* which uses the same material, had not been published when this section was originally written.) For other comments on the subject, see *Columbia Law Review*, XLII (1942), 271-282, *Wisconsin Law Review*, (1943), 118-127, and *Virginia Law Review*, XXXIII (1947), 731-739. Cf. Lester B. Orfield, *Criminal Procedure from Arrest to Appeal* (New York: New York University Press, 1947), chap. VII, sec. 22, pp. 417-428.

5. Thomas M. Cooley, *Constitutional Limitations* (8th edition, by Walter Carrington; Boston: Little, Brown and Company, 1927), I, 698; *Powell* v. *Alabama, supra,* p. 60. *Betts* v. *Brady,* 316 U.S. 455, 466 (1942); and see *supra,* chap. I.

6. Cf. *supra.,* p. 21.

7. Sir William Blackstone, *Commentaries on the Law of England* (2d edition by Thomas M. Cooley; Chicago: Callahan and Company, 1873), IV, 355.

8. *Powell* v. *Alabama, supra,* 64.

9. *Betts* v. *Brady, supra,* 466.

10. Act of September 24, 1789, c. 20, 1 Stat. 73, 92.

11. Act of April 30, 1790, c. 9, s. 30, 1 Stat. 112, 119, reenacted as sec. 1034, Revised Statutes, and sec. 563 of Title 18, United States Code (1940).

12. Holtzoff, *op. cit.,* p. 8.

13. *Ibid.*

14. *Nabb* v. *United States,* 1 Ct. Cl. 173 (1864); *United States* v. *Van Duzee,* 140 U.S. 169 (1891; dictum).

15. *Johnson* v. *Zerbst,* 304 U.S. 458, *infra.*

16. Holtzoff, *op. cit.,* p. 8.

17. 304 U.S. 458 (1938). Noted in *Cornell Law Quarterly,* XXIV (1939), 270-274.

18. 304 U.S. 458, 463.

19. *Ibid.,* 462-463, quoting *Powell* v. *Alabama, supra,* 69.

20. *Johnson* v. *Zerbst, supra,* 464 .

21. *Ibid.,* 465.

22. *Ibid.,* 468.

23. *Cundiff* v. *Nicholson,* 107 Fed. (2d) 162 (C.C.A., 4th Cir., 1939), per Parker, J. To the same effect: *Williams* v. *Sanford,* 110 Fed. (2d) 526 (C.C.A., 5th Cir., 1940), certiorari denied 310 U.S. 643; *Adkins* v. *Sanford,* 120 Fed. (2d) 471 (C.C.A., 5th Cir., 1941); *O'Keith* v. *Johnston,* 129 Fed. (2d) 889 (C.C.A., 9th Cir., 1942); *United States* v. *Steese,* 144 Fed. (2d) 439 (C.C.A., 3rd Cir., 1944); *Cooke* v. *Swope,* 28 F. Supp. 492 (D.C., W.D., Wash., 1939), affirmed on other grounds 109 Fed. (2d) 955.

24. *Evans* v. *Rives,* 126 Fed. (2d) 633 (App. D.C., 1942).

25. *Michener* v. *Johnston,* 141 Fed. (2d) 171 (C.C.A., 9th Cir., 1944).

26. *Adams* v. *United States ex rel. McCann,* 317 U.S. 269, at 277 (1942).

27. 324 U.S. 786, 788 (1945).

28. Cf. *Von Moltke* v. *Gillies,* 332 U.S. 708 (1948).

29. *Adams* v. *United States ex rel. McCann, supra,* 279; *Johnson* v. *Zerbst,* 304 U.S. 458, 468-469.

30. *Adams* v. *United States ex rel. McCann, supra,* 277.

31. *Patton* v. *United States,* 281 U.S. 276 (1930), *supra,* pp. 66-69.

32. *Adams* v. *United States ex rel. McCann, supra.* Justices Douglas, Black, and Murphy dissented.

33. *Ibid.*

34. *Mothershead* v. *King,* 112 Fed. (2d) 1004 (C.C.A., 8th Cir., 1940).

35. *Forthhoffer* v. *Swope,* 103 Fed. (2d) 707 (C.C.A., 9th Cir., 1939); *Hall* v. *Johnston,* 103 Fed. (2d) 900 (C.C.A., 9th Cir., 1939); *McDonald* v. *Hudspeth,* 108 Fed. (2d) 943 (C.C.A., 10th Cir., 1940); *Frame* v. *Hudspeth,* 109 Fed. (2d) 356 (C.C.A., 10th Cir., 1940), reversed upon consent, 309 US. 632.

36. *McCoy* v. *Hudspeth,* 106 Fed. (2d) 810 (C.C.A., 10th Cir., 1939).

37. *Buckner* v. *Hudspeth,* 105 Fed. (2d) 396 (C.C.A., 10th Cir., 1939), certiorari denied 308 U.S. 553.

38. *Sanders* v. *Allen,* 100 Fed. (2d) 717 (App. D.C., 1938).

39. *Williams* v. *Huff,* 142 Fed. (2d) 91 (App. D.C., 1944).

40. Statement by government counsel in *Holiday* v. *Johnston,* 313 U.S. 342, 346 (1941). See also *Walker* v. *Johnston,* 109 Fed. (2d) 436, 438 (C.C.A., 9th Cir., 1940).

41. *Buckner* v. *Hudspeth, supra*; *Moore* v. *Hudspeth,* 110 Fed. (2d) 386 (C.C.A., 10th Cir., 1940), certiorari denied 310 U.S. 643; *Macomber* v. *Hudspeth,* 115 Fed. (2d) 114 (C.C.A., 10th Cir., 1940), certiorari denied 313 U.S. 558. Cf. Holtzoff, *op. cit.,* 10. Robert N. Hudspeth was the warden of the Federal Penitentiary at Leavenworth, Kansas.

42. Cf. *Sanford* v. *Robbins,* 115 Fed. (2d) 435 (C.C.A., 5th Cir., 1940), certiorari denied 312 U.S. 697.

170 (pp. 115-118) REFERENCES

43. Zahn v. Hudspeth, 102 Fed. (2d) 817 (C.C.A., 10th Cir., 1939), certiorari denied 307 U.S. 462; Nivens v. Hudspeth, 105 Fed. (2d) 756 (C.C.A., 10th Cir., 1939); Harpin v. Johnston, 109 Fed. (2) 434 (C.C.A., 9th Cir., 1940), certiorari denied 310 U.S. 624; Franzeen v. Johnston, 111 Fed. (2d) 817 (C.C.A., 9th Cir., 1940); see Walker v. Johnston, 312 U.S. 275, 285 (1941). James A. Johnston was until recently the warden at Alcatraz.

44. 312 U.S. 275 (1941).

45. The use of commissioners was held to violate the statutory requirements. Holiday v. Johnston, 313 U.S. 342 (1941).

46. Walker v. Johnston, supra, 286.

47. Conley v. Cox, 138 Fed. (2d) 786 (C.C.A., 8th Cir., 1943).

48. Diggs v. Welch, 148 Fed. (2d) 667, 670 (App. D.C., 1945), certiorari denied 325 U.S. 889.

49. Bostic v. Rives, 107 Fed. (2) 649 (App. D.C., 1939), certiorari denied 309 U.S. 664.

50. United States v. Hartenfeld, 113 Fed. (2d) 359 (C.C.A., 7th Cir., 1940).

51. Achtien v. Dowd, 117 Fed. (2d) 989 (C.C.A., 7th Cir., 1941). Assigned counsel was 23 years of age and had been a member of the bar for only two years.

52. Crum v. Hunter, 151 Fed. (2d) 359 (C.C.A., 10th Cir., 1945).

53. Casebeer v. Hudspeth, 121 Fed. (2d) 914 (C.C.A., 10th Cir., 1941), certiorari denied 316 U.S. 683, rehearing denied 317 U.S. 704; Bostic v. Rives, supra.

54. Johnson v. United States, 110 Fed. (2d) 562 (App. D.C., 1940).

55. Hudspeth v. McDonald, 120 Fed. (2d) 962 (C.C.A., 10th Cir., 1941).

56. Diggs v. Welch, supra, 670.

57. Avery v. Alabama, 308 U.S. 444, 446 (1940).

58. Shores v. United States, 80 Fed. (2d) 942 (C.C.A., 9th Cir., 1935), certiorari denied 297 U.S. 705.

59. Avery v. Alabama, supra, 452.

60. Thomas v. District of Columbia, 90 Fed. (2d) 424 (App. D.C., 1937).

61. Orfield, op. cit., p. 425.

62. Burall v. Johnston, 146 Fed. (2d) 230 (C.C.A., 9th Cir., 1944), certiorari denied 325 U.S. 887.

63. Gilmore v. United States, 129 Fed. (2d) 199 (C.C.A., 10th Cir., 1942), certiorari denied 317 U.S. 631. But see United States ex rel. Mertner v. Hiatt, 33 F. Supp. 545 (D.C., M.D. Pa., 1940).

64. Thomas v. Hunter, 153 Fed. (2d) 834 (C.C.A., 10th Cir., 1946); Wilfong v. Johnston, 156 Fed. (2d) 507 (C.C.A., 9th Cir., 1946); see also Batson v. United States, 137 Fed. (2d) 288, 289 (C.C.A., 10th Cir., 1943; dictum). Kent v. Sanford, 121 Fed. (2d) 216 (C.C.A., 5th Cir, 1941), certiorari denied 315 US. 799, appears distinguishable on the grounds that the court specifically assumed the responsibility of protecting the defendant's interests and equally expressly reserved the right to recall counsel if needed.

65. Lovvorn v. Johnston, 118 Fed. (2d) 704 (C.C.A., 9th Cir., 1941), certiorari denied 314 U.S. 607; Gargano v. United States, 137 Fed. (2d) 944 (C.C.A., 9th Cir., 1943); Thompson v. Johnston, 160 Fed. (2d) 374 (C.C.A., 9th Cir., 1947), noted in Tulane Law Review, XXII (1947), 202-205.

66. Edwards v. United States, 139 Fed. (2d) 365 (App. D.C., 1943), certiorari denied 321 U.S. 769; cf. Canizio v. New York, 327 U.S. 82 (1946).

67. Glasser v. United States, 315 U.S. 60 (1942); noted in: Georgetown Law Journal, XXX (1942), 570-572, Michigan Law Review, XLI (1942), 321-323, Minnesota Law Review, XXVI (1942), 657-658, Temple Law Quarterly, XVI (1942), 439-440, University of Chicago Law Review, IX (1942), 733-737, Washington University Law Quarterly, XXVII (1942), 581-583.

68. Farris v. Hunter, 144 Fed. (2d) 63 (C.C.A., 10th Cir., 1944).

69. American Bar Association, Canons of Professional Ethics, Canon 6 (adopted August 27, 1908), in American Bar Association, Opinions of the Committee on Professional Ethics and Grievances (1947), p. 3.

70. 327 U.S. 821 (1946).

71. Ibid., 866-867. "The rule is intended to indicate that the right of the defendant to have counsel assigned by the court relates only to proceedings in court and, therefore,

does not include preliminary proceedings before a committing magistrate." Advisory
Committee on Rules of Criminal Procedure, *Notes to the Rules of Criminal Procedure
for the District Courts of the United States* (Washington: Government Printing Office,
1945), p. 41.

72. 327 U.S. 821, 892.

73. *Miller v. United States*, 317 U.S. 192, 197 (1942).

74. Attorney General of the United States, *Annual Report for the Fiscal Year ending
June 30, 1941* (Washington: Government Printing Office, 1942), pp. 3, 35.

75. Public Law 222, 78th Congress, Act of January 20, 1944, c. 3, 58 Stat. 5, United
States Code (1940), Title 28, sec. 9a.

76. Holtzoff, *op. cit.*, p. 22.

77. On legal aid work see: Reginald H. Smith, *Justice and the Poor* (New York:
Carnegie Foundation for the Advancement of Teaching. Bulletin No. 13, 1919); same
and John S. Bradway, *Growth of Legal Aid Work in the United States* (Washington:
Government Printing Office, 1936): John S. Bradway, ed., "Legal Aid Work," *Annals
of the American Academy of Political and Social Science*, CXXIV (1926); S. B.
Jacobv, "Legal Aid to the Poor." *Harvard Law Review*, LIII (1940), 940-976; and the
reports and proceedings of the *National Association of Legal Aid Organizations*.

78. See: Walton J. Wood. "The Office of Public Defender," *Annals of the American
Academy of Political and Social Science*, CXXIV (1926), 69-75; John S. Bradwav,
"Notes on the Defender in Criminal Cases," *ibid.*, CXXXVI (1928), 119-128; Smith,
op. cit., chap. XV; Smith and Bradway, *op. cit.*, chap. IX.

79. Attorney General of the United States. *Annual Report for the Fiscal Year ending
June 30, 1938* (Washington: Government Printing Office, 1939), p. 7.

80. Same, *Annual Report for the Fiscal Year ending June 30, 1940* (Washington:
Government Printing Office, 1941), pp. 7-8.

81. S. 1845 and H. R., 4782; see Robert T. Murphy, "Public Defender in Federal
Courts." *Georgetown Law Journal*, XXXVIII (1940), 037-045.

82. S. 2871, introduced by Senator Capper, and H. R. 8693, by Representative
Kefauver, both in the 76th Congress.

83. Statutory references are collected in Bradway, *op. cit.*; see also *Betts v. Brady*, 316
U.S. 455 (1942).

84. *Powell v. Alabama*, 287 U.S. 45 (1932). The case has been widely noted and
commented on. See *Boston University Law Review*, XIII (1933), 92-98; *Columbia Law
Review*, XXXII (1932), 1430-1431, *George Washington Law Review*, I (1932), 116-
117, *Iowa Law Review*, XVIII (1932), 383-384, *Michigan Law Review*, XXXI (1933),
245-255. *Minnesota Law Review*, XVII (1933), 415-418, *New York University Law
Quarterly Review*, X (1933), 389-391, *Notre Dame Lawyer*, VIII (1933), 260-261,
Oregon Law Review, XII (1933), 227-233, *St. John's Law Review*, VII (1933), 126-127,
Southern California Law Review, VII (1933), 90-96, *Texas Law Review*, XI (1933),
546-548, *University of Cincinnati Law Review*, VII (1933), 90-91, *University of Pennsylvania Law Review*, LXXXI (1933), 337-338, *Virginia Law Review*, XIX (1933),
203-204, *Wisconsin Law Review*, VIII (1933), 370-371. See also comment by Felix
Frankfurter in *New York Times*, November 13, 1932, sec. 2, p. 1.

85. Statement of the case summarized from the opinion, 287 U.S. 45, 49-58.

86. *Weems v. State*, 224 Ala. 524 (1932), *Patterson v. State*, 224 Ala. 531 (1932),
Powell v. State, 224 Ala. 540 (1932).

87. 287 U.S. 45.

88. 110 U.S. 516 (1884).

89. 287 U.S. 45, 66.

90. *Gitlow v. New York*, 268 U.S. 652 (1925), *Stromberg v. California*, 283 U.S.
359 (1931), *Near v. Minnesota*, 283 U.S. 697 (1931). The Court also referred to the
series of cases, beginning with *Chicago, Burlington & Quincy R. Co. v. Chicago*, 166
U.S. 226 (1897), in which the taking of private property for public use without just
compensation was held to violate due process of law.

91. 287 U.S. 45, 67-68.

92. *Ibid.*, 68.

93. *Ibid.*, 69. Italics added.

94. *Ibid.*, 71.

95. 297 U.S. 233 (1936).

172 (pp. 125-134) REFERENCES

96. Ibid., 243-244.
97. 297 U.S. 278, 285-286 (1936).
98. 302 U.S. 319 (1937).
99. Ibid., 323.
100. 110 U.S. 516 (1884).
101. Palko v. Connecticut, supra, 324-325.
102. Ibid., 324-325.
103. Ibid., 327. Italics added.
104. 304 U.S. 458 (1938).
105. 308 U.S. 444 (1940). Noted in Georgetown Law Journal, XXVIII (1940), 997-999.
106. (Note) Georgetown Law Journal, XXVIII (1940), 997, 999.
107. 308 U.S. 444, 446-447. The language is Mr. Justice Black's. It appears to be in marked contrast with his position in later cases, cf. Betts v. Brady, infra, and Foster v. Illinois, infra.
108. 312 U.S. 329 (1941).
109. 316 U. S. 455 (1942). See: George I. Haight, "Betts v. Brady," American Bar Association Journal, XXXIX (1943), 61-63. Cf. annotations in: Chicago-Kent Law Review, XXI (1942), 107-112, Columbia Law Review, XLII (1942), 1205-1208, Georgia Bar Record, V (1942), 51-54, Indiana Law Journal, XVIII (1943), 135-139, Marquette Law Review, XXVII (1942), 32-39, Southern California Law Review, XVI (1942), 55-56, Tulane Law Review, XVII (1942), 306-310, University of Pennsylvania Law Review, XCI (1942), 78-79. And see a letter to the editor, New York Times, August 2, 1942, sec. 4, p. 6, by Benjamin V. Cohen and Erwin N. Griswold. Most comments are critical of the majority opinion.
110. 316 U.S. 455, 457.
111. Ibid., 462.
112. Ibid., 462-463, citing Powell v. Alabama, Grosjean v. American Press Co., Johnson v. Zerbst, and Avery v. Alabama.
113. It should be noted that in deciding Powell v. Alabama the Court had made only the most perfunctory mention of this statutory requirement, 287 U.S. 45, 59, and had not drawn upon it in reaching its decision.
114. 316 U.S. 455, 464.
115. Ibid., 471.
116. Ibid., 461-462. Emphasis added in both quotations.
117. This statement is made of Betts v. Brady in Virginia Law Review, XXXIII (1947), 731,733.
118. 316 U.S. 455, 477.
119. Justice Black averred his own belief that the Bill of Rights was intended to be made applicable to the States by the Fourteenth Amendment but admitted that such was not the accepted view. 316 U.S. 455, 474-475.
120. Amrine v. Tines, 131 Fed. (2d) 827, 833 (C.C.A., 10th Cir., 1942). The sequence of the two sentences has been reversed.
121. Betts v. Brady, supra, 475, quoting from Palko v. Connecticut, supra, at 325.
122. 316 U.S. 455, 462.
123. 323 U.S. 471 (1945). Noted in Georgia Bar Record, VII (1945), 484-486; Michigan Law Review, XLIV (1945), 489-490.
124. 323 U.S. 471, 475.
125. Tomkins v. Missouri, 323 U.S. 485, 489 (1945), referring to both the Williams and the Tomkins case.
126. Williams v. Kaiser, supra, 482.
127. 323 U.S. 485 (1945).
128. Ibid., 488.
129. 324 U.S. 760 (1945). Dismissed on other grounds.
130. 324 U.S. 786 (1945). Justices Frankfurter, Roberts, and Jackson dissented.
131. 329 U.S. 173 (1946). Justices Douglas (Black and Rutledge concurring) and Murphy filed dissenting opinions.
132. 327 U.S. 82 (1946). Criticized in Columbia Law Review, XLVI (1946), 648-653. Cf. Gayes v. New York, 332 U.S. 145 (1947).
133. Murphy and Rutledge, JJ., dissented.

134. 329 U.S. 663 (1947). See also *Uveges v. Pennsylvania*, 335 U.S. 437 (1948), involving a seventeen-year-old charged with multiple burglaries.

135. *Marino v. Ragen*, 332 U.S. 561 (1947). The principal point of the decision was the availability of the writ of habeas corpus as a remedy, Justice Rutledge's concurring opinion sharply criticizing the practice under Illinois law.

135a. After protracted proceedings in the state courts, Marino was released on parole in July 1950. But he was not to enjoy his freedom: federal agents at once rearrested him for deportation as an undesirable alien. Kansas City *Times*, July 11, 1950, p. 14.

136. *Foster v. Illinois*, 332 U.S. 134 (1947); *Bute v. Illinois*, 333 U.S. 640 (1948); *Gibbs v. Burke*, 337 U.S. 773 (1949); *Quicksall v. Michigan*, 339 U.S. 660 (1950).

137. 332 U.S. 134, 136.

138. *Ibid.*, 136-137.

139. *Ibid.*, 138.

140. *Ibid.*, 138-139.

141. *Ibid.*, 140-141.

142. 333 U.S. 640, 677, 679.

143. Arthur M. Schlesinger, Jr., "The Supreme Court, 1947," *Fortune* (January, 1947), 73-79, 201-212.

144. Robert J. Harris, "Ten Years of the Supreme Court: 1937-1947; Due Process of Law," *American Political Science Review*, XLII (1948), 32, 41.

Chapter VII

1. Carl B. Swisher, *American Constitutional Development* (Boston: Houghton Mifflin Company, 1943), p. 1017.

2. *Supra*, chaps. III and IV.

3. *Supra*, chap. VI.

4. *Bushell's Case*, Vaughan 135 (1670), 6 How. State Trials 999; see *supra*, chap. I.

5. *Supra*, chap. V.

6. *Supra*, chap. VI.

7. *Adams v. United States ex rel. McCann*, 317 U.S. 269, 276 (1942).

8. Joseph Story, *Commentaries on the Constitution of the United States*; first published in 1833; (3rd ed.; Boston: Little, Brown and Company, 1858), II, 597.

9. *Loc. cit.*

10. *Ibid.*, p. 589.

11. Francis Lieber, *On Civil Liberty and Self-Government* (Philadelphia: Lippincott, Grambo and Company, 1853), I, 250.

12. *Ibid.*, p. 89.

13. *Ibid.*, p. 157.

14. *Ibid.*, p. 152.

15. *Supra*, chap. IV.

16. See the extensive bibliography in Harry E. Barnes and Negley K. Teeters, *New Horizons in Criminology* (New York: Prentice-Hall, Inc.; 1943); cf. Frank Tannenbaum, *Crime and the Community* (Boston: Ginn and Company, 1938), pp. 25-50, and John G. Thompson, *Urbanization, Its Effects on Government and Society* (New York: E. P. Dutton and Company, 1927), pp. 479-508.

17. Roscoe Pound, *Criminal Justice in America* (New York: Henry Holt and Company, 1930), p. 12.

18. Witness the work of the National Commission on Law Observance and Law Enforcement, of crime commissions in numerous states and cities; and the Crime Surveys of Illinois, Missouri, Cleveland, etc.

19. Cf. John B. Waite, *Criminal Law in Action* (New York: Sears Publishing Company, Inc., 1934), chap. XV.

20. Cf. William E. Mikell, "Criminal Procedure—Defects in Its Administration," *Annals of the American Academy of Political and Social Science*, CXXV (1926), 91, 92; Charles C. Arado, "Criminal Defense," *Chicago Bar Record*, XXVII (1946), 286.

21. E. Ray Stevens, "The Criminal and the Law," *Marquette Law Review*, X (1925), 1, 3.

22. Pound, *op. cit.*, pp. 10-11.

23. *Supra*, notes 20 and 21.

24. J. C. McWhorter, "Abolish the Jury!" West Virginia Law Quarterly, XXIX (1923), 97-108, also in: American Law Review, LVII (1923), 42.

25. Harry E. Barnes, "Trial by Jury," American Mercury, III (1924), 403, 405.

26. Barnes and Teeters, op. cit., p. xi.

27. See, e.g., James W. Garner, "Crime and Judicial Inefficiency," Annals of the American Academy of Political and Social Science, XXIX (1907), 601, 609; (Justice) Henry B. Brown, "Administration of the Jury System," Green Bag, XVII (1905), 623-626; William H. Taft, "Delays and Defects in the Enforcement of Law in This Country; The Jury System," North American Review, CLXXXVII (1908), 856-859.

28. Cf. Henry C. Caldwell, "The American Jury System," American Law Review, XXII (1888), 853-872; William Lyon Phelps in Scribner's Magazine for April 1925, quoted by John H. Wigmore, "First Aid for Trial by Jury," Journal of the American Judicature Society, IX (1925), 121.

29. See Roscoe Pound, "Jury," Encyclopedia of the Social Sciences (New York: The Macmillan Company, 1930-1935), VIII, 492, 495-496.

30. William F. Willoughby, Principles of Judicial Administration (Washington: The Brookings Institution, 1939), pp. 489-490.

31. Note, for example, that such involved issues as may arise under the anti-trust laws or under the Securities and Securities Exchange Acts may, because of the criminal features of these enactments, be placed before a jury for decision.

32. See United States v. Wood, 299 U.S. 123 (1936), Thiel v. Southern Pacific Company, 328 U.S. 217 (1946), and William L. Hickey, "Improvements of the Jury System in Federal Courts," Georgetown Law Journal, XXXV (1947), 500-516.

33. The literature of modern criminology is voluminous. Barnes and Teeters, op. cit., is a recent and readable exposition of this viewpoint and offers a select but ample bibliography of the field. Cf. also Cardozo's address "What Medicine Can Do for Law," in Law and Literature, reprinted in Margaret E. Hall, ed., Selected Writings of Benjamin Nathan Cardozo (New York: Fallon Law Book Company, 1947), pp. 371-394.

34. Hawaii v. Mankichi, 190 U.S. 197, 217-218 (1903), supra, pp. 44-47. It is suggested that Justice Murphy's apostrophe of jury trial as "fundamental," Adams v. United States ex rel. McCann, supra, 286 (dissent), is not symptomatic of any major trend.

35. Patton v. United States, 281 U.S. 276 (1930), supra, pp. 36-38.

36. The phrase is from Pendleton Howard's Criminal Justice in England (New York: The Macmillan Company, 1931), p. 406.

37. In effect such a development would place trial by jury in a similar status with reference to the Sixth Amendment which the right to counsel had prior to Johnson v. Zerbst, 304 U.S. 458 (1938), supra, chap. VI.

38. Supra, note 7.

39. Cardozo, J., in Palko v. Connecticut, 302 U.S. 319, 325 (1938; with reference to self-incrimination).

40. Johnson v. Zerbst, supra; see supra, chap. VI.

41. Tanksley v. United States, 145 Fed. (2d) 58 (C.C.A., 9th Cir., 1944); cf. supra, chap. IV.

42. 110 U.S. 516 (1884); cf. supra, chap. VI.

43. Rodney L. Mott, Due Process of Law (Indianapolis: The Bobbs-Merrill Company, 1926), pp. 159, 161.

44. Ibid., p. 165; see also Horace Flack, The Adoption of the Fourteenth Amendment (Baltimore: The Johns Hopkins Press, 1908).

45. Cf. Adamson v. California, 332 U.S. 46, 68, 71-89 (1947; dissenting opinion); Betts v. Brady, 316 U.S. 455, 474 (1942; dissenting opinion).

46. Cf. Palko v. Connecticut, supra, 324.

47. Betts v. Brady, supra; Foster v. Illinois, 332 U.S. 134 (1947); Bute v. Illinois, 333 U.S. 640 (1948).

48. Palko v. Connecticut, supra, 325.

49. Adamson v. California, 332 U.S. 46 (1947).

50. The writer recently interviewed the members of two federal grand jury panels. In spite of their recent participation in its work a majority of those questioned were unable to state the purpose and function of the grand jury. The preponderant feeling appeared to be that it was "a waste of time and money" and that nothing of practical value was accomplished.

51. *Davidson* v. *New Orleans*, 96 U.S. 97 (1878), opinions of Mr. Justice Miller for the majority and of Mr. Justice Bradley, concurring.

52. Note in this connection the increasing number of instances, as yet confined to the lower courts, in which the actual competence of appointed counsel is brought in issue. *Supra,* pp. 115-117.

Bibliography

1. *Primary Sources:*

UNITED STATES. Administrative Office of the United States Courts. *Annual Reports of the Director.* Washington: Government Printing Office, 1940-

ATTORNEY GENERAL. *Annual Reports.* Washington: Government Printing Office, 1790-   .

CONGRESS. *Annals of Congress.* Volume 1, compiled by Joseph Gales Senior. Washington: Gales and Seaton, 1834.

HOUSE OF REPRESENTATIVES, Committee on Revision of the Laws. *United States Code, 1940 Edition.* Washington: Government Printing Office, 1941-   .

DEPARTMENT OF STATE, Bureau of Rolls and Library. *Documentary History of the Constitution of the United States of America, 1786-1870.* Washington: Department of State, 1894-1905.

Documents Illustrative of the Formation of the Union of the American States. Edited by Charles C. Tansill. Washington: Government Printing Office, 1937.

HAWAIIAN COMMISSION. *Report.* (Senate Document No. 16, 55th Congress, 3rd session.) Washington: Government Printing Office, 1898.

JUDICIAL CONFERENCE OF SENIOR CIRCUIT JUDGES. *Reports.* Washington: Government Printing Office, 1923-   .

NATIONAL COMMISSION ON LAW OBSERVANCE AND ENFORCEMENT. *Report on Criminal Procedure.* Washington: Government Printing Office, 1931.

Report on Prosecution: Government Printing Office, 1931.

PRESIDENT. *Messages and Papers of the Presidents.* Edited by James D. Richardson. Washington: Government Printing Office, 1896-1899.

Revised Statutes. Washington: Government Printing Office, 1875; 2d edition, 1878; Supplement I, 1891; Supplement II, 1901.

Statutes at Large. Volumes 1-17: Boston: Little and Brown (later: Little, Brown and Company), 1848-1873; Volumes 18-   : Washington: Government Printing Office, 1875-   .

SUPREME COURT, Advisory Committee on Rules of Criminal Procedure. *Preliminary Draft of Federal Rules of Criminal Procedure.* Washington: Government Printing Office, 1943.

Notes to the Rules of Criminal Procedure for the District Courts of the United States. Washington: Government Printing Office, 1945.

NEW YORK. Judicial Council of the State. *Annual Reports.* Albany, New York: Williams Press, Inc., 1934-   .

VIRGINIA. House of Burgesses. *Journals, 1619-1658/9.* Edited by Henry R. McIlwaine. Richmond, Virginia: The Colonial Press, E. Waddey Company, 1915.

STATUTES AT LARGE. Compiled by William W. Hening. Richmond, Virginia: Samuel Pleasants Junior, 1809-1823.

ELLIOT, JONATHAN, ed. *The Debates in the Several State Conventions on the Adoption of the Federal Constitution.* 3rd edition. Philadelphia: J. B. Lippincott Company, 1835.

FARRAND, MAX, ed. *The Records of the Federal Convention of 1787.* Revised edition. New Haven: Yale University Press, 1937.

The Federalist; a commentary on the Constitution of the United States, written by Alexander Hamilton, James Madison and John Jay. Edited by Edward G. Bourne. New York: Tudor Publishing Company, 1937.

HOWLAND, ARTHUR C., ed. "Ordeals, Compurgation, Excommunication and Interdict." University of Pennsylvania, Department of History, *Translations and Reprints from the Original Sources of European History* (no date), vol. IV, No. 4.

MACLAY, WILLIAM. *Journal.* Edited by Edgar S. Maclay. New York: D. Appleton and Company, 1890.

MADISON, JAMES. *Writings.* Edited by Gaillard Hunt. New York: G. P. Putnam's Sons, 1900-1910.

STUBBS, WILLIAM, ed. *Select Charters and Other Illustrations of English Constitutional History.* 9th edition, revised throughout by Henry M. C. Davis. Oxford: Clarendon Press, 1921.

THORPE, FRANCIS N., comp. *The Federal and State Constitutions, Colonial Charters and Other Organic Laws* . . . Washington: Government Printing Office, 1909.

2. *Reference and Search Materials:*

BALDWIN, WILLIAM E., comp. *Bouvier's Law Dictionary.* Century edition. Cleveland: Banks-Baldwin Law Publishing Company, 1940.

BEAMAN, MIDDLETON G. *Analysis of the Federal Statutes 1789-1873.* Washington: Government Printing Office, 1911.

CULVER, DOROTHY C., comp. *Bibliography of Crime and Criminal Justice 1927-1932.* New York: The H. W. Wilson Company, 1934.

CULVER, DOROTHY C., comp. *Bibliography of Crime and Criminal Justice 1932-1937.* New York: The H. W. Wilson Company, 1939.

ESTRICH, WILLIS A., GEORGE S. GULICK AND WILLIAM M. McKINNEY, eds. *American Jurisprudence.* San Francisco: Bancroft-Whitney Company; Rochester, New York: The Lawyers Co-operative Publishing Company, 1936- .

Federal Digest, 1754 to Date. St. Paul, Minnesota: West Publishing Company, 1940- .

KUHLMANN, AUGUSTUS F., comp. *A Guide to Materials on Crime and Criminal Justice.* New York: The H. W. Wilson Company, 1929.

MACK, WILLIAM, AND WILLIAM B. HALE. *Corpus Juris.* New York: The American Law Book Company; London: Butterworth & Company, 1914-1932.

MACK, WILLIAM, AND DONALD J. KISER. *Corpus Juris Secundum.* Brooklyn, New York: The American Law Book Company, 1936- .

SCOTT, GEORGE W., AND MIDDLETON G. BEAMAN. *Index to the Federal Statutes 1874-1931.* Revised by Walter H. McClenon and Wilfred C. Gilbert. Washington: Government Printing Office, 1933.

SELIGMAN, EDWIN R. A., editor-in-chief. *Encyclopaedia of the Social Sciences.* New York: The Macmillan Company, 1930-1935.
Shepard's Federal Reporter Citations. 5th edition. New York: The Frank Shepard Company, 1938- .
Shepard's United States Citations. 5th edition, case edition. New York: The Frank Shepard Company, 1943-

3. Books:

AMERICAN BAR ASSOCIATION. *Opinions of the Committee on Professional Ethics and Grievances, and Canons of Professional Ethics.* N. p.: n. n., 1947.
AMES, HERMAN V. *The Proposed Amendments to the Constitution of the United States During the First Century of Its History.* Published as Volume II of the Annual Report of the American Historical Association for the Year 1896. Washington: Government Printing Office, 1897.
ARBER, EDWARD, ed. *Travels and Works of Captain John Smith.* New edition, with introduction by A. G. Bradley. Edinburgh: J. Grant, 1910.
BALDWIN, SIMEON E. *The American Judiciary.* New York: The Century Company, 1905.
BARNES, HARRY E., AND NEGLEY K. TEETERS. *New Horizons in Criminology.* New York: Prentice-Hall, Inc., 1943.
BLACKSTONE, SIR WILLIAM. *Commentaries on the Law of England.* Cooley's 2d edition. Chicago: Callaghan and Company, 1873.
BRUNNER, HEINRICH, *Die Entstehung der Schwurgerichte.* Berlin: Weidmannsche Buchhandlung, 1872.
CARDOZO, BENJAMIN N. *The Nature of the Judicial Process.* New Haven: Yale University Press, 1921.
CARPENTER, WILLIAM S., AND PAUL T. STAFFORD, eds. *Readings in Early Legal Institutions.* New York: F. S. Crofts & Company, 1932.
CHITWOOD, OLIVER P. *Justice in Colonial Virginia.* Baltimore: The Johns Hopkins Press, 1905.
CHUMBLEY, GEORGE L. *Colonial Justice in Virginia.* Richmond, Virginia: The Dietz Press, 1938.
CLARK, FLOYD B. *The Constitutional Doctrines of Justice Harlan.* Baltimore: The Johns Hopkins Press, 1915.
COOLEY, THOMAS M. *A Treatise on the Constitutional Limitations Which Rest upon the Legislative Power of the States of the American Union.* 8th edition, by Walter Carrington. Boston: Little, Brown and Company, 1927.
CORWIN, EDWARD S. *The Constitution and What It Means Today.* 8th edition. Princeton, New Jersey: Princeton University Press, 1947.
DUNBAR, SEYMOUR. *A History of Travel in America.* Indianapolis: The Bobbs-Merrill Company, 1915.
FLACK, HORACE. *The Adoption of the Fourteenth Amendment.* Baltimore: The Johns Hopkins Press, 1908.
FORSYTH, WILLIAM. *History of Trial by Jury.* New edition, prepared by James A. Morgan. New York: James Cockroft & Company, 1875.

Fox, Sir John C. *The History of Contempt of Court.* Oxford: Clarendon Press, 1927.

Green, Leon. *Judge and Jury.* Kansas City, Missouri: Vernon Law Book Company, 1930.

Hall, Margaret E., ed. *Selected Writings of Benjamin Nathan Cardozo.* New York: Fallon Law Book Company, 1947.

Haskins, Charles H. *Norman Institutions.* Cambridge, Massachusetts: Harvard University Press, 1918.

Henry, William W. *Patrick Henry.* New York: Charles Scribner's Sons, 1891.

Holdsworth, Sir William S. *A History of English Law.* 4th edition. London: Methuen & Company, Ltd., 1936-1938.
Some Lessons from Our Legal History. New York: The Macmillan Company, 1928.

Housel, Theodore W., and Guy O. Walser, *Defending and Prosecuting Federal Criminal Cases.* 2d edition. Buffalo, New York: Dennis & Company, Inc., 1946.

Howard, Pendleton. *Criminal Justice in England.* New York: The Macmillan Company, 1931.

Hull, William I. *William Penn: A Topical Biography.* New York: Oxford University Press, 1937.

Jenks, Edward. *A Short History of English Law.* 2d, revised edition. London: Methuen & Company, Ltd., 1920.

Lasson, Nelson B. *The History and Development of the Fourth Amendment to the United States Constitution.* Baltimore: The Johns Hopkins Press, 1937.

Lesser, Maximus A. *The Historical Development of the Jury System.* Rochester, New York: The Lawyers Co-operative Publishing Company, 1894.

Lieber, Francis. *On Civil Liberty and Self-Government.* Philadelphia: Lippincott, Grambo and Company, 1853.

McIlwain, Charles H. *The High Court of Parliament and Its Supremacy.* New Haven: Yale University Press, 1910.

McKechnie, William S. *Magna Carta: A Commentary on the Great Charter of King John.* 2d edition. Glasgow: James Maclehouse and Sons, 1914.

Maitland, Frederic W., and Francis C. Montague. *A Sketch of English Legal History.* New York: G. P. Putnam's Sons, 1915.

Miller, Elmer I. *The Legislature of the Province of Virginia.* New York: Columbia University Press, 1907.

Moley, Raymond. *Our Criminal Courts.* New York: Minton, Balch & Company, 1929.
Politics and Criminal Prosecution. New York: Minton, Balch & Company, 1929.

Moley, Raymond, ed. *Missouri Crime Survey.* New York: The Macmillan Company, 1926.

Moore, John B. *A Treatise on Extradition and Interstate Rendition.* Boston: The Boston Book Company, 1891.

MOSCHZISKER, ROBERT V. *Trial by Jury.* Philadelphia: Geo. T. Bisel Company, 1930.

MOTT, RODNEY L. *Due Process of Law.* Indianapolis: The Bobbs-Merrill Company, 1926.

ORFIELD, LESTER B. *Criminal Procedure from Arrest to Appeal.* New York: New York University Press, 1947.

OSGOOD, HERBERT L. *The American Colonies in the Seventeenth Century.* New York: The Macmillan Company, 1904-1907.

PAULLIN, CHARLES O., AND JOHN K. WRIGHT. *Atlas of the Historical Geography of the United States.* Washington: Carnegie Institution, 1932.

POLLOCK, SIR FREDERICK, AND FREDERIC W. MAITLAND. *The History of English Law before the Time of Edward I.* Cambridge: University Press, 1895.

POUND, ROSCOE. *Criminal Justice in America.* New York: Henry Holt and Company, 1930.

Readings on the History and System of the Common Law. 2d edition. Boston: The Chipman Law Publishing Company, 1921.

ROTTSCHAEFER, HENRY. *Handbook of American Constitutional Law.* St. Paul, Minnesota: West Publishing Company, 1939.

SAIT, EDWARD M. *Political Institutions: A Preface.* New York: D. Appleton-Century Company, 1938.

SCOTT, ARTHUR P. *Criminal Law in Colonial Virginia.* Chicago: University of Chicago Press, 1930.

SCOTT, AUSTIN W. *Fundamentals of Procedure.* New York: Baker, Voorhis & Company, 1922.

SMITH, REGINALD H. *Justice and the Poor.* New York: Carnegie Foundation for the Advancement of Teaching, 1919.

AND JOHN S. BRADWAY. *Growth of Legal Aid Work in the United States.* Washington: Government Printing Office, 1936.

SMITH, SIR THOMAS. *The Commonwealth of England.* London: Printed by R. Young for J. Smethwicke, 1640.

SPICER, GEORGE W. *The Constitutional Status and Government of Alaska.* Baltimore: The Johns Hopkins Press, 1927.

STEPHEN, SIR JAMES F. *A History of the Criminal Law of England.* London: Macmillan and Company, 1883.

STORY, JOSEPH. *Commentaries on the Constitution of the United States.* 3rd edition. Boston: Little, Brown and Company, 1858.

SWISHER, CARL B. *American Constitutional Development.* Boston: Houghton Mifflin Company, 1943.

TACITUS, CORNELIUS. *Germania.* Edited by George Stuart. Philadelphia: Eldredge & brothers, 1885.

TANNENBAUM, FRANK. *Crime and the Community.* Boston: Ginn and Company, 1938.

THAYER, JAMES B. *A Preliminary Treatise on Evidence at the Common Law.* Boston: Little, Brown and Company, 1898.

THOMPSON, JOHN G. *Urbanization, Its Effects on Government and Society.* New York: E. P. Dutton and Company, 1927.

UNITED STATES CIVIL SERVICE COMMISSION. *History of the Federal Civil Service 1789 to the Present.* Washington: Government Printing Office, 1941.
VON HASSELN, HENRY. The Work of the First Congress in 1789. Unpublished Master's Thesis, University of Virginia, 1946.
WAITE, JOHN B. *Criminal Law in Action.* New York: Sears Publishing Company, Inc., 1934.
WARREN, CHARLES. *A History of the American Bar.* Boston: Little, Brown and Company, 1911.
WIGMORE, JOHN H., ed. *The Illinois Crime Survey.* Chicago: Illinois Association for Criminal Justice, 1929.
WILLOUGHBY, WESTEL W. *The Constitutional Law of the United States.* 2d edition. New York: Baker, Voorhis and Company, 1929. *The Fundamental Concepts of Public Law.* New York: The Macmillan Company, 1931.
WILLOUGHBY, WILLIAM F. *Principles of Judicial Administration.* Washington: Brookings Institute, 1929.

4. *Articles:*
AIGLER, RALPH W. "Legislation in Vague and General Terms." *Michigan Law Review,* XXI (1923), 831-851.
ARADO, CHARLES C. "Criminal Defense." *Chicago Bar Record,* XXVII (1946), 286.
BARNES, HARRY E. "Trial by Jury." *American Mercury,* III (1924), 403-410.
BERGE, WENDELL. "The Proposed Federal Rules of Criminal Procedure." *Michigan Law Review,* XLII (1943), 353-382.
BLUME, WILLIAM W. "The Place of Trial in Criminal Cases: Constitutional Vicinage and Venue." *Michigan Law Review,* XLIII (1944), 59-94.
BOSKEY, BENNETT, AND JOHN H. PICKERING. "Federal Restrictions on Criminal Procedure." *University of Chicago Law Review,* XIII (1946), 266-299.
BRADWAY, JOHN S. "Notes on the Defender in Criminal Cases." *Annals of the American Academy of Political and Social Science,* CXXXVI (1928), 119-128.
(ed.) "Legal Aid Work." *Annals of the American Academy of Political and Social Science,* CXXIV (1926), 1-189.
BROWN, HENRY B. "The Administration of the Jury System." *The Green Bag,* XVII (1905), 623-626.
CALDWELL, HENRY C. "The American Jury System." *American Law Review,* XXII (1888), 853-872.
COLEMAN, CHARLES T. "Origin and Development of Trial by Jury." *Virginia Law Review,* VI (1919), 77-86.
"Historical Sketch of Trial by Jury." *Canadian Law Times,* LX (1920), 732-742.
"Trial by Jury." *American Law Review,* LIV (1920), 750-759.

CONBOY, MARTIN. "Federal Criminal Law." In Reppy, Alison, ed. Law: A Century of Progress 1835-1935. New York: New York University Press, 1937.

CONNOR, HENRY G. "The Constitutional Right to a Trial by a Jury of the Vicinage." University of Pennsylvania Law Review, LVII (1909), 197-215.

DOBIE, ARMISTEAD M. "Venue in Criminal Cases in the United States District Courts." Virginia Law Review, XII (1926), 287-294.

DUNBAR, WILLIAM H. "The Anarchists' Case before the Supreme Court of the United States." Harvard Law Review, I (1888), 307-326.

(SYMPOSIUM) "Extending Federal Powers over Crime." Law and Contemporary Problems, I (1934), 399-508.

FELLMAN, DAVID. "Some Consequences of Increased Federal Activity in Law Enforcement." Journal of Criminal Law and Criminology, XXXV (1944), 16-33; reprinted in: Fellman, David. ed. Readings in American National Government. New York: Rinehart & Company, Inc., 1947.

FRANKFURTER, FELIX, AND THOMAS G. CORCORAN. "Petty Federal Offenses and the Constitutional Guarantee of Trial by Jury." Harvard Law Review, XXXIX (1926), 917-1019.

AND JAMES M. LANDIS. "Power of Congress over Procedure in 'Inferior' Federal Courts—A Study in the Separation of Powers." Harvard Law Review, XXXVII (1924), 1010-1050.

FULLHARDT, FREDERICK A. "Evolution of the Petit Jury." Thought, IX (1934), 46-61.

GARNER, JAMES W. "Crime and Judicial Inefficiency." Annals of the American Academy of Political and Social Science, XXIX (1907), 601-618.

"The Right of Jury Trial in the Dependencies." American Law Review, XL (1906), 340-355.

GRANT, JAMES A. C. "Felony Trials without a Jury." American Political Science Review, XXV (1931), 980-999.

"Waiver of Jury Trials in Felony Cases." California Law Review, XX (1932), 132-161; reprinted in: Maggs, Douglas B., ed. Selected Essays on Constitutional Law. Chicago: The Foundation Press, Inc., 1938.

GREEN, JOHN R. "Liberty under the Fourteenth Amendment." Washington University Law Quarterly, XXVII (1942), 497-562.

GRISWOLD, ERWIN N. "The Historical Development of Waiver of Jury Trial in Criminal Cases." Virginia Law Review, XX (1934), 655-699.

HADLEY, HERBERT S. "The Reform of Criminal Procedure." Proceedings of the Academy of Political Science, X (1923), 396-406.

HAIGHT, GEORGE I. "Betts v. Brady." American Bar Association Journal, XXIX (1943), 61-63.

HASKINS, CHARLES H. "The Early Norman Jury." American Historical Review, VIII (1903), 613-640.

HAZELTINE, HAROLD D. "The Influence of Magna Carta on American Constitutional Development." Columbia Law Review, XVII (1917),

1-33; also in: Malden, Henry E., ed. *Magna Carta Commemoration Essays*. London: Royal Historical Society, 1917.

HENRY, ROBERT L. "The Story of the Criminal Jury." In: Radin, Max, ed. *Legal Essays in Honor of Orrin Kip McMurray*. Berkeley, California: University of California Press, 1935.

HICKEY, WILLIAM L. "Improvement of the Jury System in Federal Courts." *Georgetown Law Journal*, XXXV (1947), 500-516.

HOLTZOFF, ALEXANDER. "Removal of Defendants in Federal Criminal Procedure." *California Law Review*, XXXIII (1945), 230-247.
"The Right of Counsel under the Sixth Amendment." *New York University Law Quarterly Review*, XX (1944), 1-22.

HUDSON, WILLIAM. "A Treatise on the Court of Star Chamber." In: Hargrave, Francis, ed. *Collectanea Juridica*. London: E. and R. Brooke, 1791.

JACOBY, SIDNEY B. "Legal Aid to the Poor." *Harvard Law Review*, LIII (1940), 940-976.

JEFFERSON, BERNARD S. "Race Discrimination in Jury Service." *Boston University Law Review*, XIX (1939), 413-447.

MCCLAIN, EMLIN. "The Hawaiian Case." *Harvard Law Review*, XVII (1904), 386-399.

MCWHORTER, JAMES C. "Abolish the Jury!" *West Virginia Law Quarterly*, XXIX (1923), 97-108; also in: *American Law Review*, LVII (1923), 42-56.

MIKELL, WILLIAM E. "Criminal Procedure—Defects in Its Administration." *Annals of the American Academy of Political and Social Science*, CXXV (1926), 91-93.

MURDOCH, HECTOR B. "Jury Justice." *Juridicial Review*, XX (1908), 59-75.

MURPHY, ROBERT T. "Public Defender in Federal Courts." *Georgetown Law Journal*, XXXVIII (1940), 937-945.

NATIONAL ASSOCIATION OF LEGAL AID ORGANIZATIONS, Record of Proceedings. 1923- .

ORFIELD, LESTER B. "A Resume of Decisions of the United States Supreme Court on Federal Criminal Procedure." Published serially: *Nebraska Law Review* (1941-42), XX, 251-303, XXI, 1-25, 113-143; *Rocky Mountain Law Review*, XIV (1942), 105-125; *Kentucky Law Journal*, XXX (1942), 360-406; *Missouri Law Review*, VII (1942), 262-301; *Journal of Criminal Law and Criminology*, XXXIII (1942), 219-244; *Oregon Law Review*, XXII (1942), 60-87.

POLLOCK, SIR FREDERICK. "The King's Peace in the Middle Ages." *Harvard Law Review*, XIII (1900), 177-189; reprinted in: Wigmore, John H., Ernst Freund and William E. Mikell, eds. *Select Essays in Anglo-American Legal History*. Boston: Little, Brown and Company, 1907-1909.

POWICKE, FREDERICK M. "Per Iudicium Parium vel Legem Terrae." In: Malden, Henry E., ed. *Magna Carta Commemoration Essays*. London: Royal Historical Society, 1917.

RADIN, MAX. "The Myth of Magna Carta." *Harvard Law Review*, LX (1947), 1060-1091.

"The Right to a Public Trial." *Temple Law Quarterly*, VI (1932), 381-398.

"The Rivalry of Common-Law and Civil Law Ideas in the American Colonies." In: Reppy, Alison, ed. *Law: A Century of Progress 1835-1935*. New York: New York University Press, 1937.

REINSCH, PAUL S. "The English Common Law in the Early American Colonies." *Bulletin of the University of Wisconsin*, No. 2 (1899); reprinted in: Wigmore, John H., Ernst Freund and William E. Mikell, eds. *Select Essays in Anglo-American Legal History*. Boston: Little, Brown and Company, 1907-1909.

SCHLESINGER, ARTHUR M., JR. "The Supreme Court, 1947." *Fortune* (January, 1947), 73-79.

STEPHEN, SIR HARRY L. "The Trial of Sir Walter Raleigh." *Transactions of the Royal Historical Society*, Fourth Series, II (1919), 172-187.

STEPHENS, J. E. R. "The Growth of Trial by Jury in England." *Harvard Law Review*, X (1896), 150, 160.

STEVENS, E. RAY. "The Criminal and the Law." *Marquette Law Review*, X (1925), 1-8.

STEWART, MELVILLE. "The Right to Trial by Jury in Prosecutions for Petty Federal Offenses." *West Virginia Law Quarterly*, XXXIX (1932), 40-51.

TAFT, WILLIAM H. "Delays and Defects in the Enforcement of Law in This Country: The Jury System." *North American Review*, CLXXXVII (1908), 856-859.

VINOGRADOFF, SIR PAUL. "Magna Carta, C. 39." In: Malden, Henry E., ed. *Magna Carta Commemoration Essays*. London: Royal Historical Society, 1917.

WARREN, CHARLES. "New Light on the History of the Federal Judiciary Act of 1789." *Harvard Law Review*, XXXVII (1923), 49-132; reprinted in part in: Maggs, Douglas B., ed., *Selected Essays on Constitutional Law*. Chicago: The Foundation Press, Inc., 1938, III, 1246-1254.

WELLS, CHARLES L. "The Origin of the Petty Jury." *Law Quarterly Review*, XXVI (1911), 347-361.

WIGMORE, JOHN H. "First Aid for Trial by Jury." *Journal of the American Judicature Society*, IX (1925), 121-122.

WOOD, WALTON J. "The Office of Public Defender." *Annals of the American Academy of Political and Social Science*, CXXIV (1926), 69-75.

5. *Unsigned Law Review Comments and Notes:*

"Army and Navy—Loss of Jurisdiction by Court Martial for Failure to Observe Rights Secured by Fifth and Sixth Amendments," *Virginia Law Review*, XXXIII (1947), 505-507.

"Civil and Criminal Contempt in the Federal Courts." *Yale Law Journal*, LVII (1947), 83-107.

"Constitutional Law—Criminal Law—Trial by Jury—Power of Defendant in Criminal Prosecution to Waive Right to Jury Trial without Advice of Counsel." *Minnesota Law Review,* XXVII (1943), 533-534.
"Constitutional Law—Criminal Law and Procedure—Right to Assistance of Counsel." *Michigan Law Review,* XLI (1942), 321-323.
"Constitutional Law—Criminal Procedure—Jury Trial—Right of Defendant not represented by Counsel to waive Trial by Jury." *Southern California Law Review,* XVI (1943), 240-242.
"Constitutional Law—Criminal Procedure—Right to Counsel." *Southern California Law Review,* XVI (1942), 55-56.
"Constitutional Law—Criminal Prosecutions—Right to Counsel." *Minnesota Law Review,* XXVI (1942), 657-658.
"Constitutional Law—Deprivation of Right to Counsel by Appointment of Attorney Representing Co-Conspirator." *University of Chicago Law Review,* IX (1942), 733-737.
"Constitutional Law—Due Process—Conduct of Trial—Right to be Represented by Counsel." *University of Cincinnati Law Review,* VII (1933), 90-91.
"Constitutional Law—Due Process—Denial of Motion for Continuance." *Georgetown Law Journal,* XXVIII (1940), 997-999.
"Constitutional Law—Due Process—Right of Accused to Benefit of Counsel under Fourteenth Amendment." *Wisconsin Law Review,* VIII (1933), 370-371.
"Constitutional Law—Due Process—Right of Counsel." *Oregon Law Review,* XII (1933), 227-233.
"Constitutional Law—Due Process—Right to Assistance of Counsel —Further Abandonment of the Rule of Hurtado v. California." *Columbia Law Review,* XXXII (1932), 1430-1431.
"Constitutional Law—Due Process—Right to Counsel." *New York University Law Quarterly Review,* X (1933), 389-391.
"Constitutional Law—Due Process—The Right to Counsel in a Criminal Proceeding." *St. John's Law Review,* VII (1933), 126-127.
"Constitutional Law—Due Process—Whether the Fourteenth Amendment Guarantees an Indigent Defendant the Right to Counsel in a Non-Capital Case." *Chicago-Kent Law Review,* XXI (1942), 107-112.
"Constitutional Law—Due Process: Criminal Prosecutions—Right to Counsel." *Minnesota Law Review,* XVIII (1933), 415-418.
"Constitutional Law—Due Process and Equal Protection—Right of Counsel." *Michigan Law Review,* XXXI (1933), 245-255.
"Constitutional Law—Due Process of Law—Denial of the Right to Aid of Counsel." *Southern California Law Review,* VII (1933), 90-96.
"Constitutional Law—Due Process of Law—Failure in Capital Case of State Court to Appoint Counsel for Poor Defendant until Trial." *Virginia Law Review,* XIX (1933), 293-294.

"Constitutional Law—Due Process of Law—Right of Defendant in Criminal Proceeding to Counsel." *Tulane Law Review,* XVII (1942), 306-310.

"Constitutional Law—Due Process of Law—Right to Counsel." *Boston University Law Review,* XIII (1933), 92-98.

"Constitutional Law—Due Process of Law—Right to Counsel." *Georgia Bar Journal,* VII (1945), 484-486.

"Constitutional Law—Due Process of Law—Right to Counsel." *Iowa Law Review,* XVIII (1933), 383-384.

"Constitutional Law—Refusal of State Court to Appoint Counsel for Indigent Defendant for Non-capital Offense Not a Violation of Due Process." *University of Pennsylvania Law Review,* XCI (1942), 78-79.

"Constitutional Law—Right of Counsel—Right to Effective Counsel." *Washington University Law Quarterly,* XXVII (1942), 581-583.

"Constitutional Law—Right of Indigent Prisoner to Counsel." *Indiana Law Journal,* XVIII (1943), 135-139.

"Constitutional Law—Right of Trial by Jury—Reckless Driving as a Crime within the Constitutional Guarantee." *Harvard Law Review,* XLIV (1931), 465.

"Constitutional Law—Right to a Public Trial." *Boston University Law Review,* XXV (1945), 145-147.

"Constitutional Law—Right to Counsel." *Wisconsin Law Review,* (1943), 118-127.

"Constitutional Law—Right to Counsel." *Columbia Law Review,* XLVI (1946), 648-653.

"Constitutional Law—Right to Counsel—Habeas Corpus." *Michigan Law Review,* XLIV (1945), 489-490.

"Constitutional Law—Right to Counsel Guaranty of Sixth Amendment Not Part of Due Process of Fourteenth Amendment." *Columbia Law Review,* XLII (1942), 1205-1208.

"Constitutional Law—Right to Exclude Public from Court Room during Trial of Criminal Cases." *Temple Law Quarterly,* III (1928), 76.

"Constitutional Law—Right to Jury Trial—Petty Statutory Offenses."*Michigan Law Review,* XXXV (1937), 1377-1380.

"Constitutional Law—Right to Representation by Counsel as Comprehended by the Due Process Clause—The Scottsboro Case." *University of Pennsylvania Law Review,* LXXXI (1933), 337-338.

"Constitutional Law—Sixth Amendment—Right to Assistance of Counsel on Appeal in Criminal Cases." *Tulane Law Review,* XXII (1947), 202-205.

"Constitutional Law—Sixth Amendment—Trial by Jury—Government Employee as Juror in Criminal Prosecution." *Brooklyn Law Review,* VI (1937), 388.

"Constitutional Law—Trial by Jury—Right to Waive Presence of Trial Judge." *Michigan Law Review,* XL (1941), 113-115.

"Constitutional Law—Trial by Jury—Waiver of Right to a Jury of Twelve in Criminal Trials." *Harvard Law Review,* XLIV (1930), 124-125.

"Constitutional Law—Trial by Jury in Criminal Cases." *Georgetown Law Journal,* XVIII (1930), 374-382.

"Constitutional Law—Trial by Jury—Territories of the United States: Porto Rico." *Harvard Law Review,* XXXVI (1922), 105.

"Constitutional Law—Unless Defendant Has Clearly Waived Right to Counsel, Appointment of Co-defendant's Counsel to Represent Him Justifies Reversal because of Conflict of Interest." *Georgetown Law Journal,* XXX (1942), 570-572.

"Constitutional Law—Waiver of Jury Trial—Federal Courts." *Georgetown Law Journal,* XXVI (1938), 762-764.

"Crimes—Waiver of Jury, Effect." *Michigan Law Review,* XXVIII (1930), 1054.

"Criminal Law—Conspiracy—Constitutional Law." *Temple Law Quarterly,* XVI (1942), 439-440.

"Criminal Law—Constitutional Law—Due Process of Law—Course and Conduct of Trial—Counsel for Accused." *Notre Dame Lawyer,* VIII (1933), 260-261.

"Criminal Law—Procedure—Duty of Court to Appoint Counsel for Indigent Accused." *Texas Law Review,* XI (1933), 546-548.

"Criminal Procedure—Constitutional Law—Trial by Jury for Reckless Driving." *University of Pennsylvania Law Review,* LXXIX (1931), 640-642.

"Criminal Procedure—Presence of Judge at Trial—Substitution of Judges." *Nebraska Law Review,* XXI (1942), 171-174.

"Denial of Counsel to Indigent Defendant in State Criminal Trials as a Violation of Due Process." *Marquette Law Review,* XXVII (1942), 32-39.

"Due Process of Law—Right of Indigent Defendant to Have Counsel Appointed in Criminal Cases." *Georgia Bar Journal,* V (1942), 51-54.

"Juries—Constitutionality of Statute Making Federal Employees Eligible." *Journal of Criminal Law and Criminology,* XXVII (1937), 914-917.

"Jury—Constitutional Law—Right of Defendant in Prosecution for Reckless Driving." *Columbia Law Review,* XXXI (1931), 325-326.

"Jury—Criminal Law—Power of Defendant on Trial for Penitentiary Offense to Waive a Jury Trial." *Columbia Law Review,* XXX (1930), 1063-1064.

"The Petty Offense Category and Trial by Jury." *Yale Law Journal,* XL (1931), 1303-1309; reprinted in: Maggs, Douglas B., ed. *Selected Essays on Constitutional Law.* Chicago: The Foundation Press, Inc., 1938.

"Procedure: Habeas Corpus: Right of Accused to Aid of Counsel." *Cornell Law Quarterly,* XXIV (1939), 270-274.

"Right to Representation by Counsel." *Georgetown Law Journal,* XXXI (1943), 327-334.

"The Right to Benefit of Counsel under the Federal Constitution."
Columbia Law Review, XLII (1942), 271-282.
"The Right to the Assistance of Counsel under the Federal Consti-
tution." Texas Law Review, XXIII (1944), 66-77.
"Scottsboro Case—Constitutional and Criminal Law—Due Process
under the Fourteenth Amendment to the U.S. Constitution."
George Washington Law Review, I (1933), 116-117.
"Some Recent Supreme Court Decisions on the Right to Counsel
under the Fourteenth Amendment." Virginia Law Review, XXXIII
(1947), 731-739.
"To What Extent, If at All, Is the Right to Jury Trial Optional in
Criminal Cases in the Federal Courts?" Massachusetts Law Quarterly, IX (1924), No. 3, 61-67.

Table of Cases

Index

70
71
72
74
75
76
77
79
81
83
85
88